AGINCOURT

OSPREY
PUBLISHING

MICHAEL LIVINGSTON

AGINCOURT

BATTLE OF THE SCARRED KING

OSPREY PUBLISHING
Bloomsbury Publishing Plc
Kemp House, Chawley Park, Cumnor Hill, Oxford OX2 9PH, UK
29 Earlsfort Terrace, Dublin 2, Ireland
1385 Broadway, 5th Floor, New York, NY 10018, USA
E-mail: info@ospreypublishing.com
www.ospreypublishing.com

OSPREY is a trademark of Osprey Publishing Ltd

First published in Great Britain in 2023

A catalogue record for this book is available from the British Library.

ISBN: HB 978 1 4728 5520 6; PB 978 1 4728 5516 9; eBook 978 1 4728 5519 0; ePDF 978 1 4728 5517 6; XML 978 1 4728 5518 3; Audio 978 1 4728 5521 3

23 24 25 26 27 10 9 8 7 6 5 4 3 2 1

Plate section image credits and captions are given in full in the List of Illustrations (pp. 9–13).
Fig. 11 is available under CC BY-SA 4.0: https://creativecommons.org/licenses/by-sa/4.0/
All quotations from Anne Curry, *The Battle of Agincourt: Sources and Interpretations* (Boydell, 2000) are reprinted by permission of Boydell & Brewer Ltd.
Maps by www.bounford.com
Index by Alan Rutter

Typeset by Deanta Global Publishing Services, Chennai, India
Printed and bound in Great Britain by CPI (Group) UK Ltd, Croydon, CRO 4YY

MIX
Paper | Supporting responsible forestry
FSC® C171272
FSC
www.fsc.org

Osprey Publishing supports the Woodland Trust, the UK's leading woodland conservation charity.

To find out more about our authors and books visit www.ospreypublishing.com. Here you will find extracts, author interviews, details of forthcoming events and the option to sign up for our newsletter.

Contents

Foreword

By Bernard Cornwell

Agincourt. The name glows in England's history: a battle in which an outnumbered army, trapped by an over-confident enemy, destroys that enemy.

It is a deserved reputation. The battle, or rather its outcome, shocked all Europe. And its fame is a continuing inspiration; during the Second World War Winston Churchill asked Laurence Olivier to make a film of Shakespeare's *Henry V* – with its Agincourt centre-stage – to boost English morale before another invasion of French territory. While the French remembered the battle as 'the wretched day', for the English it stood as divine confirmation of their prowess and the rightness of their cause. No matter that that cause was never fully realised, and that the French would go on to win the Hundred Years War, the English victory at Agincourt has remained, as the great Sir John Keegan wrote, 'a set-piece demonstration of English moral authority and a cherished ingredient of a fading national myth.' In his next sentence Keegan added: 'It is also a story of slaughteryard behaviour and of outright atrocity.'

For all this, Agincourt is one of the most studied battles of English or French history. Historians have delved into archives and chronicles searching for scraps and hints of what happened that day in October 1415, and, though there are minor disagreements about the numbers of troops engaged, generations of scholars have forged a tale now generally accepted about what happened and where it happened. Visit the field of Agincourt, as I have done many times, and you will find a fine small museum, while the road that crosses the traditional battlefield is generously decorated with large cut-out figures of English archers. You will find a well-known story.

I have also been a frequent visitor to the traditional battlefield of Crécy. Yet after reading Michael Livingston's superb book on that fight – *Crécy: Battle of Five Kings* – I learned that I had been in entirely the wrong place. So I anticipated this present volume on Agincourt with some apprehension. There was no chance, I thought, that I would experience the same astonishment again. Surely everything there was to say about Agincourt had been said? Everything there was to know about the battle was known?

I had underestimated his meticulous research. Michael is a military historian who approaches his work with a tactical understanding of the ground that the opposing commanders must deal with. In my own book about the battle of Waterloo I wrote, 'The Waterloo campaign is all about roads.' And so it was, but so too were the campaigns of Crécy and Agincourt, and it is Michael's deep research into available routes and his study of ancient maps and landscapes that enables him to find new insights into long-established history – that, and a deep appreciation of what the 15th-century soldier faced in combat.

Livingston's new discoveries accentuate the story's drama, providing a fresh understanding of how a small and sick English army was trapped by a large and over-confident French foe but still managed to pull off a remarkable and overwhelming victory. That story endures, even as this astounding book fixes the myth within a more realistic frame and adds to our understanding of what led to that slaughteryard of horrors, atrocities, and, for at least one side, unforgettable glories.

List of Illustrations

are attempting to make their assault. (Photo by Historica Graphica Collection/Heritage Images/Getty Images)

Fig. 24: A gouache of the town of Azincourt, painted by Adrien de Montigny between 1605 and 1611 at the behest of Duke Charles de Croÿ (1560–1612). The viewpoint is from south of the town, on the ridgeline north-west of the *Morival*, looking north: the church of Saint-Nicholas is in the left centre of the town, the castle of Azincourt is to the right, and the road to Maisoncelle stretches out of view to the bottom left. The road to Tramecourt, and the traditional location of the battle, appears to be the line of trees through the field at the right bottom. Note that the foregrounded ridgeline and road are an artistic trope of these paintings and do not reflect reality. (Private collection)

Fig. 25: A gouache of the town of Maisoncelle, painted by Adrien de Montigny between 1605 and 1611 at the behest of Duke Charles de Croÿ (1560–1612). The viewpoint is from north of the town, on the ridgeline north-west of the *Morival*, looking south: the same position from which the gouache in Figure 24 was made. The English position in 1415 would have been in front of the village and stretching to the left. Note that the foregrounded ridgeline and road are an artistic trope of the period and do not reflect reality. (Private collection)

Fig. 26: Looking south-west down the *Morival*, the field known as *L'Anglais* is in the trees at top left, in the buildings edging Maisoncelle. The line of trees in the upper centre marks a depression in the landscape called the *Fosse a Rogne*. (Livingston)

Fig. 27: Key locations pinned to satellite imagery of Agincourt, looking west, with shadows modelled for approximately 9am on 25 October 1415 through Google Earth Pro™. Note that vertical terrain changes are here exaggerated by a three-to-one ratio in order to more strongly emphasize these features. Overlaid atop this reconstruction of the map are the minor and major medieval roads, along with potential English formations at the traditional location and the alternate location argued in this book. (Livingston)

Fig. 28: Looking east, from the air above the *Morival*, at the farmland across which the English took position, just north of Maisoncelle. (Livingston)

List of Maps

Introduction

We Happy Few

On 15 May 1944, 145 men secretly gathered at Saint Paul's School in London. Prime Minister Winston Churchill was there, as was King George VI. General Dwight D. Eisenhower, the Supreme Commander of the Allied Expeditionary Force in Europe, led the proceedings. Taken together, the extraordinary men who filed into the school's auditorium that day represented nearly the entirety of the Allied command in Great Britain.

It was a unique moment. Rarely were so many leaders gathered in one place, lest a Nazi bomb cripple the command structure by taking them all out at once. Rarer still was what they were there to decide: the final go-ahead for Operation *Overlord*, the invasion of Nazi-occupied France that has been called 'the most prodigious undertaking in the history of warfare'.[1] D-Day, if confirmed, was just a few weeks away.

Nearly four long years earlier, Churchill had famously said about the RAF in the Battle of Britain that 'Never in the field of human conflict was so much owed by so many to so few'. Here, now, it could be said that never before had the fates of so many been held in the hands of so few.

General Bernard Montgomery presented the final plans, pointing to a scale model that had been built of places whose names would soon be etched in our collective memories: Omaha Beach, Saint-Lo, Caen. He concluded with a statement of resolution: 'We shall have to send the soldier in to this party seeing red. Nothing must stop them. If we send them in to battle this way, then we shall succeed.'

Among the many who met this declaration with determined bravado was Churchill's chief of staff, Lieutenant General Hastings Ismay (Figure 1). The moment, he would later recall, reminded him of the words Shakespeare attributed to King Henry V before the battle of Agincourt: 'He which hath no stomach to this fight / Let him depart.'[2]

It should come as little surprise that Agincourt came to Ismay's mind in that extraordinary moment. History is, in a very real sense, a story that we tell ourselves about the past. And the story that the English tell of their victory over the French on 25 October 1415 is one of incomparable glory. It is the story of an army deep in enemy territory – beleaguered and outnumbered – facing a massive gathering of the 'flower of French chivalry', as the chroniclers described it. It's a story of dogged resolve and powerful leadership in the face of terrifying adversity, when a group of men who in their willingness to bleed and die together wrought an improbable but resounding victory. It's a story that stands not just as a central pillar in English history, but also as a central pillar in its nationalistic *mythology*. From the early popularity of the 'Agincourt Carol' in the 15th century to Shakespeare's *Henry V* – from the multiple film adaptations of it to its presence in John Lennon's childhood sketchbook today – Agincourt has been – and still remains – a cultural touchstone in the forging of the English fighting spirit (Figures 2 and 3).

This popularity makes it all the more essential that we attempt to reach back, beyond the myth, to try to understand what really happened on those French fields in 1415.

HISTORY AND TRUTH

I say 'try to understand' because the full truth of Agincourt is something that no one – not even the men who were there – can know. History is a story about the truth, not the truth itself.

Please understand that this should not diminish historians or the writing of history. Quite to the contrary, it should underscore the importance of the task before us: if history is never written in stone, then we can never give up the hard work of refining it.

Think about the legal system. Our laws bind us together as a society. Good or bad, for better or ill, they functionally define who we are and how we behave. Yet when it comes to our laws, one thing we can be certain about is that not everyone will follow them. Full compliance is a dream unlikely to ever be achieved. (Indeed, the very existence of a law almost assuredly depends upon non-compliance: if everyone obeyed, then there would be little point in the law existing!) Importantly, though, we do not, as a society, respond to this inevitable legal failure by abandoning our law codes in favour of lawless anarchy. Instead, we refine the laws. They won't ever be perfect, but if we mean to hold society together we must ever seek that perfection.

So it is with history, which can bind us even more forcefully than law. We don't respond to our inevitable failure to get it perfect by abandoning the effort to achieve perfection. We refine our history. Plug the holes. Close the gaps. Improve it piece by piece. History isn't dead. It's quite vigorously alive. This means, of course, that while the inaccessible truth of the past might not change, the story we tell about it – our history – can and must do so. Complaining about 'revisionist' history is truly complaining about history itself: it's always revisionist.

The work of doing this – of making and remaking history – isn't easy. There's the difficulty of the historical detective work necessary to find those holes, gaps, and improvements. But just as important is the difficulty of facing our own demons along the way: if history binds us, making even the smallest of changes to what we think we know about it can be mighty uncomfortable.

Take, for instance, what Shakespeare has Henry V go on to say *after* those lines that had come to Ismay's mind in 1944:

> This day is called the feast of Crispian.
> He that outlives this day and comes safe home
> Will stand a' tiptoe when this day is named
> And rouse him at the name of Crispian.
> He that shall see this day, and live old age,
> Will yearly on the vigil feast his neighbors
> And say 'Tomorrow is Saint Crispian'.
> Then will he strip his sleeve and show his scars.
> And say, 'These wounds I had upon Crispin's day'.
> Old men forget; yet all shall be forgot,
> But he'll remember with advantages

What feats he did that day. Then shall our names,
Familiar in his mouth as household words,
Harry the King, Bedford and Exeter,
Warwick and Talbot, Salisbury and Gloucester,
Be in their flowing cups freshly remembered.
This story shall the good man teach his son,
And Crispin Crispian shall ne'er go by,
From this day to the ending of the world,
But we in it shall be rememberèd –
We few, we happy few, we band of brothers;
For he today that sheds his blood with me
Shall be my brother; be he ne'er so vile,
This day shall gentle his condition;
And gentlemen in England now abed
Shall think themselves accursed they were not here,
And hold their manhoods cheap whiles any speaks
That fought with us upon Saint Crispin's day.[3]

It's a damn good speech. That Shakespeare fellow, I think we can agree, might well be going places.

But it's not at all true.

Had he lived to old age, 'Harry the King' would hardly have welcomed the general veterans of Agincourt coming to his palace doors to break bread with their 'brother'. And very certainly none of the common men who fought and bled for him at Agincourt were made gentlemen of England on the field or when they got home. They were simply sent on their way – if vile they came then vile they went. Whatever scars they bore, whatever stories they told, the king wasn't sharing them over flowing cups.

Not to mention that Henry V, though probably the first king of England in generations to speak English as his first language, is exceedingly unlikely to have spoken in such perfectly formed metre.

The speech is a story. A version of history that subsumed itself so deeply into the English consciousness that General Ismay, witnessing a moment on which the fate of the free world might well have hinged, saw it through this lens.

Henry V, too, saw the world through his own lenses: a view wrought of his life experiences and the storied histories of *his* past.

The sub-title of this book refers to Henry as a 'scarred king': the stories we tell ourselves about who we are can be drawn from the scars of our experiences – physical, mental, even spiritual – and I am quite certain this was the case with the man who led the English to battle at Agincourt.

None of this is truly blameworthy. We *all* see the world through such lenses. Sometimes a lens can blur the truth. Sometimes it can bring it into sharper relief. But the point on which we must be clear is that we're *always* seeing the world through a lens of one kind or another – Ismay and Henry, you and me.

SOME INITIAL LENSES (AND DEFINITIONS)

In this book I will try to be transparent, if you will, about my own lenses. One of them, you should know straight off, is that I'm often as interested in *how* we know as I am in *what* we know. So the story I want to tell isn't just a ground-shifting new history of Agincourt. It will also be a story about the making of that story. Amid the talk of blood and guts will be discussions of manuscripts and archives as well as landscape and memory. To my mind, we can't have either one without the other.

Another thing to point out at the start: I am uninterested in telling you a pro-English account of Agincourt. That tale has been told again and again and again – often by far greater writers than I could hope to be. (See Shakespeare, William.) Nor am I going to 'flip the script' and write a pro-French narrative of Agincourt. (I don't know how one would do that since the English so thoroughly kicked their tails.) I am an American, and in the present case of studying one of the most extraordinary days in the Hundred Years War I hope that this 'foreign' identity can serve as a feature and not a bug: I don't have a dog in this fight. I simply want to tell the story of the truth of Agincourt as we know it today – as we believe it was for the men who fought and died there.

It may not be the story you know.

Our understanding of what happened at Agincourt has changed dramatically in the six centuries since 1415. In truth, our understanding of the battle has changed in just the past six *years* as we continue to learn more and more about this remarkable and important battle. *Agincourt: Battle of the Scarred King* unfolds the most up-to-date story we have. So, what you're about to read is going to be different from the story I was once taught.

As I said above, it can be uncomfortable when this happens, when there's a difference between what we once believed and what is now believed. Some of what you will read in this book is likely to challenge assumptions you have had about the battle, its victorious king, and much else. I apologize in advance for the discomfort, but not for the new discoveries that cause them.

Likewise, I apologize in advance for the fact that I'll mostly be presenting the names of the people in this book in accordance with the languages of their origin. I know that many English history books refer to the duke of Alençon in 1415 as *John*, but as a Frenchman he would have been most displeased at the notion. His name was *Jean*, and as he died upon that famous ground, I feel it proper to let him keep it as he knew it.

Speaking of spellings, I'll be using the modern spellings of place-names throughout this book to aid readers wanting to follow the events on a map or in person. As one instance that you'll see quite a bit, the subject of this book is near the village we now call Azincourt: so I'll use *Agincourt* for the battle and *Azincourt* for the place. Likewise, I'll refer to Henry V marching through the modern town of Arques-la-Bataille, though in 1415 it was known only as Arques.

Once we get to the battle itself, you'll note that a great many of my translations come from a single volume: Anne Curry's *The Battle of Agincourt: Sources and Translations* (Boydell, 2000). This is a remarkable book, gathering together in translation most of the sources for Agincourt. Anyone wishing to work on the battle is enormously glad for its existence. That said, many of the translations gathered in its pages are somewhat more stilted in their language than will be preferred by the modern reader. Many of the translations also refer to arrow 'fire' or bows 'firing' – which is something that gunpowder weapons do, not bows and arrows. Still, this is the standard source text even among academic researchers of the engagement, so it seemed best to use it as the common reference point here.

WHERE WE BEGIN

It's impossible to say what moments, when and where, truly shift the course of history. A butterfly flapping its wings in Africa, as the saying goes, might birth a storm across the sea. If so, when does the story of that storm begin? Across the sea? With the flapping of the wings? With the birth of the butterfly?

Where, to my present purpose, do I begin the story of Agincourt? There's the landing of the English army in France in 1415, of course. A fine date. But really it started with the English fleet sailing from Southampton, did it not? For that matter, the sailing was the culmination of months of prior preparations, which were only happening because of the king's determination to take his army to France. And that determination, when we break it down, had a lot to do with the circumstances of Henry V's accession to the throne of England in 1413 – circumstances that were fundamentally dependent on how his father had seized that throne from a previous king and set the realm into a decade and more of internal turmoil starting in 1399.

And so it goes in history. There's no beginning. It's literally one thing after another, and everything everywhere – at some level – is related.

I can't tell it all, though. Not in ten books or twenty. I've got to break it down to what's necessary, to what most directly gets us to the fields of northern France where Henry V won his most extraordinary victory. If I'm going to trace the road to Agincourt, I've got to start somewhere.

And because Agincourt is a story with at least two sides, we probably need two starting points: one English, one French.

The first will be arguably the most fateful moment in the life of the man who would win at Agincourt: the moment that the future king of England was shot in the face with an arrow in 1403. The second will be the attempted assassination of a one-eyed man on the streets of Paris in 1392. After that, we'll jump back in time a bit to catch everyone up to the point that Henry V – recovered in body from that arrow wound, if not perhaps fully recovered in mind – set sail for France to make his claim against the crown of the king of France who had gone mad after that near killing.

Part One

Two Beginnings

O for a Muse of fire, that would ascend
The brightest heaven of invention,
A kingdom for a stage, princes to act
And monarchs to behold the swelling scene!

William Shakespeare, *Henry V*, I.Prol.1–4

I

Shrewsbury and Scars, 21 July 1403

He saw the arrow coming.[1]

No matter what else we can conclude about what happened to the future King Henry V on 21 July 1403 – and how it might have affected him all the way through to his great triumph at Agincourt – we can feel confident that on this day an arrow hurtled through the noise and the dust of battle, and that a young man momentarily lifted the visor across the front of his helm. Perhaps he meant to shout an order. Or perhaps he merely yearned for a gasp of fresh air and a glimpse of a stainless blue sky untouched by iron. But the visor went up, and he saw a flash of dark against the light of the sky. An instant later, all was red pain.

He was 16.

21 July 1403 was, we think, a beautiful English summer day. The fields outside the town of Shrewsbury had been green with abundance as the armies had marched by. Now, as Englishmen slaughtered Englishmen there, those crops were trampled into a slurry of blood, piss, and shit (Figure 5).

The battle of Shrewsbury was a sudden horror. Only two weeks earlier, King Henry IV and his son were gathering the English army to assist the earl of Northumberland against border incursions by the Scots. The king was already marching north when word came that Henry Percy, the earl's son, had rebelled against the crown alongside several other lords. This younger Percy, more famously known as Hotspur, was marching south to join his growing forces with those of his uncle, the earl of Worcester. No longer would the king be helping his countrymen. He would instead be fighting them.

The Percy call to rebellion found a ready answer in Cheshire. King Henry IV had only come to the crown in 1399 when he deposed – and probably murdered by starvation – King Richard II. Richard had often relied upon the support of the famed Cheshire archers, and many people of that shire remained fiercely loyal to him after his death. They were more than eager to take arms against the man who had taken his crown.

The Percies themselves had previously been loyal to Henry in his seizure of that crown, just as they had been loyal in supporting the new king against a wide-ranging rebellion that had broken out in Wales under the leadership of the remarkable Owain Glyndŵr. But all that had changed now. A series of broken promises from the crown – and an unwillingness to ransom a nobleman captured by Owain – had the Percies in arms. Bolstered by the men of Cheshire, with more and more fighters streaming to his banners each day, Hotspur marched on the fortified town of Shrewsbury in the hope of taking it.

King Henry IV, once he was aware of the rebellion, had acted quickly. He had changed the course of his march and called more men to arms *en route*. Remarkably, he reached Shrewsbury first, on 20 July. The two armies – each said to be 14,000 men strong – jockeyed for position before facing off across a field of peas north of the town the next morning. For much of the day, the leaders exchanged offers and insults. Soon enough, they knew there would be a fight.

Despite his son's youth, the king had set the prince of Wales in charge of the left wing of his army. The right wing was under the command of the earl of Stafford. Henry himself held the centre under his royal standard. As soon as the battle commenced, the savage efficiency of the Cheshire archers was made clear. Pierced by the arrows, Henry's men 'fell like the leaves that fall in cold weather after frost', writes the chronicler Thomas Walsingham.[2]

And now, as the battle hung in the balance – and the future of the English kingdom with it – an arrow had slipped through that blue sky and struck the crown prince in the face. According to the surgeon who ultimately saved his life, the arrow buried itself six inches deep in his head.

We don't know who shot the arrow. We don't know if it was deliberately aimed for the prince or if it was, as is more likely, simply one of the countless arrows loosed between the lines that by chance found the end of its perfectly parabolic flight here, in the face of the young man whom Shakespeare would name Hal or Harry.

The Bard, as he recounts the battle of Shrewsbury in *King Henry IV, Part I*, does his best to minimize the event. In fact, he moves the moment completely off stage. At the end of Act V, Scene iii, Prince Hal is mocking his old friend Falstaff by throwing a bottle of wine at him amid the tumult of the battle's beginnings. But when the curtain rises on Scene iv, something has clearly happened. Hal and his father enter the stage in the company of Lord John of Lancaster and the Earl of Westmoreland:

KING. I prithee,
Harry, withdraw thyself. Thou bleedest too much.
Lord John of Lancaster, go you with him.
LANCASTER. Not I, my lord, unless I did bleed too.
PRINCE. I beseech your Majesty make up,
Lest your retirement do amaze your friends.
KING. I will do so.
My Lord of Westmoreland, lead him to his tent.
WESTMORELAND. Come, my lord, I'll lead you to your tent.
PRINCE. Lead me, my lord? I do not need your help,
And God forbid a shallow scratch should drive
The Prince of Wales from such a field as this,
Where stain'd nobility lies trodden on,
And rebels' arms triumph in massacres![3]

Remarkably, the scene that Shakespeare presents isn't wholly fiction. We don't know how early people were mythologizing this moment – I suspect it was pretty damn early – but we know that from the beginning our sources speak with one voice when it comes to the prince's wound: he was struck, the men around him tried to take him out of the battle, and he refused to go.

Perhaps it was the instinctive awareness of a born leader who knew that his leaving might well cause the lines under his command to fall back in a retreat that would be likely to turn into a rout. Given Henry V's ultimate place as a nationalist English hero – due to Agincourt, the subject of this book – I suspect this ideal explanation is the one most people would assume. But some, with a slightly dimmer view of men upon the field of battle, might think his refusal to leave nothing more than that bravado that is inarguably toxic in so many social interactions – but is nevertheless of some genuine utility when it comes to convincing human beings to stride into the bloody, deadly tumult of war. Others, less critical but no less honest about the human condition, might see nothing more at work than mere shock.

At some point, someone tried to pull the arrow out. The arrow shaft came free, but the arrowhead into which it was socketed did not. This would not have been surprising. Such arrowheads were just loosely affixed to the ends of the shafts: the *intention* was for the arrowhead to come loose in the body, where its lingering presence could continue to do damage to the victim. Because of this, in combination with the presence of any barbs on the arrowheads themselves – which would catch against the fast-swelling tissues of the body's attempt to seal the entrance wound – we know that embedded arrows most often weren't *pulled* out of the victim, but *pushed*. Horrifying as it is to imagine, an arrowhead can sometimes do less damage being shoved out the other side of the body than torn back out through the original hole.

In the prince's case – whether it was the reason the arrow was pulled or not – pushing the arrow through was not an option. The 'shallow scratch' that Hal laughs off in Shakespeare was an arrow that had plunged six inches into his face and left its arrowhead lodged against his spine at the base of his skull. Pushing it further would have paralysed or, more likely, killed him.

For what it's worth, I suspect that the person who tried to pull the arrow out didn't know that just yet. I think it was the prince himself, who at the moment of impact instinctively tried to get the damnable thing out and away. I admit, however, that there is nothing to base this upon other than my own instinct and the fact that I can't imagine anyone *else* daring to yank it out in such short order – and it's hard for me to imagine the prince doing what he did next with a 30 inch-long arrow shaft sticking out of his head.

Because at this moment, the right wing of the king's army disintegrated. Its commander, the earl of Stafford, had fallen, and in short order the lines were collapsing in flight. As the wing beside it broke apart, the centre, where the king's banner yet flew, faltered.

People like to imagine medieval battles as long slogs of men pressing another to annihilation, but this sudden collapse was how most of them ended. In the Middle Ages, battles were quick things, most often ended as Shrewsbury appeared about to end: one side wavered and broke in a deadly rout as men were struck down in the mad pursuit.

Hotspur saw his moment, and he ordered his men to charge.

The rebels streamed down against the king's evaporating right and wavering centre. The royal standard bearer was struck down and killed. For a moment the battle, and Henry's crown with it, seemed lost.

And in that moment, with an arrowhead lodged against his spine, young prince Hal ordered a charge of his own. His left wing, wheeling, drove into Hotspur's charging flank.

The lines mixed as they slammed into one another. Friend and foe all looked alike upon the field. The chaos is hard to imagine. Thousands died.

In the end, Henry IV survived. Hotspur did not. The crown was saved.

Even as the king set about wreaking vengeance upon the rebel leaders – Hotspur's body was ordered to be cut up into four pieces to be displayed across England, an act for which literal receipts[4] exist – he sought help for the son who had done so much to win the day.

Surgeons on the field had no remedy. If he hadn't pulled the arrow himself, they almost assuredly pulled it at this time. Not long afterwards, the prince of Wales was taken to Kenilworth Castle, a wagon ride over bumpy roads for more than 60 miles.

Wounds kill in any age. They were far deadlier in the pre-modern world, and head-wounds were often the worst of all. In the American Civil War, penetrating head injuries had an estimated mortality rate of over 70 per cent, and those odds were not improved by a foreign object being left in the patient's body.[5] As one of the characters in Geoffrey Chaucer's *Canterbury Tales* (about 1390) notes, it was well-known in medical circles 'that unless men can grab the arrow or draw it out, a wound only superficially healed is rarely cured'.[6] Of course, in a pre-modern context, the extraction process itself could be just as fatal as the wound. The famed French surgeon Henri de Mondeville suggested that the first step in any attempted extraction was to be sure the patient had attended to his spiritual needs through confession and his earthly needs through the drawing up of a will. One couldn't be too careful.[7]

There were times, though, when surgeons had no choice but to leave an arrowhead in place. King David II of Scotland, for instance, received two arrow wounds at the battle of Neville's Cross in 1346. Two doctors from York – William of Bolton and Hugh of Kilvington – were summoned to the castle of Bamburgh to attend to him.[8] After they removed the first arrow, they determined that removing the second arrowhead in his head would be fatal, so it remained there, causing him recurrent bouts of terrible pain until his death in 1371.[9] Getting it out, though, was always the best choice if it was possible.

To this end, over the days and perhaps weeks to come, doctors from across the realm attempted to ply the young man with potions, prayers, and no doubt an array of painful manipulations. Nothing helped.

At last, John Bradmore, a surgeon from London, came to Kenilworth. Remarkably, he left us an account of what happened next in a medical treatise he wrote, called *Philomena*.

The arrow, Bradmore records, had entered 'beside the nose on the left side ... and the head of the arrow, after the shaft was extracted, stood firm in the back part of the bone of the head six inches deep'.[10] Leaving it in, as had been done with David II, was simply not an option. As it was, the prince's health was threatened by seizures owing to the arrowhead's proximity to his spinal cord: the involuntary movement they could cause might kill him in any number of ways. So Bradmore immediately began a day-and-night routine of using compresses and special ointments to try to calm the inflammation around the arrowhead while he decided the best course of action. It didn't take him long to recognize that the same proximity to the spine that was threatening seizures meant not only that the arrowhead had to be removed, but also that it couldn't be pushed through. It needed to come out the way it had gone in, which meant – horrifyingly – he needed to *enlarge* the wound in the teenager's head as wide as the widest part of the arrowhead.

There is a popular notion that medieval medicine is the height – perhaps I should say the depth – of barbarity. But while Bradmore's treatment may seem primitive by our standards, it stands on solid medical grounds. He correctly judged the problems at hand. He knew what needed to be done. And given the limited facilities and the limited fields of knowledge available to him, that he managed to do it remains truly astonishing.

He began by wrapping clean linen cloth around thin sticks made from the pith of an old elder tree. All this was, as Bradmore reports, 'saturated in rose-infused honey'. The sticks probed the wound to its bottom. The linen 'tents', as he called them, kept the wound from closing. The honey acted as an anti-bacterial. Using larger and larger tents, he gradually opened the wound until he had essentially made a tunnel into the young man's head.

Meanwhile, he designed and had built a set of tongs that had teeth on their inside and outside surfaces such that tightening a screw through the interior threads pressed the exterior teeth outwards. He inserted this device into the empty socket of the arrowhead and tightened the screw. The exterior teeth, as designed, pressed out and gripped the interior of the socket. 'Then, wiggling it to and fro, little by little', Bradmore says, he extracted the tool and arrowhead both, much to the relief of 'the diverse gentlemen and the servants of the prince standing by'. He used a syringe to cleanse the wound with fine white wine. Next, he created a paste made of boiled breadcrumbs that were strained and then mixed with barley flour, honey, and a coniferous resin (which has anti-microbial qualities). He packed this around a tent and put it back into the wound. Repeating this process every two days with smaller and smaller tents, after nearly three weeks he had cleansed and packed the wound. After this, he tended to the prince with more ointments and compresses until the flesh had healed and his spasms were no longer a threat. 'Thus', Bradmore concludes, 'thanks be to God! – he was perfectly cured'.

His treatment had taken weeks under Bradmore's care, after who knows how many days of unsuccessful treatments before the good doctor took over. It's hard to imagine the agony that the 16-year-old boy endured. Bradmore says nothing of it – no doubt not wanting to suggest any weakness on the part of his royal patient – but a reasonable assumption is that the prince of Wales was given ample doses of what they would have called Venice Treacle, or theriac: a closely guarded and very expensive concoction of 64 ingredients that included opium among its roots, leaves, barks, herbs, fruits, oils, and various other elements.

Even with the dulling effect of such medications, which were unreliable at best, it is hard to imagine the trauma – both physical and mental – that would have resulted from such an experience. Many suffered wounds in battle, it is true, but few indeed could afford the expert care that assured young Hal's survival. Others suffered and died. He had suffered and lived.

To the end of his days, he remembered what had happened at Shrewsbury. It marked him.

Part of that mark was physical. Despite Bradmore's expert work and careful ointments, there must have been a scar. Given the depth and position of the wound, I suspect this scar ran the length of the right side of Henry's nose. No one describes this. Their silence, like Bradmore's on the pain, is presumably a nod to royal status. But it's difficult to imagine that it wasn't prominent. Interestingly, the posthumous portrait of Henry V that now hangs in the National Portrait Gallery in London shows this king – and this king alone – in profile. The rest of the royal portraits show both sides of their subjects' faces, but the right side of Henry V's face is forever hidden from view.

More powerful than the physical scar, though, was the mental one.

In large measure, Shakespeare built the two parts of his history of Henry IV around the prince's journey from being Hal, who socializes with drunks and low-lifes, to being the man who, changed, could hold court and rule a kingdom. As Henry V puts it at the end of *Henry IV, Part 2*:

Presume not that I am the thing I was,
For God doth know, so shall the world perceive,
That I have turn'd away my former self.[11]

Shakespeare may have popularized the notion of Henry V's change, but he did not invent it. Chroniclers had already noted his turn from youthful frivolities to an adulthood of prayerful divinities.[12] Maturity can come from many things, but it's likely that the prince's wound at Shrewsbury was one of them.

Henry had suffered brutally, a trauma that is hard to imagine. But more than this, he had survived what perhaps no one else had survived, a triumph that is hard to comprehend. He might well have believed himself blessed by God.

He had also learned at first hand that the crown was only as strong as the man who wore it. His father's once-loyal subjects had turned against him. A countryman had loosed the arrow that had plunged into his own skull. When it came his time to lead, he would show his strength.

From this point forwards, events may have set in motion the spirit of destiny and the dedication to power-in-arms that would in time drive Henry to the fields of France. From this point forwards, though no one could know it, England was marching towards Agincourt.

2

Assassination and Madness, 13 June 1392

Just after midnight of 13 June 1392, a one-eyed man and a small party of companions made their way from the royal residence of the Hôtel Saint-Pol to the man's home in Paris. Six figures hid in the shadowed streets ahead, waiting for their moment.

Born in 1336, one year before what's usually considered the opening of the Hundred Years War, the one-eyed man had lived his entire life in a world at war. His own hands were unashamedly bloody as a result. He was known to his enemies, and to some of his friends, as the Butcher.

His real name was Olivier – named after his father, whom he would follow as lord of the château of Clisson in Brittany. Since he was the fifth person of his name to hold the title, the history books name him Olivier V de Clisson. In 1341, the duke of Brittany died, leaving behind a succession dispute between two rival claimants for the title: the late duke's half-brother and a nephew of the king of France. What would probably have been a largely internal matter in Brittany became, because of the Hundred Years War, a proxy for the conflict between England and France. Money, materiel, and men swarmed in from both sides, and what would come to be known as the War of the Breton Succession was quickly under way.

Olivier's father supported the French king's side in the matter, and in 1342 he was in charge of the defence of the important city of Vannes when it fell to an English siege. Captured, Olivier's father was eventually released on what was – at least to the French court – considered to be a lesser ransom than ought to have been paid for his freedom. The suspicion was that he had secretly cut a deal with the English, one that had involved handing them the city without a proper fight.

Afterwards, Olivier's father was invited by the French to participate in a tournament, where he was arrested for treason. And although no evidence was provided to the public – historians haven't found much, either – he was found guilty and beheaded in 1343. His head was placed on a pike in Nantes as a warning to any Bretons thinking of aiding the enemy. What remained of his body was hung by its armpits on the highest level of the Gibbet of Montfaucon: 16 stone columns atop a hill outside of Paris, with at least two tiers of beams for hanging victims between them.

Olivier was seven.

His mother took him and his younger brother to Nantes to see their father's head rotting in the sun. She made them swear vengeance for the death.

For the next 17 years, Olivier learned how to fight, while his mother raised what was essentially a pirate fleet to prey on their enemies, earning herself the nickname 'The Lioness of Brittany'. It was awful business. At the age of nine, Olivier watched his little brother die of exposure after one fight left the two of them and their mother adrift at sea for five days. He lived for a time in the court of King Edward III of England – the man who had effectively started the Hundred Years War by declaring himself the rightful king of France. When he was old enough, Olivier took up arms for the English cause and fought in his home country, spilling French blood.

These were dark years for France. A dramatic loss to Edward at the battle of Crécy in 1346, followed by the English seizure of Calais in 1347, gave the English a momentum that was slowed only by the sudden arrival of the Black Death, which tore through Europe and left fewer people to fight and less money to pay them with. When the pandemic slowed and war began anew, there were more crushing blows for the French, including a loss at the battle of Poitiers in 1356, in which King Jean II of France himself was captured.

France's treasury was by now depleted, and her spirit wounded. Tens of thousands had died in enormous battles like Crécy and

Poitiers. We have no way of knowing how many more French died in the smaller, untold skirmishes between those grand stages, or in the agony of starvation, exposure, or the other grievous harms that inevitably followed so much conflict. England had won great wealth in the fighting, but it was also burning through money at an unsustainable rate. Foreign wars are expensive. Edward's ability to continue the conflict, despite his successes, was not inexhaustible.

Like two weary, battered warriors, France and England finally came to an agreement to end the fight. The Treaty of Brétigny, signed in 1360, set the ransom for the imprisoned king of France at three million crowns and put roughly a third of France under the control of Edward's son and heir, the Black Prince.

Looking back, it's remarkable that this peace lasted as long as it did. The Treaty of Brétigny was, after all, made under extreme duress with extreme terms. The land given up was of incalculable value both economically and socially. More calculable, but no less daunting, was the enormous balance due for the French king's ransom. The three million coins owed to England – they are often called *crowns* today, but at the time they were specifically *écus à la chaise* (literally 'Shields of the Throne') – each contained roughly 4.5 grams of gold. As I'm writing this book, market price for gold has been roughly 60 US dollars a gram for a couple of years, meaning that in gold content alone we're talking something in the order of $800,000,000 today.

That's a *lot* of cash.

It was so much cash that France had a great deal of trouble coming up with it. Though the French claimed to be shaking the cushions for every last cent, even at the signing of the treaty in 1360 it was clear that they wouldn't have enough to get their king out of hock.

Meanwhile, Edward was chafing at the cost of his royal peer's elaborate upkeep. Prison for such men was hardly the dungeon of Hollywood imagination. Those didn't really exist for common people, much less for men of status like the king of France. Jean was instead maintained in relative luxury in the king of England's palaces. Being a king had to count for something.

To help raise the money for his ransom – and, quite honestly, to get him off Edward's account books – the king of France was allowed to return home. In his place, 40 high-born French were swapped with the English to guarantee the terms of the treaty. Among them was one of the king's sons. At the time, it was thought they would be in prison for six months.

Three years later, his father's ransom still unpaid, the French prince escaped an English prison and returned in secret to France. His father, already ashamed that his realm hadn't paid the promised sum to his captors, was aghast at the dishonour of his son's escape. So in early 1364 the king sailed for England, volunteering himself for imprisonment to restore his good name. King Edward had no choice but to take him back.

No matter the niceties of his captivity, though, a few months after he returned to England, the king of France took ill and died.

In France, his eldest son took the crown. His name was Charles V. He had been managing most of the administration of the realm already, but his rule was now official. Among other fires he had to deal with immediately, the war was still raging in Brittany. It wasn't going well, and our man Olivier de Clisson had a lot to do with it.

At the battle of Auray in 1364 a Breton–English army defeated the forces of the French-backed claimant, who was killed in the fight. It was the end of the War of the Breton Succession, with the English-supported side the victor. Olivier had lost an eye in the battle, but he had won a growing reputation: the plan that had seized the victory was said to have been his.

Like so many other men who faced the looming peace in France and now Brittany, Olivier looked elsewhere to ply his trade. In 1367 he was under the command of the Black Prince in what is now Spain, the latest proxy battleground between the English and French, when the English won another devastating victory at the battle of Nájera.

The new French king, to say the least, hadn't been dealt the best hand. But if we can say one thing about the man, it's that Charles would prove a very good gambler: he knew when and on whom to make his bets.

First on his list was Bertrand du Guesclin, who had been captured by the English at both Auray and Nájera, but who was nevertheless widely regarded as a brave, loyal, and smart leader. He was made constable of France, a title that meant power and wealth: being in charge of the king's army gave him the ability to sway policies foreign and domestic, and to enrich himself on war booty.

Charles also called upon Olivier, the man who had faced Bertrand in both of those battles and beaten him. The king offered Olivier choice lands in Normandy to buy his allegiance.

So Olivier, some 26 years after he had made an oath to avenge his father's death, joined the French cause and quickly became a very trusted lieutenant for Bertrand.

Together, they would often have met with the king at the Hôtel Saint-Pol, which Charles had recently built as a palace for himself and his family just outside Paris. It was quieter than it was within the bustling medieval city. The air was certainly far cleaner. Here, they coordinated a steady push back against the English, which will be discussed in the next chapter.

When Bertrand died in 1380 – after a long and successful career as constable of France – there was no question as to who would replace him. Only a few months later, Charles V died. His son, who took the crown as Charles VI, was just shy of 12. Olivier loyally stood by him as an advisor and a steadying hand on the tiller of military affairs. They became quite close. Olivier, already in possession of substantial income from his lands, had by now added to them considerably. He was one of the most powerful men in the realm.

No surprise, then, that after spending the day of 13 June 1392 at the Hôtel Saint-Pol, attending Corpus Christi festivities with a king who was known to many of his subjects as Charles the Beloved, the house that one-eyed Olivier was returning to on this night in June was no ordinary Parisian domicile. It was, plainly put, a mansion. It still exists today, much updated over the centuries, but still whispering of what a glorious place it was even in Olivier's day. By the strange turns of the world, it now houses the museum of the National Archives of France.

Pre-eminent men tend to make enemies, and Olivier was no exception.

Which is why, on this quiet, summer night, six men were planning to kill him.

The would-be assassins were led by Sir Pierre de Craon, a violent nobleman who had recently been banished from Paris. We don't know what had happened, exactly, but we know that he had fled to Brittany. The duke there, despite owing his position to Olivier, had nevertheless grown to detest him. He had convinced Pierre that Olivier was to blame for his troubles. Now, Pierre had snuck back into Paris to take his vengeance with the help of some friends.

The attack came just minutes after Olivier left the palace in the company of a handful of friends and some servants bearing torches against the darkness. As the party passed by a darkened alley, Pierre and his men burst out of the shadows, weapons in hand, shouting for Olivier's death. The assailants were on him almost immediately. The torches were thrown to the ground as Olivier's companions and servants fled.

The men attacking him had swords. Olivier had only a dagger. But he used it well, plunging and slashing as his horse reared in the commotion. He took multiple wounds across his legs as the men assaulted him, but his mail shirt turned the blades that would otherwise have taken his life on the spot. At last, he was heaved from his horse. Whether it was from a blow to his upper body or his horse's panic – or, as I suspect, a combination of the two – he was thrown head-first into the door of a bakery. Knocked unconscious, he hit the stones and didn't move.

Thinking him dead, Pierre and the others fled into the night.

THE MADNESS

The commotion in the street woke the townspeople and alerted guards. The king himself rushed to the scene with a crowd of courtiers and soldiers. To his relief, his constable was alive. While we can't envy Olivier the headache he had, he'd been lucky. His wounds were superficial.

The king's relief, though, quickly turned to rage. His constable might have survived the attack, but the attempted assassination of a man so close to the crown was not something that could go unanswered. Despite the dark, Olivier had recognized Pierre's face among his attackers. So the hunt to find him and the others was on.

Pierre, racing away from Paris, soon found out that Olivier had survived and identified him as one of the assailants. He fled to

Brittany, looking for protection. The duke did not offer it, though he allowed Pierre to move on. Several of Pierre's accomplices were meanwhile caught and beheaded. His lands and property were seized or destroyed.

Olivier was convinced that the duke of Brittany had been behind the whole enterprise and might even now be hiding the fugitive. Charles was more than willing to listen to his constable's insistence on the duke's guilt. Other leaders at court were likewise interested in taking Brittany down a peg whether the accusations were true or not. In July, the king made his decision: he would raise an army and march against the duke. Olivier loaned him the money to make it happen as soon as possible.

This was not normal. Though people might imagine medieval monarchs as beholden to no one, the truth is that their power was dependent upon an intricate web of relationships. A crown, without the backing of others, wasn't much more than a fancy hat. A king's rule required the obedience of the ruled, which meant that the king needed others in positions of power to consent to his decisions, most especially the decision to go to war. In England, this meant that a king needed the agreement of Parliament and his ruling nobles for any significant act. France had essentially the same thing. But what Charles now did – declaring war against one of those ruling nobles – he did without the united agreement of the ruling classes.

There were quite a few of these nobles who ought to have been consulted, but we need only address three here, as they or their heirs will continue to play roles in the pages that follow. The first was Charles' younger brother, Louis, who at the age of 20 had just been elevated to the position of the duke of Orléans. The other two were uncles to the king, and they had worked hard to direct the governance of France after the death of their brother until Charles had been old enough to take control in his own name in 1388. The first of these was Philippe II, duke of Burgundy. Known popularly as Philippe the Bold, he was a powerful figure with enormous wealth in the Low Countries – the name given to a patchwork quilt of medieval administrative regions centred largely on what is today the Netherlands, Belgium, and Luxembourg. One of the largest and wealthiest of these regions was the county of Flanders, and Philippe was its count. This powerbase meant that he always had an eye towards England: the riches of Flanders were inherently tied to the English wool trade, so any disruption to that economic engine – such as a war – was a disruption to Philippe's treasury. The other important uncle was Jean, the duke of Berry.

When Charles announced his intention to march against the duke of Brittany, Louis of Orléans quickly fell in line. As many inexperienced men are, he seemed anxious to get to the business of making war. Jean of Berry quietly disapproved, but Philippe made no secret at all of his fury. He was gravely worried that any action against the duke of Brittany would result in greater friction with England, to the jeopardy of all.

Charles would hear none of it.

The king was now in his early twenties. After a childhood under the thumb of his uncles, he was excited to stake his own claim to authority. So he ignored them and pressed on.

He was, however, in the most clinical meaning of the term, *anxious*. It would be later said that he had not been sleeping well and was suffering recurrent fevers. They were the first signs that something serious was wrong, though no one on the campaign would have suspected it.

On 5 August, as Charles was leading his army through a forest near Le Mans, his anxieties took a far more serious turn. The king had what can only be described as a psychotic break.

Jean Juvénal des Ursins, a French chronicler writing in the 1430s or 1440s, tells us that a man dressed in rags – himself probably not of sound mind – abruptly ran out of the woods in front of the king. He grabbed the bridle of Charles's horse and began screaming of treason in the king's ranks, warning him not to go further lest he fall into a trap laid by his enemies. The man was driven off, but not long afterwards a page accompanying the king grew drowsy in the summer heat and let drop a lance. The clanging of it startled Charles, who 'entered into a great and extraordinary frenzy, and he ran to and fro. He attacked anyone who came near and killed four men. Others immediately grabbed him and constrained him, and he was taken to his lodgings.'[1] Other writers give more detail – whether from rumour or their own imaginations, we don't know – about how he killed the page first, and that Louis of Orléans had tried to stop his older brother and barely escaped the king's manic sword-swinging (Figure 4). The king could only be approached after his sword had been broken, some said, at which point he was wrestled to the ground. He fell into a coma and was rushed back to Le Mans.

Charles the Beloved had become Charles the Mad.

In the immediate hours and days, while the king lay catatonic, Louis of Orléans tried to take control of the situation, but he was quickly pushed aside by Philippe the Bold with the support of the duke of Berry. The king's uncles saw to it that the Brittany campaign was immediately cancelled. Soon enough, whether planted or rising organically, rumours began to swirl that Charles was the victim of a supernatural malevolence. The devil had targeted the crown of France, and it didn't take long for it to be suggested that the constable of France and other 'evil' counsellors were to blame. Remembrances of how Olivier had once been aligned with the English didn't help his defence. Soon enough, even after the king was awake and semi-lucid, Olivier found himself on the run, condemned by the French parliament. The dukes of Burgundy and Berry took over control of the realm in the absence of clear governance from the king.

Many modern writers have tried to diagnose the king's condition from the stories that were told about it: that it came and went, that sometimes he refused to bathe, that sometimes he couldn't recognize his queen, that sometimes he thought his bones were made of glass ready to shatter. This latter condition – sometimes called 'the glass delusion', with Charles its first known victim – comes from the autobiography of Enea Silvio Piccolomini, who became Pope Pio II in 1458. He wrote that the king 'sometimes thought that he was glass, and could not be touched. He inserted iron splints into his clothes and armoured himself in many ways so that, falling, he would not be broken.'[2] It is fascinating, even salacious stuff, but we can't know if any of it is really true. No one in government had much incentive to share the specifics of the king's condition, so the little information that has come down to us is as liable to be unsubstantiated guesswork as it is to be substantiated fact. Perhaps it was, as many think, paranoid schizophrenia. Perhaps it was something else. In the end, the precise nature of the king's psychosis just isn't known.

Whatever its exact nature, it was real. And, because Charles was king, it had a grave impact on the kingdom. The whole point of the monarchy was to have all authority passing through a single individual: if that individual suffered from a debilitating condition, the entire system faltered. Worse, the system of governance had no real mechanism for dealing with a problem such as this. A king's death had precedent. By the extension of that precedent, a king's permanent mental incapacitation might have been a hill easily climbed: there would have been a power struggle over who would be the permanent regent until the king's passing, but it would probably have resolved itself quickly. In the case of Charles VI, though, the realm was dealing with the worst of all possibilities. The king was a young man with many years to live. And the worst bouts of his madness came and went. When he was lucid – or believed to be lucid – he was the king in all his power. When he was not, those around him had no choice but to maintain the fiction that he was still in charge, because there was no telling when he might be once more in control of his faculties.

The result was a struggle over the king's authority. Those close to the levers of power wanted to have a handle on them when the king wasn't lucid, so they aimed to convince him – during those times when he was relatively stable – that they and no one else ought to be allowed full control.

For the decades that followed the attempted assassination of Olivier V de Clisson on the darkened streets of Paris, the crown of France wavered and shook. Its ruling elites attacked each other more than they did France's enemies. By the time that Henry V invaded in 1415, he was marching against a realm that had dissolved into on-and-off civil war.

It would have disastrous consequences.

Part Two

A Brief History of the Hundred Years War

As God hears me, my lords, the English are so filled with their own greatness and have won so many big victories that they have come to believe they cannot lose. In battle they are the most confident nation in the world. The more blood they see flowing, whether it is their enemy's or their own, the fiercer and more determined they grow.

Olivier V de Clisson, constable of France,
1373, according to Jean Froissart[1]

3

Crécy and the Model Glory, 1337–77

From the beginning, the intermittent mental problems of the king of France could have been a clarion call for attacks by his enemies – England foremost among them. France was fortunate, therefore, that Richard II, the king of England when Charles' madness first started, had little interest in pursuing the Hundred Years War. It's important to understand why this is so, which means understanding the Hundred Years War from its beginning.

On a fundamental level, the Hundred Years War happened because English kings held part of France in the form of Gascony and could theoretically make a claim to the throne of France – and the men who happened to *be* on the throne of France weren't great fans of either notion. This is true, but it's also not the full story. Wars are very rarely about just one thing.

The countries involved in the D-Day assaults in 1944, for instance, were not all fighting for the same cause. They were fighting the same enemy, it's true, but exactly *why* they were fighting that enemy didn't always line up – not between them as nations and very certainly not between the hundreds of thousands of individuals engaged in the undertaking.[1]

So it was with the Hundred Years War. There were many social, economic, and ultimately even religious issues that drove England and France to war and kept them at it across so many years. Aside from that, the war that began wasn't the same war that ended over a century later. Assuming its traditional dating is accurate – dates that are, at the very least, fluid – the Hundred Years War had been going on for 78 years at the time of the battle of Agincourt and would continue for another 38 years after it. As generations succeeded generations in the conflict, the war inevitably metastasized like a horrific cancer through the body politic of both countries. It was, in the end, about a *lot* of things.

For that matter, one of the truths most often forgotten about the Hundred Years War is that it was never just about England and France – any more than the Cold War was just about the United States and the Soviet Union. The conflict had two primary belligerents, but it inevitably drew in almost everyone around them as other leaders were forced to choose sides. We've already seen this in the career of Olivier de Clisson, who had fought in the proxy wars in both Brittany and Castile.

This isn't the place for a complete history of the Hundred Years War. Our focus here is on the battle of Agincourt, a victory so pronounced, so famous, that it makes most forget that the English actually lost the war. But context matters, so let's at least start with the essential skeleton of the thing and add the muscles and sinew as needed.

At a most basic level, the immediate cause of the Hundred Years War was the fact that in 1337 the English crown had claim to a sizeable portion of what we now think of as France in the form of Gascony, the south-western corner of the modern country. The primary reason for this is that the extraordinary Eleanor of Aquitaine, who inherited those lands, married the man who became King Henry II of England in 1152 – a man who himself held claim to huge swathes of land in Normandy and elsewhere in France. Together, their combined holdings were roughly half the lands of modern France. Short-term, these lands plus those of England formed the Angevin Empire. Long-term, they set up the conditions for the Hundred Years War, because the English lands in France didn't *belong* to the English in the modern sense. They *belonged* to the king of France. The English only *held* them.

You can think about this like the difference between buying a house with a mortgage. The mortgaged house doesn't truly belong to you, but to the bank. You are renting-to-own, and the bank is meanwhile allowing you to live in the house so long as you follow their rules regarding payments, insurance minimums, and other requirements.

In the case of Gascony, the rules of the bank – here, the king of France – were that the person holding the land needed to pay homage for it. This was a formal ceremony that served as a public acknowledgment that the land truly belonged to the king, with all the social, political, and cultural connotations that this implied. It was an acknowledgment that the king was, in truth, the lord in charge.

There were other factors and complications, but even at this simplified level we can see the fundamental issue with the English lands in France: to hold his lands in Gascony, a king of England had to acknowledge that a king of France was his lord. The degree to which this theoretical problem became a real problem came and went depending on whether the players involved wanted to make a big deal of it. But it is certainly not a stretch to say that it was an ever-present strain between the two countries.

The situation between these geopolitical powers deteriorated further at the end of the 13th century as local disputes in Gascony stoked the fires of greater conflict and pushed the two kingdoms into a war that was ended by the Treaty of Paris in 1303. One of the many stipulations of the peace would be that the rival kings – Edward I of England and Philippe IV of France – would marry their children to each other. Edward I died in 1307, but his son, the newly crowned Edward II, went ahead with the agreed marriage to Philippe IV's daughter, Isabella. For a brief window, it looked as if all might turn out well between the powers, but Edward II's reign faltered, and Isabella helped lead the effort to depose him in favour of their son, Edward III, who took the throne in 1327.

Meanwhile, in France, Philippe IV had died in 1314, as had his son and heir, Louis X, in 1316. Louis' son was crowned at birth but died five days later, at which point the crown went to the second son of Philippe IV, who ruled as Philippe V until he died without a male heir in 1322. This brought the third son of Philippe IV to the throne: Charles IV, who also died in 1328, once more without a male heir.

It was a remarkable string of bad luck, and it left the kingdom of France in something of a bind. Philippe IV's bloodlines had all died out but one: the line of Isabella, which was most vigorously alive in her son. But given that he was Edward III, the king of England, few in France were interested in things going that way. So instead of giving the crown to the English nephew of the dead Charles IV, they gave it to Charles' French paternal cousin, who became Philippe VI, the first of the kings from the family Valois.

It was inevitable that more disputes would arise between the English and the French, and eventually it happened that when Philippe VI called upon Edward III to do his required homage for Gascony, the English king refused to do so. Philippe consequently declared the English lands in France to be forfeit – rather like the bank evicting you for not paying your mortgage – to which Edward responded by declaring war ... and in the process declaring himself the rightful king of France through his mother's bloodline (Figure 6). If he owned the bank, he couldn't be evicted.

Just like that, the Hundred Years War was off and running.

CRÉCY, 1346

The first years of the war saw the French attacking English coastal towns and positions in Gascony, and the English twice attempting invasions from the lands of their allies in the Low Countries – with whom they shared an extremely lucrative wool trade. The events of these years were *enormously* important in historical terms, but when it comes to the subject of this book they were background noise compared to what exploded in 1346. In that year, Philippe gathered a massive army and sent it against the English in the south-west of France under the command of his son and heir-apparent. This invasion ran up against the fortified town of Aiguillon and, beginning in April, laid siege to it. Though they held out, the outnumbered English sent out a call to England for reinforcements.

Here we'll need to slow down and get into the weeds a bit, because Henry V *very* much had the events of this year in mind when he invaded France in 1415. He was, I think, trying to replicate them.

On 12 July 1346, Edward landed in France with an army of some 15,000 men. Interestingly, they came ashore not in Gascony, but in Normandy on the Cotentin peninsula. With so much of the French military might engaged in the south, the English landing at the town of Saint-Vaast-la-Hougue was almost completely unopposed. By coincidence, it was a stretch of shoreline that would have been known to General Ismay and the other men gathered to discuss D-Day nearly 600 years later: Utah Beach was just over 15 miles south at the base of the peninsula.

Edward's invasion would come to be known as the Crécy Campaign, but its namesake battle would not be fought until 26 and 27 August. Between the king's arrival and that great victory lay hundreds of miles of French roads, countless skirmishes, and several near disasters.

The first major event in the campaign was the sacking of Caen on 26 July. The historical heart of Normandy, Caen was a large and prosperous city when the English army marched towards it. The townspeople knew they were coming: in the two weeks since their arrival Edward and his men had blazed a steady path of destruction along the roads down the spine of the Cotentin peninsula. Towns were pillaged and often burnt. The French refugees would have been a stream of despair ahead of the English army.

With the main French force still besieging Aiguillon in Gascony, Philippe and his remaining commanders were working hard to spin up a second army to meet the English, but they needed time. Caen was a chance to buy them some: a large, walled, well-provisioned city, it could surely hold out for quite a while.

It didn't.

The city of Caen spread out beyond the protection of its walls, and its defenders made the surprising decision to attempt a defence of these outskirts rather than leaving them to be looted and fired. The militia and townspeople marched out and lined up at the edge of the town to stop the English. Edward, in response, ordered his men to array for a fight.

The sight of the English army would have been daunting to even the most professional and prepared soldiers. To these people who had gathered to defend their homes it must have been pure terror. When the English archers sent up an initial volley – a cloud of shafts whose high-pitched whistle was a song of death – the defenders broke and ran for the safety of Caen's walls.

Edward, perhaps fearing some kind of entrapment, tried to keep control of his men. When they started to run after the townspeople, he ordered them to stop. But nobody was listening. They stormed the streets, entering the city before the gates could be closed.

For five days the proud city screamed.

Edward wrote in a letter that 'a great number of nobles, knights, gentlemen, and militia were slain' on the French side, without bothering to make a count of the total dead, which must have run into the thousands.[2] The chronicler Jean le Bel, one of our earliest accounts of the moment, gives grim details of what he described as a 'great slaughter': 'it was pitiful to see the townsmen and their women, daughters, children: they didn't know which way to turn, and had to watch their wives and daughters raped, their houses smashed open, and all their belongings plundered.' There were 120 nuns taking shelter at the Abbaye aux Dames, he reports, along with 40 lay sisters. 'They were all raped', and their abbey 'virtually razed to the ground along with a large part of the town'.[3]

While the sacking of Caen was a vicious, brutal horror for the French, it was an enormous windfall for the English: so much was looted from the city that they simply couldn't carry it. Edward, changing his plans, had the wealth sent back to England on the ships that had ferried him across the English Channel. He had to be thrilled by both the much-needed financial boost – he had been treading perilously close to bankrupting the realm – and the propaganda coup of the victory.

Edward must also have been thrilled by how little effective resistance he had encountered up to this point. The riches he sent home were accompanied by letters ordering reinforcements of men and supplies to meet him at Le Crotoy on the mouth of the River Somme. It was over 150 miles away across enemy territory, but Edward apparently anticipated little problem in conducting a march there, raiding and pillaging as he went, a tactic that historians call a *chevauchée*. Once at Le Crotoy, he could resupply, offload plunder, and either pull out of France or connect with a smaller allied army that had invaded French holdings from the Low Countries.

If Edward thought things would continue to be so easy, he was gravely mistaken. By the time the English army had marched out of Caen and reached the south bank of the Seine at Rouen, Philippe was already gathering a second French army on the north bank. The bridge between them had been shattered.

Edward marched up-river, seeking a way across the water, but Philippe had wisely ordered all the crossings – from Rouen to Paris – destroyed or heavily garrisoned. The further the English marched, the more precarious their situation became. By 13 August, Edward had been forced all the way to Poissy, just west of Paris. Philippe was in nearby Saint-Denis, strengthening his position. Letters of challenge were sent back and forth between the kings. Two days later, Philippe believed that an agreement had been made to meet in battle on a field south of Paris at Antony. But as he marched his army there, English engineers completed the rebuilding of a bridge across the Seine. Rather than meet his enemy, Edward crossed the river under cover of night. Then he bolted north, trying to reach the reinforcements he had ordered to the mouth of the Somme.

A frustrated Philippe pursued, with fast riders pushing to get ahead of his quarry. They succeeded, and by the time Edward reached the Somme he found that the French had once more destroyed or garrisoned the bridges. The English army was again stopped by a river, and this time they had the French army – roughly twice the size of their own – bearing down on them from behind.

Edward bought time by retreating towards Saint-Valery, his situation going from bad to worse as the enemy closed in. At one point, the stories say he fled one encampment so quickly that the king of France was able to eat his dinner.

Then, a stroke of absolute luck. Someone – probably a prisoner of war – informed him of a little-used local ford between the walled town of Abbeville and the sea. Blanchetaque it was called, meaning 'white stain' and probably referring to a bed of chalk – solid footing for those attempting to wade through the waters, passable only at low tide.

The chance of successfully making such a water crossing, with enemies in all directions, was not good. But it was also the only chance they had. Philippe's forces were only a few miles away.

On 24 August, the English camp got up before dawn and marched for the river as quietly as they could. They left behind lit fires and no doubt a good many of their tents and other supplies in an attempt to convince the French scouts they were still in camp. Around 6am the English were poised on the river bank, impatiently watching the water level as the tide slowly drained out to sea.

By the light of the rising sun, the English were spotted. French forces quickly began coalescing on the far bank. By the time the water was low enough for an attempted crossing, the defence on the other side was significant. The first Englishmen drove into the water anyway.

We don't know what speech Edward might have given his troops. It was, I suspect, something like what Montgomery said to those planning for the D-Day assaults.

Go in seeing red. Stop for nothing.

They had no other option. If they stayed on the south bank of the Somme, they would surely die there. Their only chance was to fight their way first through the water and then through the enemy on the other side. Many would fall, but no one could stop. The only way was forward.

It was awful work. The river would have been a froth of water and blood. A natural ford like this would not have been wide. There were only so many English who could engage, and they were fighting both the current of the river and the enemy on the high ground of its far bank.

But Edward and his men were desperate, far more desperate than the French trying to hold them off. They fought like wild dogs. As soon as one man fell, another came behind him. Bodies piled up, but a toe-hold became a foot-hold. Soon the English were defending a veritable beachhead. And still more fighters were surging through the river.

The French defenders broke and retreated to Abbeville. Edward ordered the rest of his army over with all speed. And just in time: Philippe arrived as the last of the English wagons were floated across the Somme, the tide streaming in behind them.

Edward had managed the impossible. It's overshadowed in our memory due to the fact that the battle of Crécy was mere days away, but the battle of Blanchetaque ought to be better remembered. It is one of history's greatest military escapes.

The French king moved a few miles up-river to the bridge crossing at the walled town of Abbeville. Edward had frustrated him, but he was confident that he could still bring the English army to heel. Philippe had perhaps twice as many men, all of them better rested and better fed. His army counted four kings among their ranks: himself, King John of Bohemia, his son Charles, the king of the Romans, and King James III of Majorca.

And there were no ships waiting for the English off the shore at Le Crotoy.

With nothing but bad choices, Edward took what he thought would be the best of them: he ran for the allied army from the Low Countries that he believed was besieging Béthune. It was probably the right call, but it didn't work. Philippe, moving on better roads, got ahead of him and cut him off. Trapped up against the dense Forest of Crécy, the English took the best position they could.

The battle of Crécy was a two-day affair, beginning late in the day on 26 August. The English had taken some slight high ground and surrounded it with a field fortification made from tipped-over wagons we call a *wagenburg*.[4] The French, streaming in to meet them by multiple roads, were not well organized. Worse, they didn't recognize that the English weren't sitting ducks. Edward still had some tricks up his sleeves.

The first trick was the topography, which appeared to be a relatively even stretch of gently rising ground to the English lines. In fact, it dipped down just before reaching the English position, meaning that as the initial French lines were coming into contact with the enemy, they were out of view of the French behind them. The full impact of what was unfolding wasn't clear until a person was in it.

The second trick was the technology. There were a few early cannon used on the English side – mainly employed to break up cavalry charges by spooking the horses with smoke and thunder – but the real surprise experienced by the French at Crécy was the same horror that the townspeople had experienced at Caen: the effect of massed archers. Compared to the ranged weapons used on the French side, the English longbow had better range, could loose arrows at a much quicker rate, and had a wider dispersion of death in the form of the two 'wings' of thousands of archers that Edward had hidden behind his wagons and in the trees and hedges flanking his position.

Philippe first sent in a host of Genoese mercenary crossbowmen. Because no one knew about the presence or the power of the English longbows, these crossbowmen were sent in without their shields and armour. They marched forward – probably dipping out of view of their French commanders thanks to the topography – and loosed their first shots. The English, hunkered behind their wagons, let the wood take the bolts. Then the archers stood or stepped out from their hiding places. They pulled and loosed.

Screams rose into the August sky.

The French commanders already had a cavalry charge on the gallop, rolling forward to follow behind those crossbow shots. The screams, they probably thought, came from English throats. They couldn't see until it was too late. The Genoese, trying to flee, ran pell-mell into the cavalry charge. In the collision of horses and men everything was thrown into chaos and disorder. The English pulled and loosed again. At this point, they could hardly miss.

Edward's wagenburg didn't completely surround his forces. He had placed a gap at its centre. This single way in or out was an open invitation to an assault, and he baited it still further: stretched out across this opening was his dismounted vanguard – his most able knights standing with their colourful banners flapping above them. At their centre was one of the greatest prizes of all: King Edward's son, the crown prince of England.

Though I'll refer to him by his later, famous title, he wasn't yet known as the Black Prince. At this point he was a young man of 16 years – interestingly, the same age the future Henry V, his grand-nephew, would be when he took the arrow at Shrewsbury. And though Edward had knighted him when the army landed in Normandy, he had never seen a combat quite like this one. There were tens of thousands of men and horses on the field. Arrows buzzing angrily through the air. Thunderous booms from the newfangled cannon. Screams and shouts. Horror and death.

To this point, the Black Prince would have had a front-row seat for it all. Astoundingly, he would have seen that the losses had been almost entirely on the French side. His father's plan was sound. The wings of archers were pushing any assault from the French towards that open centre where he stood surrounded by the high lords of England, gleaming in their armour. Wave after wave of the French had tried to charge them, to punch through them, but looking across our sources it seems that few if any of them had even reached them. The future Black Prince and the older warriors around him were simply watching them die, row after row.

It was, as I said, a good plan.

And the kid was about to screw it up.

Because the dismounted English vanguard – which was under the Black Prince's command – inexplicably left their position at the front of the wagenburg. They advanced.

We don't know why. My personal suspicion is that the young man was eager for glory. Seeing the standards of the French lords being mowed down, he wanted his piece of the action.

Unfortunately, though, entering melee combat was about the worst thing he could have done. It meant that the archers could no longer simply shoot into the mass of men. No Englishman dared hit the crown prince. Worse, almost anything could happen in the mad chaos of close-quarters fighting, where chance often prevails over skill.

On this day, chance meant that the crown prince of England, having pushed too far out from his lines, was surrounded and taken prisoner.

For this brief moment, the Hundred Years War hung in the balance. The prince of Wales would bring a literal king's ransom: riches, no doubt alongside the relinquishing of any claim to the throne of France. As long as the Black Prince was in French hands, the war was effectively over.

The Black Prince surrendering to the French isn't the picture most of us have of this man or this moment. The popular image of Crécy is instead fixed by later writers like Jean Froissart, who in the various revisions of his chronicle – written at the end of the 14th century – told ever more complimentary stories about how the English were worried for the prince's safety and asked his father to help him. Edward, watching the battle from a windmill, responded that the boy should be left alone to 'earn his spurs' as a knight. When concerned fighters went to help the young man anyway, they found him resting, awaiting the next wave of French fighters to kill.

A damn good story.

But a false one.

The young man was captured. While his captors bickered over who would get credit for the ransom – one early source has them greedily killing each other over it – an English contingent led by the bishop of Durham fought its way through the chaos and rescued him. His father, meanwhile, rather than disdainfully leaving his son to sink or swim in his own, left the windmill and rode out from the wagenburg in a panic in order to help secure his safety. It makes sense that he would. Edward was no fool.

The battle continued until there was no light by which to continue the killing. At some point, Philippe left the field. His commanders took him to the castle of Labroye, from which he would ride to Amiens the next day. Apparently, he left in such haste that he never signalled a general retreat. The abandoned survivors of his army took refuge in the nearby ditches and brush, waiting to see what the morning would bring. Edward, fearful of what might lie ahead in the dark, ordered his men to stay in place, ready to fight at any moment. No one really knew what had happened.

Fog covered the countryside, so thick that when the sun came up it still wasn't clear what had happened the previous day or what the future might hold. Eventually, Edward allowed some of his men to ride out in groups to reconnoitre: was Philippe gone? Was he gathering for another attack?

Groups of English riders set out into the gloom. Frenchmen, thinking they were countrymen, waved them down to ask what was happening. 'When they saw the English coming against them,' the chronicler Jean le Bel tells us, 'they approached them because they thought that they were their own men, and the English were among them like lions among sheep, and they killed them at will.'[5]

There was another French army coming, though. Because Philippe and the other leaders had fled in a different direction, a second force marching up from Abbeville didn't know what had happened. They stumbled upon Edward's position and were destroyed.

As the fog burned off, it became clear that the battle of Crécy was two days of disaster for the French. But Edward's mind was focused on how nearly it had come to defeat. That morning, according to the account of a citizen of Valenciennes, the king of England had his son brought forward. He asked him 'if it was pleasing to him to enter and be in the battle, and if it was a good game. And the Prince silenced himself and was ashamed.'[6]

That the story I've just told doesn't match the popular depiction shouldn't surprise us. After all, this isn't the story the English wanted told. What they wanted was nothing less than the greatest victory the English had ever won – at least until it was overshadowed by Agincourt.

And this is a key point for us. Because what *we* know about Crécy is very probably not the same thing that Henry V would have known about it when he went to the fields of France in 1415. He probably didn't fully understand what happened to Edward III because he was too close to the propaganda of what had happened there. History is often like this: it may seem a paradox, but the more disconnected from events we are, often the better we understand them.

What did Henry know of Crécy? Probably it was the story as it had been told and retold by the English themselves. There was no room for the Black Prince's mistakes in this story. There would be no sense of desperation. That things hadn't gone according to plan was best set aside. Instead, it was all winning. The great riches to be had in sacking a major city in France. The outfoxing of the enemy in crossing the Seine. The improbable crossing of the Somme at Blanchetaque. The astounding victory at Crécy.

Glory. Beginning to end.

This was the model. And almost 70 years later, in 1415, Henry would try to follow it.

Back in 1346, though, Edward had a decision to make. He had broken Philippe's army in the field. Among the dead were the king of Bohemia, the duke of Lorraine, and the counts of Alençon, Blamont, Blois, Chaumont, Chemille, Flanders, Harcourt, Salm, and Sancerre, along with a huge number of lesser lords and many thousands of ordinary men. For a moment, all paths were open to him.

He chose to march north, to the great port city of Calais. On 4 September he placed it under a siege that would last one month shy of a year: on 3 August 1347, after Philippe had proven incapable of dislodging the English, the city surrendered. Six of its wealthiest citizens were made to march out from the gates, nooses upon their necks, accepting their own executions in order to spare the lives of their fellow citizens – a moment poignantly captured in Auguste Rodin's magnificent statue *The Burghers of Calais* (1889).

Only the pleas for mercy from Edward's wife prevented the king from carrying out the deed.

Philippe's inability to raise the siege was a crippling blow to his already shaken authority. He tried to gather more money to raise more fighting men, but it was like trying to squeeze water from a stone. His treasury was dried up, and few of his people had the stomach for further fighting.

A few weeks after the burghers of Calais were spared and the English had begun repopulating the city with their own citizens, the Pope orchestrated a peace between Edward and Philippe. The Truce of Calais, as it came to be known, heavily favoured the English. They were granted all the lands they had gained – including precious Calais – and much else besides.

The turn of fortune was remarkable. Three times Edward had been in the jaws of defeat since he had come to France – on the Seine, then at Blanchetaque, and finally with the capture of his son – and each time he had turned it to victory. And now, a year later, he had gained one of the important cities of France. And not only did Calais offer an enormous amount of much-needed booty, but it also gave him a vital base of operations on the Continent – one that, unlike Gascony, was within easy reach of London and the Low Countries both. It was a strategic, geopolitical, and economic boon. And it set the stage for what would have seemed one long parade of English victories.

For 30 years Edward III and the men under him saw success after success. Some improbable. Some inevitable. The Black Prince learned from his mistakes at Crécy and won an enormous victory at Poitiers in 1356 – the fight that brought the French king into English hands and left the Black Prince ruling in Gascony as duke of Aquitaine (Figure 8). Then came another huge victory at Nájera in 1367. It was an amazing run.

But in the ten years following Nájera, almost all of it would be erased.

ALL UNDONE AND ALL BUT FORGOTTEN

If there are any PhD students reading this who are looking for dissertation topics, the period from 1367 to 1377 is one that deserves far more attention than it has received, especially in English. The main reason for this may be that most scholars writing in English have tracked the war through an English lens – and this was simply not a great time for the English cause. The same is true for the end of the Hundred Years War, as it happens, which means that a great many English-language histories of the period tend to run something like this: *Crécy! Poitiers! Nájera! ::mumbling:: Agincourt! ::mumbling:: The End!*

We don't have time here to give a full examination of the unravelling of the English gains in the decade after Nájera, but I do want at least to give an overview of it. Because it really is shocking.

On 6 January 1367, just weeks before he headed off on the campaign that would culminate at Nájera in Castile, the Black Prince had become, at the age of 36, the father to a baby boy named Richard. He was the prince's second son: Edward had been born in 1364. So as he marched south towards this proxy war with France, the crown prince of England had good reason to smile. He was widely respected as both a warrior and a leader: the man who had won at Poitiers and held a good half of the lands in France. He had two sons who could carry on his name and, eventually, his crown. He now rode at the head of an army without compare, almost entirely paid for out of his own rich treasury. The moment they crossed the Pyrenees, they were the strongest force on the Iberian peninsula. And then he won – and won big – at Nájera.

It was perfect.

There was just one fly in the ointment, though the English didn't know it yet. The claimant to the throne of Castile that they had defeated ... had escaped.

Worse, the claimant for whom they had won the great victory had promised the English vast sums of money if they put him back on the throne. Now that they had done so, however, he dithered on paying what was owed. The relationship between the two powers soured.

As the months passed and the Black Prince and his army sat in the sweltering Spanish heat waiting for the promised payment to show up, dysentery blazed through their ranks.

Devastated, the English army limped homeward to Bordeaux, its base in Gascony. The English chronicler Henry Knighton claims

– with some exaggeration, one hopes – that 'so many of the English died in Spain of dysentery and other diseases that scarce one man in five returned'.[7] And those who *did* return, angry that they had not been paid, turned to brigandage within English holdings.

The Black Prince was also taken ill. We don't know exactly with what and we don't know exactly when: the chronicler Froissart says the illness first hit him in Spain, meaning he had probably been seized by the same dysentery that riddled his army, but other sources say he didn't show signs of illness until several months after his return home.[8] Dysentery tends to kill quickly, whereas the Black Prince's health would slowly decline for years until his death in 1376. Whatever his illness, his poor health made it more and more difficult for the Black Prince to take to the field effectively.

Meanwhile, the claimant whom they had tried to keep from the throne of Castile came back in force and took the crown for good, defeating his half-brother at the battle of Montiel on 14 March 1369. King Charles V of France now had a vital ally in the south. In light of that, combined with the deteriorating health of the Black Prince, Charles was confident he was in position to make great gains against the English. In May of that year, he set the Treaty of Brétigny aside after nine years of official peace.

The Hundred Years War was back on.

In 1370, Charles named Bertrand du Guesclin constable of France. Bertrand had been on the losing side at Nájera, but he had learned much from the experience. He made rapid gains against the English not by engaging in pitched battles but by keeping to smaller skirmishes and encouraging rebellion among English subjects. Patient and methodical, it was death by a thousand cuts rather than a single blow.

In response, the ailing Black Prince resorted to more and more rash actions. The most infamous among them occurred in August 1370, when the town of Limoges, which had been subject to English control, gave itself over to the French. The Black Prince swore vengeance and placed it under siege. After a few days, the town was stormed in what is called the Sack of Limoges, an event that fundamentally tarnished the Black Prince's reputation. Whatever the extent of the horror – whether 'three thousand persons, men, women, and children, were dragged out to have their throats cut', as Froissart claims, or 'only' 300 civilians died, as many modern historians claim – it was a public relations disaster.[9] For the people of France, it was one more instance of English cruelty, one more reason to cast them out.

The Black Prince returned to Bordeaux to find that his eldest son had died of the plague. The loss did nothing to help his worsening health, and the prince was advised to sail for England. He did so with his wife and his younger son, Richard, in January 1371. He would not return.

With the Black Prince gone, Bertrand du Guesclin – now aided by the one-eyed Olivier de Clisson – continued to chip away at the English holdings. In 1372, the French laid siege to La Rochelle, a major seaport on the western shore put into English hands by the Treaty of Brétigny. Its location between England and Gascony meant that securing it for France would put enormous strain on English efforts to transport men, materiel, or anything else between them. Bertrand wasn't the only one who recognized the critical nature of the port, as the English sent a fleet to its defence. The French called on their newly victorious friends in Castile, who sent a powerful fleet to assist in the effort. The Castilian and English ships clashed off La Rochelle on 21 and 22 June. The English ships were either sunk or captured. Adding insult to injury, the Castilian fleet captured another four English merchant ships on their way home.

Disaster piled on disaster. La Rochelle fell to Bertrand in September, and he wasted no time in leveraging the victory not just to take more lands back, but to cripple English shipping.

With the Black Prince still ill in England, defence of English holdings on the Continent was the responsibility of his younger brother, the duke of Lancaster, better known as John of Gaunt. As a younger son, he was unlikely to wear the crown of England himself, but that did not mean that he didn't still covet a realm of his own. In 1371, he had married the daughter of the defeated claimant to the throne of Castile in order to give himself a theoretical claim on that crown himself. The loss of La Rochelle made it unlikely that he could sail there directly, and for many years he would be unable to do much more than style himself a king and try to make people address him as such.

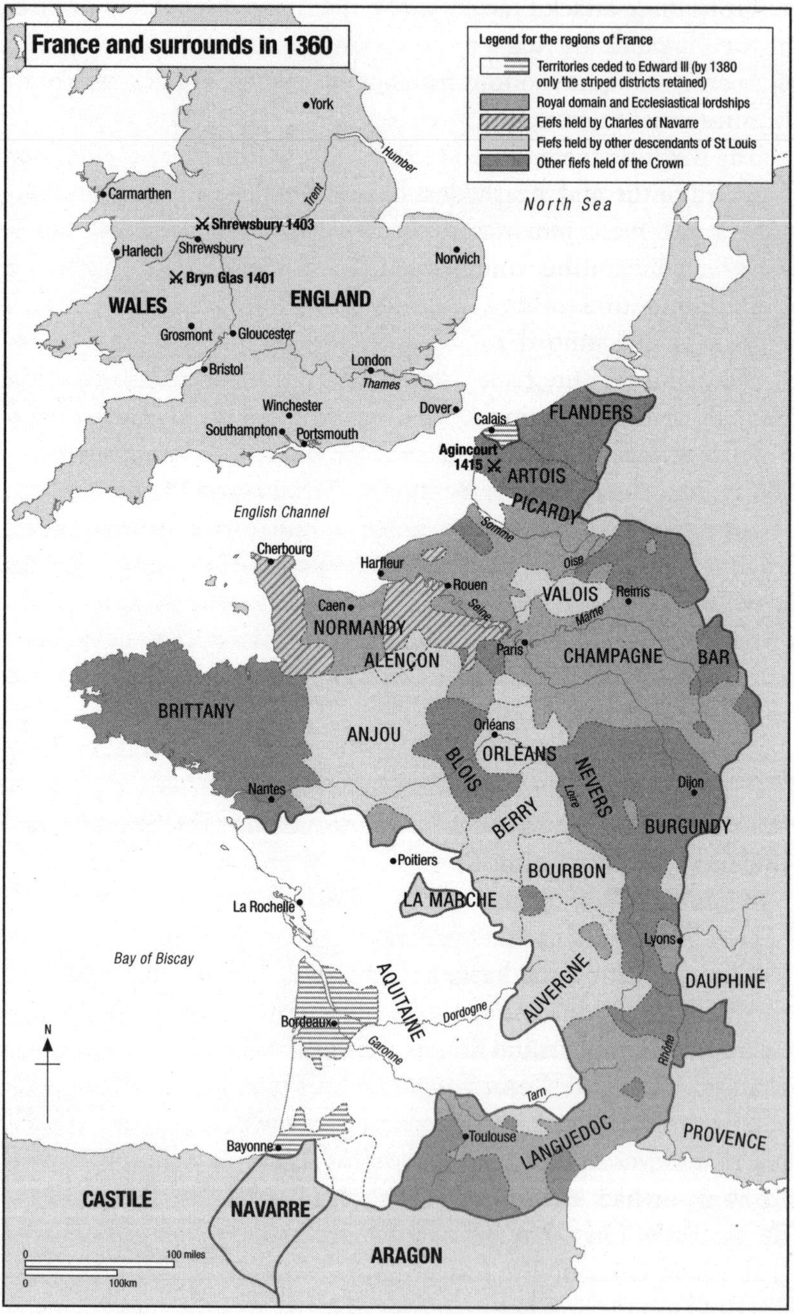
France and surrounds in 1360
Legend for the regions of France
Territories ceded to Edward III (by 1380 only the striped districts retained)
Royal domain and Ecclesiastical lordships
Fiefs held by Charles of Navarre
Fiefs held by other descendants of St Louis
Other fiefs held of the Crown
York
Humber
Trent
Carmarthen
Shrewsbury 1403
Harlech
Shrewsbury
Bryn Glas 1401
Norwich
North Sea
WALES
ENGLAND
Grosmont
Gloucester
Bristol
London
Thames
Winchester
Dover
Southampton
Portsmouth
Calais
FLANDERS
Agincourt 1415
ARTOIS
PICARDY
English Channel
Somme
Cherbourg
Harfleur
Rouen
Oise
Caen
VALOIS
Reims
Seine
Marne
NORMANDY
Paris
CHAMPAGNE
BAR
ALENÇON
BRITTANY
ANJOU
Orléans
ORLÉANS
BLOIS
NEVERS
Loire
Dijon
Nantes
BERRY
BURGUNDY
Poitiers
BOURBON
LA MARCHE
La Rochelle
Lyons
Bay of Biscay
AQUITAINE
AUVERGNE
DAUPHINÉ
N
Bordeaux
Dordogne
Garonne
Rhône
Tarn
Toulouse
LANGUEDOC
PROVENCE
Bayonne
CASTILE
NAVARRE
ARAGON
0
100 miles
0
100km

Map 1

But he *could* attack France from the still-secure English holdings on the Channel. In August 1373, he departed Calais at the head of an army of some 9,000 men. Their aim was a *chevauchée* across the entirety of France. If they couldn't sail to Gascony, they would bloody well ride there.

Five months and nearly a thousand miles later, they reached Bordeaux. It was a remarkable journey across enemy territory.

But not a victorious one.

According to Froissart, a third of Gaunt's men had frozen, starved, or succumbed to disease. Another third was killed by the French who were happy to raid them without ever offering a pitched battle – chipping away at the army, just as Bertrand had done to their lands. The third of the men who were left – ragged and exhausted – reached Bordeaux only to find it wracked with the plague and low on the supplies it needed to sustain its own people much less the 3,000 men who had stumbled in from the cold. Even more English died.

And unlike his older brother's *chevauchées* that had brought home wagonloads of riches and – on the Poitiers campaign – royal prisoners, Gaunt had won nothing.

It was a total failure. Gaunt had hoped to live up to his brother's vaunted reputation. He would weaken the French and perhaps win a Poitiers or a Nájera of his own. Instead, he was forced to return to England with only coffins to show for it.

France had been a rat's nest of problems at the beginning of Charles V's reign in 1364. In just 11 short years he had resolved most of them, remaking the kingdom in the process. France's treasury was once again full. And, thanks to the brilliance of men like Bertrand du Guesclin and Olivier de Clisson, English interests were in retreat across the Continent. They still held Calais, Cherbourg, and Brest along the English Channel, but the rest of Normandy was under ever tighter French control. And the great holdings of Gascony – which encompassed nearly half of France following the Treaty of Brétigny – had been reduced to the immediate surrounds of the port cities of Bordeaux and Bayonne. Little else was left. Charles wanted the English gone from France entirely, but he was also a practical man who knew that taking the cities that were left would be a difficult, expensive, and deadly undertaking. Better to secure what had already been won than to try to take it all now and risk losing his newfound gains.

Negotiations for a new peace began in Bruges, on 25 March 1375. A couple of months later, the two sides agreed to a truce while negotiations continued. Neither side wanted to back down, but neither side wanted to keep fighting forever. One year later, the truce was renewed.

Talks for something permanent were still ongoing in June 1377 when they were shaken by news from across the English Channel. Edward III, after a reign of more than 50 years, was dead.

4

Young Kings, 1377–99

The Black Prince never recovered from his illness. He died on 8 June 1376, and was interred in Canterbury Cathedral. So when his father died the next year, the crown skipped a generation and came to Edward III's grandson – the lad who had been born to the Black Prince on the eve of the Nájera campaign. He took the throne as Richard II.

He was ten.

TWO POPES, TWO KINGS

The young king of England inherited a tumultuous throne. Not only was the English cause in France limping badly after the recent French successes in the Hundred Years War, but there were new fractures opening across Europe. Few among them were as terrifying as the Western Schism, which saw two popes claiming to hold the authority of the Vicar of Christ on Earth.

Today we speak of Roman Catholicism as just one of several denominations of the Christian faith, but through much of the Middle Ages in Europe it was more or less the only game in town. To be a mainstream Christian in Europe was to be Roman Catholic: for the vast majority of these Christians, the pope was the central authority of their belief structure, the literal voice of God on Earth and the arbiter of their fates in Heaven and Hell.

The term 'Roman' Catholic is used because of the traditional association between this branch of the faith and the specific place of Rome and the Vatican within it. But from 1309 to 1377 the seven men who had held the title of pope had held court not in Rome but in Avignon, France. The last of them, Pope Gregory XI, returned to Rome – whether he was doing so to solve the problem or not is debated – and he died there in 1378.

Powerful forces were intent on keeping the Papacy in Rome, and under their influence – some would later talk of threats – the College of Cardinals chose the Rome-connected Pope Urban VI. Not all the cardinals were happy, however. Soon enough a group of them disavowed the election, got together on their own, and elected Pope Clement VII. Two men now held the same title.

Complicating matters even further, Clement quickly withdrew to Avignon, where he was supported and protected by the king of France. Fairly or not, this meant that a question of sacred authority within the Church had a very secular pertinence within Europe: Christians were forced to choose between the 'Roman' pope and the 'French' pope. They did so in peril of their souls, as the rival pontiffs excommunicated the followers of their rivals. The Western Schism would last until 1417.

Europe, already divided by political differences, now saw its separations underscored in the dogmatic terms of Heaven and Hell, good and evil. Predictably, as the French welcomed Pope Clement VII in Avignon, the English took up the cause of Pope Urban VI in Rome.

The Hundred Years War had become a holy war.

Between both the spiritual enthusiasm that he could now call upon and the youthful inexperience of the English king, the brilliant King Charles V of France was in a position to be able to further his advance against the remaining English holdings on the Continent. But it wasn't to be. On 16 September 1380, the French king died at the age of 42. He was succeeded by his son, crowned as Charles VI, who was one month less than 12 years old – 13 months younger than the king of England.

History is full of coincidences. Among them is the fact that both of these young men, almost simultaneously, would face internal revolts.

SMITHFIELD AND THE PEASANTS' REVOLT

The first of these calamities struck England: The Peasants' Revolt of 1381.

There is rarely just one cause for any revolt, but it's not a stretch to say that the Peasants' Revolt began as a disagreement over taxes. Specifically, it was a disagreement about taxes in a number of small villages around the town of Brentwood in Essex: people in the area believed that they had paid their fair share, but the government believed they had not. When the tax collector tried to arrest the man representing the little town of Fobbing, things came to blows. The tax collector fled. Several of those assisting him did not make it out. This brought a further threat of violence from government representatives anxious to re-establish their authority ... which only served to fan the flames.

News of the local disobedience spread quickly. Soon enough, a great many people across the countryside of England were rising up to join the citizens of Fobbing – not just against taxation, but also against social class stratification and many other complaints. This happens often in revolts: one act shakes the bottle, but when the cork pops loose any number of issues spill out. Within a couple of days, there were thousands of angry people taking to the streets, all over England.

By 11 June 1381, one massive assembly of these rebels was marching on London. Richard II, less than a week past his 14th birthday, retreated to the formidable Tower of London. Two days later, the rebels were within the city walls, seething as they searched for those they claimed had wronged them. Many of the heads they sought were government officials.

By this point, the main group of rebels was led by a man named Wat Tyler, of whom far too little is known. Whether by his doing or not, they had adopted as a rallying cry that they were – present revolt aside – the true subjects of the crown. Richard would certainly take their side, they seem to have thought. The problem was the king's advisors, who stood between their cries and the boy-king's ear: an administration more intent on enriching its members than in providing for the good of the king's people as he no doubt desired.

Their biggest target was John of Gaunt. The king's uncle was perhaps the richest man in the realm. He had a massive palace of his own along the Thames, called the Savoy, and he certainly hadn't helped his reputation with his inability to bring great renown home the way his elder brother, the Black Prince, had done. And although there is little indication that he was acting in any overt way to make his nephew some kind of puppet under his control, it was an accusation that was all too easy to believe.

Fortunately for him, he wasn't in London. But the Savoy still was. The rebels seized it and set it alight, along with the duke's precious treasures. They weren't robbers, they said.

The flames lit the sky all night.

Terror swept through London. Foreigners, so easily scapegoated for any imagined slights or ills, were killed in the streets in the name of peace. Prisons were broken open in the name of justice.

The king had no great military force to call upon in the city. Most of his fighters were in the far-flung borders of his realm, like his holdings in France. Holed up in the Tower, he had only a few hundred men at his disposal. Around him was an angry mob of thousands.

On the morning of 14 July, Richard II left the Tower and went to Mile End to meet the rebel leaders. His aim was to discuss their issues and hopefully come to terms.

Behind him, the Tower's gates were left open so he could make a hasty return if needed. There were awful consequences: a different group of a few hundred rebels stormed the open gates and got in. Archbishop Simon Sudbury, the Lord Chancellor, and Sir Robert Hales, the Lord High Treasurer, were both dragged out to Tower Hill. Alongside several other high-ranking men of the realm, they were beheaded. The Tower itself was ransacked.

This same day, the rebels found Henry Bolingbroke, the eldest son of John of Gaunt. Like his cousin King Richard, Henry was just 14. Henry and Richard knew each other well: both had been made members of the prestigious Order of the Garter at the age of ten. Through the aid of a royal guard, the young Henry's life was spared.

With the Tower fallen, Richard retreated to Blackfriars. Plans were made to meet with the rebels outside the city walls, at a place called Smithfield.

The next day, 15 June, the king took his time getting there. He first rode to Westminster Abbey, where he prayed. Then, returning to the city of London, he headed north from the Thames, probably skirting the city walls, and in the late afternoon reached the Priory Church of St Bartholomew the Great, which sat at the east end of Smithfield. The angry masses were spread out to the west. No one knew what was going to happen.

Smithfield is still there today, though it has changed quite a bit. Its name, contrary to expectation, doesn't derive from the word *smith*, which might imply iron-working and other trades. Instead, it derives from the word *smooth*: Smithfield was a broad, flat field in the Middle Ages, running from the priory to the bank of the River Fleet. Because this grassy ground had become a focal point of the livestock trade, in 1381 it would have been hemmed in by pigsties, corrals, and stockyards, along with the heavy scents of the butcher's trade. The remarkable 19th-century meat market that dominates this space today – a building designed by Horace Jones, who also designed Tower Bridge – is the modern evolution of this millennium-long tradition. Of course, it wasn't the meat trade that made Smithfield the logical place for the king and the rebels to meet. It was just an open space that could fit a large number of people.

This same open quality meant that Smithfield had already been the site of a number of important events. In 1305 the Scottish rebel William Wallace – of *Braveheart* fame – was gruesomely executed here: the crown had wanted his death seen by as many people as possible.

Today, though no one knew it, another rebel leader would die.

The king was on the eastern end for several reasons. For one, this was the area closest to his route of approach – and his route of flight, should it be necessary. Flies were buzzing around the heads of an archbishop and a high lord who had been dragged out from the Tower of London by the rebels. Wat Tyler and other rebel spokesmen might have been saying a great deal about how they were acting in the king's interest, but as far as the king's guard was concerned, all bets were off. Everyone had to be ready for violence. The eastern end of Smithfield was also the higher ground, though not by much. But, for a 14-year-old boy wanting to be seen and heard over the crowd, every inch would help. For that matter, it isn't entirely certain whether the king spoke to the crowd from horseback or if he dismounted and used a raised platform – or even some aspect of the priory's buildings – in order to project his presence. Last but hardly least, it was forbidden to commit violence on holy ground. Instances of it – like the murder of Thomas Becket in Canterbury Cathedral – were met with near universal horror.

Richard called Wat Tyler forward. The previous day, while the Tower was being raided, the king had made a number of agreements with the rebels and he wanted to know why this had not been enough to get them to disperse in peace. Tyler seems to have come prepared for another bargaining session – one in which both men were approaching the bargaining table with an equal hand. This is borne out by the account that Tyler greeted the king as a 'brother'.[1] The royal party's shock and revulsion at the idea is no doubt akin to what Henry V himself would have thought of Shakespeare's 'band of brothers' speech at Agincourt.

Sifting through all this is a bit of a historical minefield. There is no rebel account of the events at Smithfield. All we have are sources representing the royal position. They describe Tyler as rudely demanding refreshment, for instance. Was this so? The Bible makes frequent reference for the need to show hospitality to one's guests, and was not Tyler being invited into the presence of the king, and at a house of worship no less? For that matter, what does it mean for him to be rude? Did he speak with condescension? Did he humble himself but not sufficiently enough for those casting the judgement? Did he speak in English, which was considered lowly and therefore rude to the French-speaking royals? We know the answers to none of these questions, and there are countless more we could ask about that single word alone, much less of the whole of the scene. As historians we extrapolate what we can out of the scattered puzzle pieces left to us. We do so knowing that while we cannot ever complete the puzzle – too many pieces are gone forever – we must do what we can to see what we can.

What we make of the puzzle often says as much about ourselves as it does about the past. When I picture this scene, for instance, my instinct is to see Richard and his party as haughty and proud, looking down on Tyler and the rebels with disdain. To such men, the very notion of Tyler speaking to the king *at all* – to the king! as if he had the right! – might be reason enough to call him rude, no matter his tone, his posture, or anything else. My instinct, in other words, is to align myself with Tyler and the peasant rebels against the king and his party: I was raised to see through a lens that has me wondering how many meals the king could have bought for his starving veterans if he had sold his second-fanciest cloak.

However we perceive Tyler's approach to the king at Smithfield, the broad strokes of what happened next are clear. After his refreshments, Tyler turned to leave. Why or where he was going, we don't know.

Words were exchanged between Tyler and some of the royal retinue. The Lord Mayor of London jumped into the middle of a quickly heating argument. Tyler said something or did something that was perceived as a threat towards the king. Someone called for Tyler's arrest, at which point the rebel leader apparently attacked the mayor, who responded with a blade. In the commotion, the king's squire came forward and repeatedly stabbed Tyler with his sword.

Very little of this could be seen by the rebel masses. About the only thing that was clear – what spread with the speed of shouts – was that *something* had happened. Something bad.

The rebels tensed, took in a great, collective breath as they readied to surge forward with violent force.

The 14-year-old king did something extraordinary. He rode out into the midst of the rebels. It was astonishingly brave. For all their talk of rebelling to save their king, in this moment there might well have been many in Smithfield now willing to do him harm.

He declared himself their leader. That's what they had said he was, and he accepted it as loudly as he could. They had done him a service, he declared, and then he asked them to continue to follow him as he set off towards Clerkenwell Fields, further north – away from London, and away from where Tyler lay dying.

They followed. They began to disperse.

Behind, officials seized control of the scene and soon the city. Tyler's head was removed and put on display. Richard had saved his crown.

ROSEBEKE AND THE REVOLT

By a remarkable coincidence, Richard II's contemporary, Charles VI, faced down a popular revolt at nearly the same time: for him, it was the Flemish Revolt, which brought about the battle of Rosebeke in 1382.

As with everything else about the Hundred Years War, there was no single reason for Flanders to be involved in the conflict. That said, if there was one reason above all others that it and the rest of the regions in the Low Countries were repeatedly pulled into the fight, it was sheep.

Wool was by now medieval England's greatest export, and the Low Countries were home to its greatest importers, including the highly prosperous cities of Flanders: enormous riches were made for the English crown and Flemish coffers as merchants brought English wool into an increasingly large and busy textile industry. These riches fostered new, upwardly mobile classes of Flemings whose economic livelihoods were dependent on England, and whose political leanings followed suit. For centuries, Flanders was only a semi-autonomous state. Politically, it was tied to France, not England. The counts of Flanders ruled under the thumb of the kings of France, who by the end of the 14th century had a keen interest in syphoning off tax money for their own purposes. As Flemish tax revenues increased, so did French interests, a reality that only infuriated those who saw it as a kind of theft: they might be making their money with England and other countries, but France was taking the profits. Unsurprisingly, there were numerous Flemish attempts to shake the yoke of French influence – attempts that the English often supported either openly or tacitly. The 'of Gaunt' in the name John of Gaunt, for instance, refers to the city of Ghent: he was born there in 1340 when King Edward III was working to secure alliances.

As it happens, it was Ghent that sparked the revolt that caused problems for Charles VI. In 1379, the city felt threatened when the rival Flemish city of Bruges, facing the silting of its access to the sea, decided to dig a canal to the River Lys. The Ghentenaars responded with violence. Count Louis II of Flanders, often called Louis de Male, responded with swift reprisals, but Ghent didn't back down. It elected as its leader Philip van Artevelde, the son of a political leader who had led a pro-English uprising at the outset of the Hundred Years War. Louis came down hard on the city and its allies, but Philip managed to defeat him and capture Bruges at the battle of Beverhoutsveld on 3 May 1382. The count of Flanders fled, only to find that his failure to put down the uprising in Ghent meant that similar uprisings against his rule were erupting across his lands.

Louis' son-in-law was Philippe, the duke of Burgundy since 1363. The fourth son of King Jean II, Philippe had been 14 when he and his father were captured by the Black Prince at Poitiers in 1356 – it was in that battle that the young man had earned the epithet 'the Bold', by which we will refer to him to help keep our characters straight. Since 1380, Philippe the Bold and the other remaining brothers of the dead King Charles V had governed as regents for their nephew, the young Charles VI. They were experienced enough to know that the trouble in Flanders was not just a problem because Louis of Flanders was Philippe the Bold's father-in-law. Revolution in Flanders was, in the end, a fight against traditional power structures – the very underpinnings of their own authority. Worse, it was the kind of threat that could spread like wildfire. Already there were popular uprisings against taxation in several cities in France, including Paris, that were looking expectantly at Flanders.

In short, Ghent had to be made an example of.

Though Charles VI, now 14, was nominally in charge of the response, it was Philippe the Bold who took the lead role in organizing the effort alongside another of the king's uncles, the duke of Bourbon. By November, they were all marching north with an army of roughly 10,000 men. It might have been fewer men than van Artevelde had raised in the meantime, but the French were well organized and under highly capable military leadership. On 27 November, the two forces met each other in the battle of Rosebeke, just outside the modern town of Westrozebeke in Belgium.

As we've seen, the future Henry V was 16 years old when he took the field at the battle of Shrewsbury in 1403. One of the men he would go on to defeat at Agincourt in 1415 – the man, in fact, who is credited for coming up with the French battle plan that fateful day – was likewise 16 years old when he came to fight at Rosebeke. His name was Jean II Le Maingre, though like his father before him he would come to be known to history as Boucicaut, meaning 'the Brave'. He was in the retinue of the duke of Bourbon – another of the king's uncles – who knighted him on the eve of the battle.

According to an anonymous and extremely flattering biography of Boucicaut, written in 1409, this freshly knighted young man made a great name for himself in the fight:

> Boucicaut, with characteristic bravery, determined to measure himself hand-to-hand against a tall, sturdy Fleming; he attempted to fell him with his two-handed battle-axe. The Fleming saw that Boucicaut was relatively small, and took it that he was no more than a child; contemptuously, he struck the haft of Boucicaut's axe so brutally that the weapon fell from his hands, and the Fleming sneered: 'There's something for you to suckle, child! The French must be short of decent men if they have to enlist children ...!' Boucicaut, anguished by the loss of his axe, heard the sneer and drew his dagger and slipped under the Fleming's guard; he thrust the dagger below his enemy's breastplate and between his ribs, and the Fleming fell to the ground overcome by pain – nor could he do Boucicaut any further damage. And Boucicaut said, mockingly, 'Is this a game for Flemish children?'[2]

The battle itself lasted less than two hours, according to an Italian eyewitness named Buonaccorso Pitti, and it was as just as one-sided as this great story: though the French were outnumbered four to one, they killed 27,500 of the 40,000 Flemings.[3] The French battle plan was laid down by the one-eyed Olivier de Clisson, and it was a good one. While the Flemings charged the French lines from the front, French cavalry swung around to attack their rear. Those of the Flemings who didn't break off in rout were encircled. It was, in some respects, much like what had happened at the earlier battle of Poitiers, except that the French had little interest in giving quarter or collecting ransom. Those who didn't suffocate in the press of men were slaughtered. The chronicler Froissart tried to give a sense of what it was like, beginning with the image of

French men-at-arms – professional soldiers in full military gear[4] – attacking the largely untrained enemy:

> Men-at-arms set about beating down Flemings lustily. Some had sharp axes with which they split helmets and knocked out brains, others lead maces with which they dealt such blows that they felled them to the ground. Hardly were they down than the pillagers came slipping in between the men-at-arms, carrying long knives with which they finished them off. They had no more mercy on them than if they had been dogs. So loud was the banging of swords, axes, maces, and iron hammers on those Flemish helmets that nothing else could be heard above the din. I was told that if all the armourers of Paris and Brussels had been brought together, plying their trade, they would not have made a greater noise than those warriors hammering on the helms before them.[5]

The biography of Boucicaut claims that 60,000 Flemings died, though that is probably more than twice as many as were there. Froissart says 26,000 died. Casualties, in any case, were incredibly high. Among them was van Artevelde.

After the battle, the young king asked to see the Flemish leader, dead or alive. It took time to find him, as the dead were already being stripped of their armour and anything else they might have of value. But his body was eventually found. It was dragged to the expensive tent in which Charles waited. There, the French king and his lords examined his corpse. As Froissart says:

> He was turned over to see if he had died of wounds, but there were no wounds such as could have caused his death. He had been crushed in the press and had fallen into a ditch, with a great mass of Ghent men on top of him. When they had looked at him for a time they took him away and hanged him from a tree.[6]

YOUNG MEN IN BATTLE

Whether it is Henry V at Shrewsbury, Richard II at Smithfield, or Boucicaut and Charles VI at Rosebeke, we have been seeing a lot of men participating in a lot of violence at very young ages. If this is shocking to us, it is because most of us are – quite thankfully – a long way from the hard realities of the Middle Ages.

I don't want to overstate the violence of the period. Hollywood is all too eager to paint for us a picture of almost ceaseless, senseless killing. To be medieval, they seem to think, means to be dirty, cold, and fighting in colourless landscapes of ignorant desolation.

The truth wasn't nearly so grim. The Middle Ages could be full of love and laughter, life and vibrant colour, brilliant insights and stunning landscapes. People weren't unaware of baths. They didn't walk around killing each other all the time.

At the same time, people in the Middle Ages were familiar with death in a way that most of us probably are not.[7] For many people today, death is more distant, the pain muted by the drip of soothing drugs, the moment of passing hidden away behind hospital curtains, the rictus grin reshaped to serene calm for the wake. Medieval, ancient, or even earlier people may not have viewed death as a welcome friend, but it was certainly an ever-present companion.

Far too many knew they would see it in battle, where the great questions of life boiled down to a single binary choice: to kill or be killed. This was especially true of men of title and their immediate retinues: they had to assume, one way or another, that they would be called upon to defend their way of life from those who would take it. Boucicaut was one of these men. And his biography describes the degree to which he devoted himself to training to ensure he would be on the winning end of the fight when it came:

> He would train himself to leap fully armed onto his horse's back, or on other occasions he would go for long runs on foot, to increase his strength and resistance, or he would train for hours with a battle-axe or a hammer to harden himself to armour and to exercise his arms and hands, so that he could easily raise his arms when fully armed. Doing such exercises gave him a physique so strong that there was no other gentleman in his time who was so proficient – for he could do a somersault fully armed but for his bascinet, and could dance equipped in a coat of mail.

Among his other abilities described are powerful feats of jumping, an ability to climb between two walls built closely together, and this: 'fully armed in a coat of mail, he could climb right to the top of the underside of a scaling ladder leaning against a wall, simply swinging from rung to rung by his two hands – or without the coat of mail, by one hand only.'[8]

Although his biography is rather worshipful, and its point is to paint these as extraordinary efforts on the part of its hero, the evidence of existing medieval training manuals points to this being a difference of degree rather than a difference in kind. Fighting with heavy weapons under the encumbrance of armour is an enormous physical challenge that requires strength, stamina, and skill. When it came to the field of battle, the men who were engaged in combat would either be up to the challenge or they would die. Boucicaut wasn't alone not just in being raised to fight, but in working hard to excel at it.

The same, we will see, was true of Henry V, the man who would ultimately defeat him and take him prisoner at Agincourt.

RICHARD AND THE LANCASTRIANS

Richard II of England and Charles VI of France may have both put down rebellions, but they were both still young. Not surprisingly, older men were more than happy to take advantage of the rulers' relative inexperience to try to fill their own pockets or strengthen their own grip on the reins of power.

In England, the older men included John of Gaunt, who was pounding the benches for any way to make good his claim on the throne of Castile, as well as other leading figures who were pushing to aid Ghent in its struggle against France – the Ghentenaars may have been defeated militarily at Rosebeke, but they weren't defeated in spirit. Parliament and the young king ultimately backed this second cause, and they appointed the bishop of Norwich, Henry le Despenser, to lead the effort.

The choice of a bishop was extremely appropriate, for this wasn't just a proxy fight of the Hundred Years War. The Papal Schism ensured that it also had the trappings of a holy war: the Ghentenaars and the rest of the Flemings joined the English in supporting the pope in Rome, whereas their French-aligned enemies supported the pope in Avignon. The effort is called both Despenser's Crusade and the Norwich Crusade.[9]

Regardless of the label, it was a disaster characterized by disorganization, corruption, and a lack of experienced military leadership. The fact that it had received so much support from the government and its people – Norwich had raised a great deal of money from the populace by promising them eternal rewards – was a major scandal.

Richard's decision to back the disastrous Despenser Crusade rather than his own Castilian aspirations left John of Gaunt livid. Within a couple of years, the relationship between uncle and nephew had soured to the point that John of Gaunt quit England in 1385 to push his Castilian claims on his own.

In his absence, other men tried to leverage the young king for their own ends, which led to a splintering between those lords who were loyal to Richard and those who sought to remove some of the king's favourites through the old legal process of appeal – for this reason, they were called the Lords Appellant. Among their number was John of Gaunt's son, Henry Bolingbroke.

We don't need to get too deep into the weeds of this political fight, except to say that things escalated quickly. By December 1387, the Lords Appellant were taking arms against loyalist forces, and they won an important fight at the battle of Radcot Bridge, forcing the king to back down. Some of his favourites fled the country. Others were executed in 1388 by what became known as the Merciless Parliament.

Richard claimed that the problems plaguing his reign so far were due to a series of poor counsellors. In 1389, now 21, he proclaimed that he was going to rule in his own name. That same year, John of Gaunt returned to England – his Castilian dream unfulfilled – and took on the role of elder statesman.

As part of this fresh start, Richard tried to bring a final peace to the Hundred Years War. With their own king moving in and out of lucidity, representatives of the French government were willing to listen. In 1393 there was an offer on the table to restore a significant part of Gascony to the English, if only Richard would pay homage to the French king. It was the same old hurdle that had started the war in the first place, and it remained insurmountable: the English wouldn't do it, and the French wouldn't back down until it was done.

In 1396, Richard took the next best deal: he agreed to a truce with France that was supposed to last until 1426. One of the leading voices for this peace on the French side was Philippe, the duke of Burgundy and count of Flanders. As part of the agreement, Richard agreed to marry Charles VI's daughter, Isabella. He was 29. She was six.

A year later, Richard felt secure enough in his position to take long-delayed vengeance against the Lords Appellant. Several were executed. Some were exiled. Others were deft players of the political cards they had in hand: Bolingbroke, for instance, supported the crackdown against his former fellows and came out with a greater title than he started with. That December, however, Bolingbroke got into a fight with another former Lord Appellant that resulted in Parliament deciding they should engage in a trial by combat. Richard, perhaps suspecting that whoever won might be a greater threat for their display of armed prowess, exiled them both instead: Bolingbroke for ten years and his adversary for life.[10] Bolingbroke made his way to France, where he was welcomed by the court and installed in the Parisian mansion left empty when Olivier de Clisson had been run out of town by the king's uncles after the king went mad.

In February 1399, John of Gaunt died. Rather than allowing the exiled Bolingbroke to succeed to his father's vast lands and enormous wealth as duke of Lancaster – both of them potential threats to his own position – Richard seized it all and extended Bolingbroke's exile for life. It was a staggering and shocking overreach of the king's authority. He provided no rationale for doing so.

It might have seemed a safe bet. Bolingbroke was an exile in France, whose king had little interest in provoking the English king. Richard must have thought he had at last put an end to the pesky threat of the powerful house of Lancaster.

How very wrong he was.

5

Civil Wars, 1399–1415

Few in France considered deposing the mad king to be a viable option. Though it was not as clearly defined as it would be in later centuries, the basic concept of a divinely ordained monarchy was already well in place in medieval France: Charles was king because God wanted Charles to be king.

That said, no one was blind to the problem that his kingship now presented. His wife, Queen Isabeau, knowing full well the dangers that her husband's periods of madness posed for the realm, helped to form a small council to help maintain a semblance of order. Initially this group was dominated by the king's uncles, the dukes of Burgundy and Berry. They had been supporters of peace with the English.

They were not the only power players, however. The mad king's younger brother, Louis, the duke of Orléans, was increasingly pushing himself into the mix. He hated the duke of Burgundy in particular, to the point that he instinctively fought against pretty much anything his powerful uncle wanted to do.

Their dispute would result in bloodshed.

SOURCES AND CIVIL WARS

In the introduction I talked about the 'lenses' through which we see the world, and how careful we must be as historians to be aware of these innate biases. It's not necessarily our fault that they are there, but it is absolutely our responsibility to account for them.

To put it simply, everyone has an axe to grind.

Because this applies to everyone all the time, it becomes a real problem when we're looking at the sources on which we rely for information about the past. Chroniclers, poets, story-tellers, even folks as innocuous at court administrators are all providing information that might be unreliable for one reason or another. As the historian E.H. Carr put it in a 1961 lecture:

> No document can tell us more than what the author of the document thought – what he thought had happened, what he thought ought to happen or would happen, or perhaps only what he wanted others to think he thought, or even only what he himself thought he thought.[1]

There are many ways to grapple with this issue, but the first step to all of them is to identify the potential problem.

I bring this up now because so many of the sources we need to use for the remainder of this book come from times of deep polarization in both England and France. The fracturing of these realms profoundly infiltrates our sources from the time, because pretty much no one stood at an objective remove from the struggles for power. To use the example of France, the years moving forward would see people writing accounts – chronicles, poems, and all the rest – that provide an enormous amount of the little information we have about this time period. But the polarization of the realm meant that they often ignored the sins of their own side while highlighting – or simply making up – the sins of the other.

Take Queen Isabeau, for instance, who for centuries was regarded as a lustful, power-hungry spendthrift. Even through much of the last century this was generally regarded as established fact, with many accepting the idea that she was carrying on an affair with her husband's younger brother, Louis of Orléans. However, once historians began investigating the matter closely – rather than just accepting the stories that had been handed down – the affair turned out to be nonsense. Even the vaguer ideas of her being a poor queen rely almost entirely upon a handful of remarks from the chronicle of a man known as the Religieux of Saint-Denis – most likely identified as Michel Pintoin – probably written around 1420.[2] Its early date and popularity mean that his chronicle had an enormous influence on shaping our understanding of French history for the first quarter of the 15th century. It's an important text.

Trouble is, the Religieux was very much a supporter of the duke of Burgundy in his fight against the duke of Orléans. He took every chance possible to tarnish the duke of Orléans, the queen, and anyone else who stood against what he thought best for his country. Looking at the evidence more objectively, Isabeau seems to have been doing everything she could to hold the realm together so that her son, the dauphin, would have a throne to ascend to when the mad king died. This is precisely what she *ought* to have been doing. The fact that the men vying for power viewed her instead as an obstacle or a pawn for their own political machinations says more about them than it does about her.

The chronicle of the Religieux is not alone in having these question marks hanging over it. In a realm divided, every writer sought to shape the story of the world in which they were living. And what those writers had to say often set the foundations for the history that we might have built upon them, wrongly assuming they were objective reporters.

Historians have to work hard to verify their evidence, then re-verify what they used for that verification. I'll largely spare you the long and tedious process of this, but I don't want you to forget that it's there, behind the scenes throughout any book like this. It will be absolutely essential when it comes to locating and reconstructing the battle of Agincourt as we think it was fought in 1415. For now, it's enough to know that fractured realms leave fractured records.

As for Burgundy and Orléans, their fight over who ought to be in charge of the realm during the king's absences was a clash of kingship models, but it was also a clash of personalities and personal interests. The duke of Burgundy had been instrumental in negotiating a peace with Richard II because it supported a stable economy that was much to his benefit. The duke of Orléans, on the other hand, had a personal interest in expanding his reach into Gascon lands that were still under English control.

THE RISE OF LANCASTER

Little surprise, then, that few welcomed the exiled Henry Bolingbroke to France more warmly than the duke of Orléans. In early June 1399, mere weeks after the death of John of Gaunt, news reached them in Paris that Richard had decided to take his army and his most loyal supporters on campaign to Ireland. Bolingbroke quickly began planning for his own return. He and Louis entered into a pact of mutual support. The exiled English lord received a blessing from the abbot of Saint-Denis and with his supporters took ship for England.

No one stopped him.

He landed in Yorkshire at the mouth of the Humber. Lancastrian holdings there quickly welcomed him. In mid-July he met with Henry Percy, the powerful earl of Northumberland, and his son, who had the same name as his father. We can be exceedingly grateful that the younger Percy is more commonly known by the nickname 'Hotspur', which he had earned during many years of fighting on the borders of Scotland. It will save us some confusion.

Bolingbroke told them he had returned to England only to reclaim the property that ought to have been his by right. They bought it, and many of the other lords left in England followed suit. Bolingbroke soon found himself leading an army of the disaffected. Few were interested in fighting for the unpopular Richard. A few nobles who did so quickly lost their heads.

Many of the lords left in England saw this as a chance for a regime change. Before long, Bolingbroke was calling for exactly the same thing.

Richard returned from Ireland in the middle of August. He was met with hostility and accusations of tyranny. On 19 August he was forced to give himself over into Bolingbroke's control at Flint Castle in Wales. After they rode to London, Bolingbroke imprisoned him in the Tower.

One month later, on 1 October, Richard was formally deposed by Parliament. And less than two weeks after *that*, Bolingbroke took the crown as Henry IV – the first Lancastrian king.

The speed of Richard's fall was staggering. In one month, Bolingbroke had taken his throne – and he had done it with remarkably little bloodshed.

Watching all of this was the poet John Gower. A friend of the more famous Geoffrey Chaucer, Gower was around 70 at this point. Just a year earlier he had taken up rooms at Saint Mary Overie's Priory in Southwark. He was largely retired now, but in earlier years he had been a prolific writer of poetry in English, French, and Latin. His most famous work in English was the *Confessio Amantis* – 'The Confession of the Lover' – a sprawling, 33,000-line poem weaving together a series of shorter tales and stories in order to teach its listener about the right way to order one's life and mind. It had been first written, so Gower said, because of a chance encounter he'd had with Richard II. The fact that the poet went on to dedicate the work to the king has left many wondering how much we ought to identify the poem's confessing lover with Richard and its instructing confessor with Gower. At some point, though, Gower had a change of heart. We think it was late in Richard's reign, as the king was falling more and more into authoritarian mindsets that fitted poorly with the advice of restraint that the poet was more apt to counsel. Whenever it was, Gower decided to revise the *Confessio*, and in so doing he replaced his dedication to King Richard II with one to a not-yet-exiled Henry Bolingbroke. It was a prescient move: with Bolingbroke now becoming Henry IV, Gower probably became something of an initial poet laureate to him. This is a plausible explanation for the fact that the poet was roused from his relaxations to write a new poem in English, either upon the occasion of the coronation or close to it.

This 385-line poem is entitled *In Praise of Peace*, and it sees Gower once more giving advice to a king. Richard, he must have thought, never listened. He hoped Henry would.

The poem begins:

O worthy, noble king, Henry the Fourth,
Upon whom the good fortune has befallen
To govern the people upon this earth,
God has chosen you to comfort us all:
The honour of this land, which was crestfallen,
Now stands high through the grace of your goodness,
Which every man is meant to bless.

The high God of His justice alone,
The right that belongs to your regality
Has declared in your person to belong –
And no man can justify more than God has done.
Your title is founded upon your ancestry.
And the land's people have your right affirmed.
So stands your reign by God and man confirmed.[3]

Gower is careful to construct a kind of legal framework upon which Henry's crown might rest. There was the fact that he had a claim to the throne through his father, John of Gaunt, who was a son of Edward III. This was a precondition for rule, though it must be said that he did not have the best claim by the standards of the age. Richard had that. But after Richard the next best claimant would have been Edmund Mortimer, the earl of March, who was descended from Edward III's second son, whereas Henry's father had been Edward's third son. For this reason, Edmund had been the presumptive heir to the childless Richard. He was eight.

Still, the point for Gower and the others who supported Henry taking the crown was that he qualified *at all*. Beyond that, the poet points to the fact that Henry was chosen by both God and the people. To this he adds the fact that Henry had taken the crown by force. This, too, was on the minds of many. Some, it seems, viewed Henry's speedy conquest as a sign of greatness to come: he would be, for them, a new Alexander the Great. Gower was aware of the comparison. Speaking of Alexander, he admits how 'The world he won, and did it with conquest'. But he immediately rebukes such an enthusiasm for violence:

But though it happened that way back then,
That everything Alexander wanted he achieved,
This sinful world was all pagan then.
No one in the high God believed.
It's no wonder that the world was aggrieved.
Though a tyrant his purpose may win,
All was vengeance and unfortunate sin.

But now the faith of Christ has come to have a place
Among the princes of this earth here.
It well befits them to have pity and grace.
But yet it might be tempered in good measure:
For as they find cause in the matter
At hand, whatever may afterward occur,
The just law shall not be set aside.

Gower draws a fine line. Alexander's rule by outright conquest was wrong, because violence begets violence. It may have served a 'pagan' king for a time, but it could not serve a Christian one now. At the same time, whatever violence had been done – or would have to be done – to bring a new stability to the Christian realm of England was acceptable. Peace might be the goal of justice, but justice could not be dispensed through peace.

If the coronation was a moment of hope for Gower, he would be disappointed. Henry IV's reign immediately ran into trouble.

The first problem was what to do with Richard. At his surrender at Flint Castle, Henry had promised to protect his life. But just two months into his rule, a large group of lords met at the Abbey house in Westminster to hatch a plot to return the crown to the former king. While Henry was celebrating the feast of Epiphany in Windsor, they would seize him and kill him.

Unfortunately for the conspirators, the new king found out.

The conspirators fled. Here and there they tried to encourage the English to rise up in a general rebellion against Henry, but they found no takers. Throughout January, lords on the run were captured and executed, one by one, across the country. Henry had thwarted the plot, but it was proof of what he surely already knew: so long as Richard was alive, his crown would never be secure.

The month after the Epiphany Rising, as it came to be called, Richard died in Pontefract Castle. It's likely, but not certain, that he starved to death, and that it was not by his choice. If Henry had killed him, he would have had the blood of a king on his hands. But if he ordered him held without food, then the timing – and, he might argue, the responsibility – of the death would be in the hands of a higher power. God, all-powerful and all-knowing, could have shattered the door of Richard's prison, sent angels bearing food, or miraculously spirited him away to safety. None of this happened, so it stood to reason that God wanted the man dead. Belief in the supernatural, it turns out, is a handy 'get out of jail for free' card – or, at least in this case, a 'starve a man to death in jail for free' card.

Richard's body was put on display at St Paul's Cathedral – in large measure to prove to any who still supported him that he was dead – before Henry had it transported for burial at King's Langley Priory in Hertfordshire.

Across the English Channel in France, the news of what had happened was met with shock and horror. The deposition of a king was a frightening prospect given the status of their own monarch. More than that, it was strongly suspected that the peace that had been negotiated with Richard might not last under Henry. The duke of Berry wrote to his brother the duke of Burgundy: 'Truth to tell, my dear brother, it is a great tragedy and a signal misfortune for our country. For as you well know, Lancaster governs by the will of the English people and the English people like nothing better than war.'[4]

REVOLT IN WALES

Despite the duke of Berry's worries, Henry IV did not have the money or the means to invade France. For now, the truce of 1396 held. But that did not mean that the Lancastrian king wasn't going to war. The Scots saw in an unsettled England the perfect opportunity to advance their interests in a series of cross-border raids. Henry responded in the summer of 1400 by leading a campaign into Scotland.

It was a large undertaking, perhaps the biggest English army gathered since Crécy, but it accomplished little: the English did not manage to besiege, much less seize, any cities, and the Scots carefully avoided pitched battle. What the Scots were doing, in fact, was the very thing that Philippe VI had tried to do to Edward III during the Crécy campaign: whittle the enemy down with time and the attrition of dwindling supplies, diminishing morale, and inevitable disease. While Edward had improbably managed to beat this strategy in 1346, it had served the French remarkably well in the years since. When Henry's father, John of Gaunt, had orchestrated his great *chevauchée* across France in 1373, this was the very thing that had left him limping into Bordeaux with only a starving and broken fraction of his men left. The Scots, allies of the French, were just as well versed in the art. Henry's invasion of their lands was surely meant to show his authority to his warlords while filling the crown's coffers with war booty and ransoms. It did nothing of the sort.

Worse, at least according to some stories, when the calls were going out to gather men for the invasion, Lord Grey of Ruthin saw fit to prevent them from reaching the Welsh lord Owain of Glyndyfrdwy – today called Owain Glyndŵr, though the English sources often name him Owen Glendower – due to a dispute the two men had about their property lines. Because he failed to bring men to the Scotland invasion, Owain was branded an enemy of the crown. Lord Grey's intention in the whole affair, no doubt, was to have the king seize the Welshman's lands and turn them over to him, thus enriching himself while ridding himself of a rival. But this petty dispute lit the fuse of an explosive disaster. Rather than turning tail and running, Owain – who could claim descent from the Welsh ruling lines of Powys, Deheubarth, and Gwynedd – was proclaimed the prince of Wales by his supporters on 16 September 1400 (Figure 7).[5] Because there already *was* a prince of Wales – Henry's son and heir, the future Henry V, who had turned 14 that very day – this was a declaration of open rebellion. It was the start of a crisis that would eat up much of the next eight or more years of Henry's reign.

The Glyndŵr rebellion hasn't received as much attention in English histories as it deserves. Because the truth of the matter is that it shook England to its core.

Owain's first move is often called a *chevauchée*, though it must be pointed out that insofar as it was a running raid through the countryside – in this case, northern Wales – it wasn't destroying everything it encountered in quite the same way that Henry's *chevauchée* to Scotland had just tried to do. Instead, it was a sequence of *targeted* raids. Owain was hitting English targets in Wales – including the lands of his old adversary, Lord Grey of Ruthin – and leveraging the fact that English lords in Wales were, from the perspective of the native Welsh, occupiers.

Henry struck back with a three-week campaign through Wales to try to hunt down the rebels and show his strength. All he managed to do was execute eight suspected rebels, which only served to infuriate the Welsh even more. Across the mountains and valleys of Wales, Owain's rebellion became synonymous with Welsh freedom.

Castles began to fall, including Conwy Castle on 1 April 1401. Henry responded by ordering his highly experienced and respected Northumbrian ally Hotspur to take command of English forces in north Wales and bring the rebels to heel. By the end of May, Hotspur was able to report that he had beaten back a Welsh force – supposedly with Owain leading it – which had to be welcome news at court. Alongside it, though, Hotspur also reported that he had seized a ship off the coast of Milford Haven that contained 35 well-armed Scots.[6] Owain's cause wasn't just capturing the hearts of his fellow Welsh. It was also garnering the attention of England's other enemies.

That summer, Owain defeated a larger force of English at the battle of Hyddgen, one of a sequence of worrying events that inspired Henry to send in another army intended to punish the rebels in a show of force.[7] He executed many suspected rebels and destroyed the beautiful abbey of Strata Florida because some of the monks were believed to be aiding Owain. The Welsh leader responded by sending letters to the lords of Ireland and Scotland, asking for their help in the common cause of beating the English.[8] And then, in an act that spoke to Welsh prophecies and what we might today call a kind of nationalism, he began to fly the standard of the golden dragon of Uther Pendragon. The great Welsh poet Iolo Goch, one of Owain's earliest supporters, wrote of:

> The fair, brave, and fear-inspiring weapon of Glyndyfrdwy,
> Owain, bright bloody blade, ferocious defender –
> To contend with many shields in a host.
> The golden sword of the people, mighty lord,
> Terrifies men with his bravery.[9]

Every move Henry made seemed to worsen his situation. It had to seem as if he was fighting the Lernaean Hydra, which grew back two heads for every one that was cut off.

And then, in 1402, a sequence of absolute disasters struck.

It began early in the year, when Owain captured Lord Grey of Ruthin in an ambush. The Welsh leader hurried his prize away into the mountains, demanding a sizeable ransom from Henry for his release. Then, in June, he raided the borderlands between Wales and England. Among his targets was the town of Knighton.

The English lord who came to the aid of Knighton was Sir Edmund Mortimer. He was a man of wealth and great connections, a great-grandson of Edward III and, through the marriage of his sister, a brother-in-law to Hostpur. He was also uncle – and guardian after the lad's father died – to the young Edmund Mortimer who had been Richard II's heir-apparent. Despite this, he had never shown the slightest hint of disloyalty to his cousin, Henry IV. When he heard of Owain's assault on Knighton, he marched out at once. On 22 June, he brought Owain to battle near a hill called Bryn Glas, which rises beside the small hamlet of Pilleth today.[10] The result was a complete and total victory for the Welsh. The English forces were destroyed. Mortimer was captured and spirited away to join Lord Grey in prison.

The blow sent shockwaves through England. Bored monks often etched graffiti into abbey choir stalls, and at St Albans just north of London – 200 miles away from the battle – someone carved into the wood a Latin prayer: 'Christ, Splendour of God, I beg you, destroy Glyndŵr.'[11] In London, an aging and potentially blind Gower was roused from retirement to pen a seven-line poem in Latin decrying the state of the kingdom. Among its plights, the poet says: 'An insidious people terrorizes the king's roads.'[12]

Henry tried to blame the loss at Bryn Glas on a lack of loyalty from Mortimer: the fact that his nephew was a rival claimant to the throne, it was thought, might have meant that he had been in cahoots with the Welsh and helped lead the English forces into a trap. Accordingly, although he paid 5,000 marks to free Lord Grey, the king refused to ransom Mortimer.[13]

Among those who were disturbed by Henry's refusal to ransom Mortimer was the man's brother-in-law, Hotspur, who had fought hard against Owain himself. And then, in September, a further wedge was driven between the king and the Northumberland warlord when Hotspur and his father decisively defeated a Scots army in the battle of Homildon Hill. A range of rich ransoms were taken from the Scots leaders, but Henry – who was in desperate need of money – insisted they be given to him. This didn't seem the least bit fair to Hotspur and the men of the north who had actually taken the prisoners.

Only weeks later, Henry seized Mortimer's estates on the accusation that he had been a traitor to the crown. To be sure, there is no hint that Mortimer had ties to Owain before Bryn Glas. All evidence is to the contrary. But it's also true that almost as soon as Mortimer was accused of being Owain's ally, he actually *was*: in November of 1402 he married Owain's daughter, and on 13 December he openly announced his defection to Owain's cause: 'if King Richard is alive, his crown will be restored to him, and if that is not so, my honored nephew, who is by right heir to the said crown, will be king of England, and the said Owain will have his right in Wales.'[14] Most historians have viewed this as Mortimer being pushed into alliance with the enemy once Henry decided to abandon him, but it may be that there is a missing piece of evidence that would tell a very different story. This lack of certainty is in some sense the tragedy of history, though it holds within it the teasing possibility that tomorrow will bring a discovery that could change what we think we know of the past.

We don't know, but concern that Hotspur's allegiances might be at cross-purposes could be part of the reason that on 8 March 1403, Henry put his son, Prince Hal – the future Henry V – in charge of the royal response in Wales. There exists a letter that he wrote to his father, on 15 May, reporting that he had gone straight to Owain's home in Glyndyfrdwy:

> And there we torched a beautiful home in its park, and all the land around it. We camped there all that night, and some of our men issued out into the countryside and seized a significant gentleman of that place who was one of the chief supporters of Owain. He offered five hundred pounds for his ransom, and he promised to pay the full sum within two weeks if we would spare his life. We did not accept, and he was put to death. Many of his companions – taken on that same raid – suffered the same fate.[15]

The prince was 16.

This is the same period during which Shakespeare depicts the young man as a lay-about, drinking and whoring with John Falstaff and refusing to take the reins of government.

Why did Shakespeare represent Prince Hal this way? For starters, we should note that he was not the first to do so. Other sources also held that the young man had undergone a major change from the days of his youth to the responsibilities of adulthood.[16] Shakespeare knew that the idea of a changed man made for a good story. And *that*, more than anything, was what interested him. We may think of Shakespeare as a vaunted poet and artistic genius – and he was these things – but he was also a man who wanted to make money. He needed to sell tickets, to get, as we say today, bums on seats. Telling the truth about history might not accomplish that. Telling a story about history would.

Less than two months later, Hotspur and his father – the elder Henry Percy, who was earl of Northumberland – rebelled against Henry IV. On 21 July, at Shrewsbury, Hotspur was killed and the future Henry V took an arrow to the face.

Though the king was busy cleaning up the detritus of rebellion – and his son busy recovering from the horrific wound he had taken in that cause – Owain never ceased his struggle against the English. And while the hint that he might get help from Scotland was bad enough, it was soon looking a lot worse. At the end of summer, a couple of hundred French and Breton soldiers under the command of Jean d'Espagne arrived in South Wales. With their help, Owain's rebellion made considerable headway, including the taking of Harlech Castle the following spring.

In May 1404, d'Espagne's force returned to France, and it did not go alone. In addition to loot, it brought two Welshmen: Owain's brother-in-law and chancellor.

It was part of an audacious plan, cooked up in France and Wales, that could radically change the course of the Hundred Years War. An official peace had been kept between England and France by the yearly renewal of the truce dating to the time of Richard, but Louis of Orléans and others were anxious to see it undone.

It is fascinating that it was Orléans who, more than any of the other great lords of France, had so radically soured on the man to whom he had once made promises of support. Undermining the peace was one more way he could undermine the duke of Burgundy, of course, but Louis was also anxious to exploit the weakness of the English crown for his own end. His lands were right up against English holdings in Gascony, and he believed that a concerted French assault could push them out. To help push the realm to war, Louis had even gone so far as challenging the English king to a duel in August of 1402. Henry had replied by publicly reminding him of his earlier promises of support – an effort intended to make him look duplicitous in the eyes of the French – before pointing out that a duel was beneath him: 'What a king does, he does for the honour of God and the common good of his realm and of all Christendom, not for mere bombast and greed.'[17] The duel didn't happen, but Louis didn't stop pushing his realm harder and harder to reopen war with England.

So in the spring of 1404, the truce was not renewed. And as Owain held an independent parliament in Machynlleth, his men in France were negotiating with Charles VI and his designated advisors. The French recognized that what was good for the Welsh was bad for the English – and thus good for France. Like Brittany and Castile before it, Wales was fast becoming a proxy fight in the Hundred Years War. The result, in July, was the signing of agreements between Owain and Charles, who further directed King Henri III of Castile to aid the Welsh cause.[18]

And even *this* wasn't the worst of it.

At the end of April, Philippe the Bold died. His son, Jean the Fearless, took the title of duke of Burgundy, but he was not immediately in a position to act as a check on Louis of Orléans' efforts to conduct the affairs of France for the oft-absent king.[19]

Orléans had been spearheading several efforts to attack English interests. Plans were drawn up for summer assaults on Calais and Gascony, while an army was sent to Wales to support Owain and limit the English king's ability to assist his continental holdings. But for all his bravado, Orléans could not translate his dreams into effective reality.

Still, there was movement. The first days of 1405 saw a confederation signed between France and Wales.[20] And then, on 28 February, Owain, his new son-in-law Mortimer, and Hotspur's father, the earl of Northumberland, signed a document that historians call the Tripartite Indenture. It was a remarkable agreement. Clearly drafted by the Welsh, it outlines a pact that would have broken England in three after disposing of Henry: Owain would rule an expanded Wales in the west, while the other two men would have split the remainder, Mortimer to the south and Northumberland to the north. It was a plan to end England.[21]

They would hardly have agreed to such ends if they had not thought that achieving them was possible. Henry was on his heels, and the French were now preparing to land in force.

Unfortunately for Owain, the signing of the Tripartite Indenture marks the high point of the Welsh revolt. In the immediate months after that agreement was struck, the Welsh suffered a series of setbacks in battle. In March, a Welsh force reported to be some 8,000 strong fell upon the town of Grosmont and set it ablaze. The English prince, now back in command in Wales, responded by sending a rapid response force. The result was a major victory for the English. As the young man wrote to his father, the king, his men:

> were only a very small force in all, but it is very true that victory is not in the numbers of men, and this was well shown there: in the power of God and by the aid of the blessed Trinity your men won the field and vanquished all the said rebels and killed by reliable account on the battlefield at their return from pursuit, some say 800 and some 1000, on pain of their life.[22]

The numbers – both in terms of the total Welsh force and its casualties – seem high, but the prince was undoubtedly anxious to press the news of the success on both personal and political levels. They both knew the fragile nature of Henry IV's hold on power. There had been Shrewsbury, of course. But just the previous month Constance of York, the countess of Gloucester, had abducted Edmund Mortimer – the young man who had been Richard's designated heir before Henry's usurpation – and tried to spirit him away in an effort to use him as a figurehead for a new rebellion. She didn't get far before she was caught. The best guess is she was trying to take the boy to Wales.

As if the point needed to be underscored, at the start of May an uprising began in Yorkshire. It may be that the earl of Northumberland had received news of the Welsh loss at Grosmont and recognized that he needed to take the heat for his western allies. Towards the end of the month, Richard Scrope, the archbishop of York, gave support to the cause of overthrowing Henry. It ended disastrously when he was arrested by loyalist forces. After a trial in June, he was beheaded. Northumberland fled for Scotland.

Meanwhile, things had gone from bad to worse for the rebels in Wales. In a fight outside Usk in May, as a Welsh chronicler wrote, 'the turn [of fortune] began for Owain and his men'.[23] A different writer, Adam of Usk, provides details of a Welsh defeat and ruinous retreat:

> Gruffudd, the eldest son of Owain, attacked Usk castle with a great host on the feast of St. Gregory – an evil hour for him; however, the defences there had been considerably strengthened, and Lord Grey of Codnor, Sir John Greyndour, and many more of the king's soldiers were there, and they made a sortie in force from the castle and captured him and his men, driving them relentlessly through the river Usk, where many of them – most notably the abbot of Llantarnam – were killed either at the point of a sword or by drowning in the river, through Monkswood, where Gruffudd himself was captured, and on to the mountains of Upper Went. Of those whom they took alive, three hundred were beheaded in front of the castle, near Ponfald, although some of the nobler ones, including Gruffudd, were sent as prisoners to the king. This Gruffudd remained in captivity for six years, eventually dying of the plague in the Tower of London; and from this time onwards, Owain's fortunes began to wane in the region.[24]

Such was the situation when the French expeditionary force finally showed up in July.

The French invasion was led by Jean de Rieux, marshal of France, and several other lords. The Religieux says that they arrived in Milford Haven aboard 32 ships, though another source tells us it was 140 vessels.[25] It was at least 2,800 men strong.

After some initial successes in Wales, the combined army of these Frenchmen and Owain's rebels marched for England. On 7 August, a suitably worried Henry IV ordered his forces to gather in Hereford to repel the invasion.[26] He made all haste to get there himself.

What happened next is something of a mystery. Apparently, Henry deployed his forces upon high ground at Great Witley about ten miles from Worcester. The Franco-Welsh army took position on opposing high ground. Threats were exchanged. A few knights engaged in duels or jousts between the armies. And then, for reasons that remain unknown, the Franco-Welsh force retreated back to Wales.

If a deal had been struck, we don't know of it. Our sources are remarkably silent on what transpired – far more silent than is to be expected given the depth of the incursion into English lands. Indeed, there are those who question whether the French invaded beyond the Welsh borders at all. Such an endeavour ought to have left a major mark upon the landscape of texts, and the landscape of towns and countryside, too.

The French wintered over in Wales. Their presence now was a negative: they were more mouths to feed and more bodies to house in a land stripped of resources.

The next spring, Owain tried to pick up the pieces. In March 1406, he wrote to France, promising to change the allegiance of the churches in Wales from the pope in Rome to the pope in Avignon. He only needed to garner further support for his cause. The Pennal Letters, as they are called, went unanswered.

France had problems of its own.

THE MURDER OF LOUIS OF ORLÉANS

In 1404, Jean the Fearless had inherited from his father the vast wealth and power of Burgundy. From his mother, he had received Artois and Flanders. He was, quite quickly, one of the most powerful men in France. And it was clear from the outset that he did *not* like Louis of Orléans, who had used the death of Philippe the Bold to take a firmer grip on the levers of power whenever the king succumbed to madness.

But Jean was a cunning man. During one of the king's periods of madness, Jean managed to secure for himself the position of guardian to the dauphin – also named Louis, but we'll call him by his title to help keep things straight – and the other children of Charles. It was a brilliant, if Machiavellian move. Louis of Orléans was furious. The rivalry between Burgundy and Orléans was not just reopened, it was massively intensified. The two men were raising private armies. Major bloodshed loomed.

In 1407, the elderly duke of Berry stepped in and tried to get cooler heads to prevail. In a brokered meeting, the two men agreed to peace and gave solemn assurances that they would do nothing rash.

It lasted three days. On the night of 23 November 1407, Louis of Orléans was murdered on the streets of Paris. The assassination had been planned long before Jean the Fearless was making his shows of peace-making. Having made those shows, he made no effort to call off the attack.[27]

The assassins rented a house near the Hôtel Barbette, the royal residence of the queen, where Louis often dined. On the appointed evening, just after eight, Louis was falsely summoned to meet the king at the Hôtel Saint-Pol. Taking a mule, he started out with three companions and four attendants bearing torches. The duke was, eyewitnesses would later report, in fine spirits.

As he passed the rented house, a dozen men rushed out of the dark, crying murder. Louis was dragged off his mount. One torch-bearer was killed immediately, another put near to death. The duke's page played dead as the rest of his companions bolted. Louis, on the ground, asked what was happening. Then they set upon him (Figure 9).

The attempted assassination of the constable Olivier de Clisson on the streets of Paris in 1392 had led to the crippling mental illness of the king. That illness had now led to a successful assassination on those same streets.

It was fitting that the current constable, Charles d'Albret, was one of the first men on the scene after the duke's assassination. An axe had taken Louis' left hand. His right arm, raised to defend himself, had been shattered. His face was beaten in, his skull burst open. His brains were strewn across the street.

The rented house of the assassins was in flames – an attempt to cover their tracks.

Jean the Fearless pretended to be shocked when he was told what had happened. He wept. He helped escort the duke's coffin to burial.

All the while, the Provost of Paris was investigating. In a remarkable *tour de force* of medieval detective work, he put the pieces together in just two days, announcing to the gathered lords of the realm that he needed to question them. Jean balked and, taking the dukes of Berry and Anjou aside, admitted to them that he had orchestrated the assassination. A day later, Berry told the council. Jean fled Paris.

The murder set off what is now known as the Armagnac–Burgundian Civil War – though clearly the roots of this conflict stretch much further back. On one side were the supporters of Jean the Fearless, the duke of Burgundy. On the other side were the supporters of Louis of Orléans' son, Charles, who received the early support of the count of Armagnac. What is considered modern France was split between them, but the nature of medieval lordships and titles meant that there was no contiguous border between the belligerent parties. The country was a jumbled mix of allegiances, all loosely bound by their ties to a mad king. And along the kingdom's edges – at Calais and in the sliver of Gascony that remained in their hands – the English were still lurking.

A PRINCE RAISED IN BATTLE

At least in the first years of the civil war, however, there was no English power ready to take advantage of this new weakness. Henry IV was still struggling to contain Owain and the Welsh. That revolt might be dwindling, but it still continued to syphon away time and resources. Good news came in 1409, when Harlech Castle – a significant fortification that had been seized by Owain's forces – was at last recaptured for the crown, and the elder Mortimer, who had gone over to the Welsh cause after his defeat at Bryn Glas, died in the process.

So at least *some* threats to the crown were drying up.

At the same time, however, Henry's health was failing. In the decade since he had become king, he had known nothing but threats. It was bound to take its toll on his mind and body.

Unlike in France, though, where an ailing king brought the instability of competing forces seeking greater control, in England there was little debate about who would help step into the void. It would be the young Prince Hal, who after recovering from his wounds at Shrewsbury had gone back into the field to lead the fight against Owain and the Welsh.

His years in Wales were formative for the future Henry V. It was a struggle that had begun when he was 14 and lasted into his twenties: he had become a man on the battlefield, and it had taught him a great many lessons that would carry him through to Agincourt.

One hard-won lesson was how important it was to hold fortified sites against the enemy, and what a difficult slog it was to retake them if lost. The castle at Aberystwyth, for instance, was taken by the Welsh in 1404. The prince had to lead extensive efforts to drive them out, including a long-term siege that did not recapture the castle until 1408. Harlech had taken another year to recover. Fortifications were built to dominate the landscape and enforce political will. They were essential to any hope of establishing lasting control over a region.

There, too, he had learned the necessity of money in war: men had to be paid and fed, engines of war had to be built and maintained. Despite the prince's repeated calls for financial backing, it was several years into the rebellion before he began receiving what he considered the necessary monetary support for the fight. Up to then he had been working with a 'shoe-string' budget, which meant taking extra care with every coin. Fiscal responsibility became something of a habit for the young man. It would not have been lost on him that as soon as he had the resources he needed, the war began to turn around for the English. Investments in war, he must have concluded, paid dividends on the field.

These years also taught him the value – and volatility – of personal loyalty. Our records make clear that he heavily relied upon and rewarded a core group of soldiers who followed him throughout his career. At the same time, the rebellions of Hotspur and others of his countrymen would never have been far from his mind. For that matter, the rebellion in Wales was, in the most literal sense, a rebellion against him personally: the lands there were, from the point of view of the English, *his*. So Prince Hal had both a good reason to distrust his fellow men and an undeniable need to hold close those who earned his faith.

Above all, he was a man who had learned to put his ultimate trust in God.

As I said at the outset of this book, it is hard not to see Shrewsbury as the key determinant of this mentality. The prince had experienced first hand the grim costs of war, and he had survived. He might well have carried this confidence as a sense of divine blessing. Those who followed him might have felt likewise.

If so, that faith would be tested soon enough.

THE NEW KING

Prince Hal was 26 when he became King Henry V on 20 March 1413 (Figure 10). Separating the man from the myth of Henry V is difficult. His victory at Agincourt just two years into his reign – and the legend of greatness that came with it – recast him into an incomparable and inaccessible figure. His mistakes were moulded into mysterious strategies. Even his quirks became examples of excellence.

Reports that he would 'rebuke even notable captains for looking him in the face when talking to him', for instance, are related in a positive light – the king had 'a forbidding public presence' – rather than negatively because he was the successful Henry V and not, say, the floundering Henry IV.[28] We see this kind of spin again and again not just in the history books, but in our original sources, too. It makes sense to expect this in the English sources, which tend to sanitize their victorious monarch whenever possible. But it shows up in the French sources as well, where the political blocks that were bickering and jockeying for power used Henry as a contrast to their rivals. If they wanted to blame the French loss on disorganization, they would paint Henry as the most organized king possible. If they blamed the French king for not being present at the battle, they made sure to emphasize Henry's warrior status. If the loss was God's will, on the other hand, they wanted to paint Henry as something akin to a priest-king.

Of all the characterizations of Henry, I suspect that this last one is the most accurate. His life to this point had certainly angled him towards devotion. A Frenchman who spent a week at court in the run-up to the Agincourt campaign thought the king 'better suited to be a churchman than a soldier'.[29] Still, the real Henry remains something of a cypher. Again and again, we run into those lenses of history, those axes to grind.

We can never know his exact thoughts, but we can be certain of his actions. It is clear that he was extremely sensitive to his family's tenuous hold on power. His father's usurpation of the throne from Richard II had frayed the fabric that held the country together. Revolt after revolt had nearly torn it apart. As prince he had witnessed it all. He had taken that arrow to the face at Shrewsbury facing Hotspur. He had ordered men's deaths in Wales. He had watched the kingdom's coffers empty and its prestige evaporate. It is little surprise that, as king, he was determined to stabilize the realm.

One of his first acts, therefore, was to issue a general amnesty to those who had rebelled against his father. Soon after, he had the remains of the deposed king disinterred from the smaller church where Henry IV had ordered him buried. With ceremony, Richard II's body was moved to his tomb in Westminster Abbey. Both were respectful gestures, attempts to heal old wounds, but we can't ignore their practical political value: behind every rebellion had been rumours that Richard might still be alive. Henry was, in the name of honouring the king, making it quite clear that he was not.

Smart moves, but they weren't enough. Henry knew all too well that nothing created unity quite so efficiently as a war. It was the primary reason his father had gone to Scotland in 1400 at the outset of his own reign. That campaign hadn't quite gone to plan, of course, but his son had bigger dreams. Where his father had looked north Henry V cast his gaze in the other direction.

South.

As the king of England turned his eyes to France, the eyes of the competing factions there were likewise turning their eyes to him.

The duke of Burgundy had, by 1409, rationalized the assassination of Louis of Orléans as an act of tyrannicide: the king's brother had been justifiably killed for his sins and his efforts to acquire power. With the Treaty of Chartres that year, Jean the Fearless was formally absolved of wrongdoing, welcomed back into court, and made to reconcile with Louis' son Charles, who had taken up his father's title as duke of Orléans. It was a public resolution, but by no means was it an end to the private scheming.

With a new king on the throne of England, the duke of Burgundy saw a chance to flex his muscles in the French court and lead negotiations for a new peace that would keep his own interests safe while countering the interests of the rival Armagnacs. That same spring and summer, though, the duke misplayed his hand in Paris by supporting the Cabochien revolt. He had hoped to use this popular uprising to pass new ordinances that would shift more control of the kingdom into his hands, but the revolt – after a few riotous and bloody months – had to be put down by force. Once again, the duke was forced to flee to his holdings in Burgundy. From there, he still tried to conduct negotiations with Henry V, but he had few cards to play. He offered the English king the hand of his daughter, but the Armagnacs now back in control of the French court were offering up marriage to Charles VI's teenaged daughter, Catherine.

Henry eventually agreed that he would not undertake any attack against France until February 1415. This truce gave him time to build up his strength. It also gave him more time to play the sides in France against each other. He was angling for a broad settlement in English favour, something like the reinstatement of the old Treaty of Brétigny. No one on the French side had much interest in that. From what they could tell, Henry might not be long for the throne anyway: recent English history was nothing but a sequence of rebellions. As if to drive the point home, in October 1413 Sir John Oldcastle, a veteran soldier who had faithfully served Henry in Wales only to be declared a heretic for supporting a Christian reformation movement popularly termed Lollardy, escaped from the Tower of London and worked to foment an uprising that would take down church and crown. It didn't come to much, as those who gathered for the planned uprising in January were decisively beaten by royal forces, but Oldcastle himself escaped and would remain at large – with fresh calls to rebellion only a rumour away – until his capture and execution in 1417.

THE LETTERS OF THE DAUPHIN

At the end of 1413, Jean the Fearless declared that he had received letters, supposedly written by the dauphin himself, claiming that he and his mother the queen were being held prisoner in Paris at the Louvre. For the sake of France, the dauphin was begging for rescue. Only the army of the good duke of Burgundy could save them.

Nothing about this seems to have been true.[30] No originals of the letters exist. They were, almost assuredly, forged on the orders of the duke of Burgundy, who was anxious for a pretence that would allow him to march on Paris. He had failed to take the regency of the kingdom by assassination. He had failed to take it by popular rebellion. So he would try to do it at the head of an army.

In January 1414, the dauphin made public pronouncements that the letters were a lie. He and his mother were doing just fine, thank you. But still there were many who believed – or wanted to believe – that Jean the Fearless was coming to the rescue of the crown. North of Paris, the army of Burgundy began to gather. The Armagnac forces did the same in response.

By early February, Jean the Fearless and his army had taken position at Saint-Denis, just beyond Paris. Inside the city, Armagnac supporters were attacking anyone they suspected of supporting the Burgundian side. The bickering of the political elites trickled down onto the streets, sparking all manner of crimes.

Jean the Fearless didn't have a chance in hell of breaching the walls of Paris if they stood against him. His only hope was that the citizens themselves would open the gates to him. But the public declarations of the dauphin – the young man he was ostensibly there to save – were doing nothing to help his cause. Worse, the king, who had been 'absent' up to this point, apparently recovered his wits long enough to make public appearances and to make declarations in favour of the Armagnacs. The gates of Paris were locked, and it was clear they were going to stay that way. On 16 February, the duke retreated.

The next day, he was declared a traitor. Within weeks, the Armagnacs were turning their strength from defence to offence. By the start of April, they were marching north out of the city, a momentarily sane Charles VI at their head, the sacred French battle flag called the *Oriflamme* held aloft. They were marching on Burgundy. All that month they steamrolled north. The destruction was enormous. In the sacking of Soissons, the Armagnac forces reportedly killed some 1,200 of their countrymen.

The fighting dragged through the summer, as Jean the Fearless tried to slow down the Armagnac advance, losing city after city. And all the while messengers were on the move in a triangular dance between the Armagnacs, the Burgundians, and the English. Everyone knew that their opponents were talking to each other. Everyone wanted to end up with the winning hand.

But wars cost real money, and Burgundy was out of it. The Armagnacs were scraping the barrel, too. Foodstuffs were running out. In the Armagnac camp besieging Burgundian Arras, dysentery was rampant. And everyone, even Jean the Fearless, was beginning to think the English might be coming with no cause to help *any* of them.

At the start of September, the dauphin negotiated an agreement to end the siege of Arras and, with it, the Armagnac attack on the duke of Burgundy. The Armagnac leaders were not consulted in this, and they were livid. Charles of Orléans, who had come to get vengeance on the man who had assassinated his father, only swore to uphold the agreement when forced to do so by the dauphin.

TO FRANCE

The ink was hardly dry on the settlement between the Armagnacs and Burgundians outside of Arras when Henry V decided he was ready to bring war to France.

Shakespeare famously attributed Henry's determination to an insult: in the summer of 1414 the dauphin had sent him a gift of tennis balls, implying that the new English king was immature and unready for real games of war. Offended and enraged when he received these at Kenilworth Castle, Henry retorted that he would send back English cannonballs by attacking France. The story goes back to within a decade or two of the supposed event, so it may have some truth.[31] The heart of it, though, was nothing so petty. Henry clearly didn't think that the newly forged peace in France would last. And the timing with his own ambitions and his own administration was ideal.

Despite Oldcastle's attempt at an uprising in October 1413, Henry was clearly feeling more secure in his own lands. By 1 December 1413, Owain's imprisoned daughter, the wife of Mortimer, was dead, along with their daughters.[32] It had been a long time since anyone had heard from the Welsh rebel himself, and up north the Percies were pushing up the daisies. The following May, Parliament officially declared the Welsh rebellion over. The threat from the west had passed.

For years, France had been crippled by the madness of its king. Now it stood even further divided by the fighting between the Armagnacs and Burgundians. All that time, England hadn't taken advantage of the French weakness.

That was about to change.

It was God's will.

Henry had, of course, agreed to a truce until early 1415. But that did not mean that he couldn't begin the preparations for war that winter. Everyone knew that many months of lead time would be necessary. The army the king was building was massive.

In June 1415, French ambassadors arrived in England, still hoping to stave off war. There had been no secret of the military build-up across the Channel. They knew what Henry planned to do, even if they didn't know the where or the when.

When Henry received the ambassadors at Wolvesey Castle in Winchester on 30 June, one of the first things he did was to ask after their king's health.[33] It was a none too subtle slight. He then told them that they would get to business soon.

The ambassadors had safe conduct until 7 July, so their anxiety must have increased as they were left cooling their heels day after day. They could do nothing but watch the comings and goings of military men. Henry clearly had an eye for drama, as he made it clear that he was too busy preparing to invade their country to talk to them.

On 2 July, talks began, but little headway was made. The English made clear that Henry was coming for his rightful lands unless the French gave them to him. On 4 July, the French put an offer on the table that would let the English king hold the lands that had been given over in the old Treaty of Brétigny and taken back by the French in the years since – and even more in the region of the Limousin. It was a wildly generous offer. No one in France would welcome it. But no one in the weakened and divided country wanted a war, either. Henry told the ambassadors that he would think about it.

It was a lie. He knew his answer.

Holding lands wasn't the answer. This was the problem that had caused the Hundred Years War in the first place. He would *have* the lands, or he would have war.

Still, he made them wait.

For two days.

While the ambassadors waited, on 5 July, Henry offered to pardon his old adversary, Owain Glyndŵr.[34] It was, undoubtedly, one more measure to ensure peace at home while he prepared to go abroad. The rebel – if he was still alive, he would have been about 57 – never responded to the offer. What happened to him, no one knows. He was never caught. His burial place is as unknown as the date of his death. Many in Wales say that he never died. He's just waiting, like Arthur, for the time to be right for him to return and once more raise the banner of the golden dragon to the sun. It's good to dream.

The next morning, the French were provided with a counter-proposal. Henry would give them a truce to be counted in decades in return for the lands he demanded and the hand of the French king's daughter – with an accordant pile of treasure for a dowry. It was nothing the ambassadors had authority to give. More discussions were had in the quiet rooms of Wolvesey Castle through the day, but no concessions were being offered. It was, in retrospect, one grand act of theatre.

That evening, the ambassadors were brought to the great hall. Henry was enthroned in triumph, surrounded by his great lords. It was a sight to inspire both awe and dread. Reading from a prepared statement – of which copies had been made to hand out to the stunned Frenchmen – the archbishop ran through the laundry list of England's many attempts to keep the peace and Henry's magnanimous offers to try to prevent war. Denied justice, the king of England had no choice but to go to war. The ambassadors were dismissed. Henry took horse towards Southampton, where his army and the fleet that would take them to France were gathering.

As the French ambassadors were being escorted back to Dover, one was overheard telling a colleague that Henry ought to have been more receptive to negotiating, 'if he wanted to be secure' on his throne. It was widely understood, after all, that 'the king had many rivals in his own kingdom', including many who thought another man ought to have the crown, like the earl of March. If instead the king continued raising an army for war with France, the Frenchman mused, 'he would expose himself to dangers both within and without. Internally, what happened to King Richard could happen to him.' That is, Richard's campaign in Ireland had given Bolingbroke the opening he needed to seize the country, and Henry's campaign overseas could result in someone doing the same to him:

> If the king made only a brief incursion into France and then quickly came back, he would have accomplished nothing and spent a lot of money doing it, which would anger his people when he returned. If instead he stayed a long time – two or three months, perhaps – then the armed forces of France would have assembled, and they were far better trained in arms than the English were used to, and the lords of France would by then be at peace and united, putting the king himself in grave danger. [35]

When it came to France, in other words, Henry was courting trouble no matter what he did, so he would be better off staying at home and leaving the matter alone.

The fact that the king was still not in complete control of his kingdom was clear on 31 July, when the earl of March came to Henry and admitted that he had been party to a plot that intended to unite Oldcastle's disaffected followers with the resuscitated dream of the Tripartite Indenture – that coordination to destroy the monarchy and split it up between the Welsh, the Mortimers, and the Percies. It was a complicated plan that involved, among other parties, the earl of Cambridge, a man who was pretending to be the dead Richard II, and one of the king's own advisors, Henry Scrope. Within days, all those in reach of the king were arrested. The ringleaders were quickly tried and executed.

Would more men try to steal away his throne while he was away in France? Henry couldn't know. But at this point there was no backing down. The die had been cast.

On 11 August, he sailed for France.

Part Three

The Agincourt Campaign

Owre Kynge went forth to Normandy
With grace and myght of chyvalry
Ther God for hym wrought mervelusly;
Wherefore Englonde may call and cry
Chorus
Deo gratias!
Deo gratias Anglia redde pro victoria![1]

The Agincourt Carol

6

The Siege of Harfleur, 13 August–22 September

There was no means for Henry to prevent news of the gathering fleet in Southampton from reaching French ports. Merchants plied the Channel with regularity. So did spies and other informants. No surprise, then, that the French had information well in advance that the English were bringing a massive army to their shores. On 3 June, the royal council in Paris had written to officials in Normandy warning that the English planned 'to enter our kingdom and make war with all their might by land and sea'.[1] The French knew the English were coming. The question was *where exactly would they land*?

The man initially in charge of the French defence was 30-year-old Jean I, duke of Alençon. He knew – as everyone did – the playbook established by Edward III in the Crécy campaign, which involved a landing on the Cotentin peninsula itself. Working off the assumption that Henry's invasion was to some degree modelled on that of his great-grandfather, Alençon reinforced the garrisons there, as well as those across the entire Lower Normandy coast, from Valognes to Honfleur. If Henry attempted to land on the Baie de la Seine, he would meet intense resistance.

At a basic level, Alençon was not wrong. To understand what Henry V was doing invading France in 1415, we really do need to look back to the model he was probably seeking to emulate: Edward's Crécy campaign in 1346. This was the victory that had brought Calais into

English hands, the English victory that was arguably greater than any other in the Hundred Years War, the ideal by which everything else was judged. Henry wanted a Crécy of his own, and it seems clear that he intended to get it by following in Edward's footsteps as closely as possible. By concentrating his defence in Normandy, Alençon was making a well-informed, solid bet.

But even the best bets can lose.

Because while Henry may have sought to emulate the glories of Crécy, he also wasn't ignorant about Edward's troubles in getting there. In 1346, Edward faced a great number of difficulties. Some of these, like the king's desperation at Blanchetaque or the Black Prince's capture on the battlefield, had long since been spun into triumph. There is little trace of the far harder truths in the popular English understanding of the campaign by Henry's time. Henry's plan, it seems, was to try to follow Edward's footsteps from the Somme to Calais. That route had been nothing but glory, the stuff of legend. But the Seine ... well, the Seine was hard to spin into any kind of positive. It had ended well – or at least hadn't ended in the disaster it could have been – because Edward had managed to sneak across the river at Poissy and escape. But Philippe VI's holding of the river in 1346 could not be looked upon as some kind of three-dimensional chess that the *English* had been playing. If Edward's engineers hadn't managed to rebuild the bridge, if his army hadn't managed to sneak across at night, if Philippe hadn't thought that the English king had agreed to meet him on the field of battle south of the city, then the history books would tell a very different story of the events of 1346: a story of Philippe's strategic brilliance and Edward's staggering blunder in marching his army to ruin in the shadow of Paris.

Setting off in 1415, Henry was determined not to make the same mistake. He would have Edward's glory, but he would do it without the risk of crossing the Seine. He didn't land on the Cotentin peninsula, as Edward had. Nor did he come ashore on any of the other Normandy beaches where Alençon expected him. All of these points were on the wrong side of the Seine and would require him to fight his way across that wide and well-guarded river. Instead, he would come ashore on the *north* side of the river.

Otherwise, though, Alençon was right to expect Crécy 2.0. Edward had seized a French city – Caen – then marched across the Blanchetaque and on to Calais. Henry would take a French city – Harfleur – then march across the same ford and to the same city. Edward had met the French *en route* and defeated them in battle. Henry, no doubt, was certain he would do likewise if it came to that.

And so he did.

Just not at all in the way he expected.

HENRY'S ARMY

The army that Henry had raised relied on both the carrot and the stick. At one level it called upon men of rank whose positions were linked to their oaths to fight for the crown. If they refused to uphold these oaths, those positions could be forfeit. Other men fought for pay and potential further earnings in the field via looting and the taking of ransoms.

Most of the hired soldiers served under captains, who made contracts agreeing to provide a certain number of men, who would be paid a specific amount of money from the state treasury depending on where the expedition might go. These contracts were written out twice on a single sheet, which was then separated into two individual copies by a random, jagged cut, forming unique 'teeth'. Because the Latin word for teeth is *dentes*, the contracts are known as indentures. The point of the cut was to create a means of establishing authenticity: a valid indenture would have a perfect fit with its corresponding half. The text would match, and so would the jagged edge. Matching text meant neither party had attempted to alter the agreement. Meshing teeth meant only one copy of the agreement could be executed.

The continued existence of so many of these indentures, along with the further records that were needed to keep track of the whole enterprise – including the muster rolls listing the names of the men who took their places in the army[2] – means we may know more about the English army that set sail for France in 1415 than we do about any other army in the Middle Ages. The accountants and record-keepers were diligent in their work. Careful management of financial resources, we might remember, is one of the habits Henry had learned in Wales.

That so many records exist is wonderful, but it also makes how little we know about the army upsetting.

Let's start with what we do know.

The indentures suggest a ratio of the types of soldier that the English were gathering in 1415: there would be three archers for each man-at-arms. Many armies of the previous century had a relatively equal ratio between these troop types, but the recent garrisons in Wales had moved towards the inclusion of an ever-greater number of archers. This build-up coincides with the appointment of the young Prince Hal to command in Wales.

Some have seen this as a coincidence, pointing out that archers were cheaper to outfit. Since 'the Lancastrian kings were frequently short of funds', this made their presence 'a useful ploy'.[3] This is true enough, but I don't think we can set aside the timing. Archers had *always* been cheaper to field, and they had more than proven their worth in Edward's Crécy campaign and elsewhere. Cost-effectiveness was just one of many reasons to favour an archer-dominated army in the nearly seven decades since 1346.

But it hadn't happened until Henry was in charge.

He was the difference, and little surprise that he was: a man who had not just seen the longbow in action at the battle of Shrewsbury, but nearly been killed by one.

Regardless of why he brought the archers, we have a fairly good idea of how many of them Henry brought. He had roughly 12,000 fighting men in total. Of these, 9,000 or more would fight with bows.[4] It wasn't quite the 14,000 men – half archers – that Edward had brought for his Crécy campaign, but it was a massive army nonetheless.[5]

And it wasn't just fighters. A medieval army of this size brought with it everyone – and everything – it might need. There were men to make and maintain weapons, but there were also men to make and maintain the carts and wagons that would carry them and the mules and packhorses that pulled the same. The fact that so many of Henry's men were mounted – men-at-arms and archers alike – meant a whole swathe of saddle-makers, blacksmiths, and grooms. There were also carpenters, masons, stone-cutters, leather-workers, wranglers, and a large company of miners – this last group highly specialized in undermining walls to bring them down in a siege. There were tent-makers to help house the men, and a whole slew of camp-followers to feed them, do their wash for coin, and tend to any other needs they might have. And the king had to be kept in royal style, even on campaign: that meant kitchen staff, chamberers, people to tend to his wardrobe, and even his own chapel and minstrels.

Much of this non-fighting component was as it had been on other campaigns before (and after) this one. But there were differences.

One difference was the surgeons. Lots of them. The English army of 1415 had a *bona fide* surgical corps. A surgeon had saved Henry's life after Shrewsbury, and now the king brought not only his own personal surgeon, but two other lead surgeons – Thomas Morstede and William Bradwardine – at the head of dozens of additional medical staff and a significant supply of medical stores, including copious amounts of medicinal honey.[6]

Another new feature was a sizeable artillery train of largely small and medium-sized guns.

All of these men, plus an equal or even greater number of horses, in addition to the non-combatants, the supplies, the livestock ... when everything was put together the tonnage that had to be shipped across the English Channel was enormous. The crown had to put its full fleet into the effort – including Henry's own 540-ton flagship, the *Trinity Royal*[7] – as well as a great number of ships hired out from the Low Countries and English ports. There were an estimated 700 ships, with 14,000 men aboard once the non-combatants were added, and up to 20,000 horses as well.[8] Everything and everyone was gathered at Portsmouth. The Solent became a forest of masts.

On 11 August, the time had come.

The fleet set sail, bound for France.

THE LANDING AND THE *GESTA*

It took two days for the ships to cross the English Channel. Their destination was the Cap de la Hève, west of the target city of Harfleur. The coastline north of this point was rough cliffs, so the landing point would have been around the southern shore, on the coastline below the town of Sainte-Adresse. Today, the beautiful

Villa Maritime Museum looks out upon the sea over wide and inviting beaches, but in 1415 the coastline was strewn with rocks at or just below the water-line that were ready-made to sink a ship.

The source of this information is a detailed recounting of the campaign composed by a chaplain close to the English king's household. Not only is it an eyewitness account, but it appears to have been completed by the spring of 1417, when memories of what had happened would be fresh. It is today known by its Latin title, *Gesta Henrici Quinti* – 'The Deeds of Henry V' – and it is widely regarded as the most reliable story of the English side of the invasion.

It doesn't come without question marks, though. Eyewitness accounts are tremendously useful in history, just as they are in courts of law today, but they are always biased to one degree or another. The anonymous author who wrote the *Gesta*, for instance, made no secret of his adoration of Henry V – to the point that many believe the work to be written for the king himself.[9] Even accounting for this, we find again and again that the Chaplain, as I'll refer to its author, blesses us with important details that consistently check out against the other streams of information that we can bring to bear: other chroniclers, administrative accounts, even the very ground itself. Though a great many sources will be cited throughout the rest of this book, the *Gesta* will be the bedrock to which we will return again and again.

As the English ships arrived off shore on 13 August, for instance, the Chaplain informs us that Henry summoned his war council to his ship the *Trinity Royal* – a communication managed by unfurling a banner – where they discussed whether to begin the landing at once. They all knew they needed to establish a beachhead, and they all knew that the faster this was done the less likely it would be that the French could repel the effort. But it was by this point late in the afternoon, and the rocky shoreline meant that the landing would be slow and laborious. The larger English cogs that had brought most of the army over the Channel had to keep in deeper water, so the vast majority of the men, horses, and supplies would have to be transferred from these big ships to smaller ships before they could be transferred to shore. If they started now, only a few men would be ashore before nightfall, which could leave them in a precarious position should the French attack.

These concerns suggest that the English hadn't chosen their landing point to avoid Alençon. They didn't know that he was stretched out across Lower Normandy on the other side of the Seine. They had chosen to be on the north side of the river for their own purposes, and Alençon had guessed wrong. The lands that were about to be overrun with English were almost entirely undefended. Harfleur's garrison at that moment comprised only 34 men-at-arms and a gathering of crossbowmen.[10]

Early the next morning, the English began their landing. It took them three days. The *Gesta* reports that Henry sent out a slew of orders organizing his men for the campaign. The army would be in three primary divisions, often referred to as 'battles': the vanguard at the front of the march would be under the command of the duke of Clarence; Henry himself would command the centre; and the rearguard would be under the earl of Suffolk. If they arrayed for battle, the vanguard would be at the king's right and the rearguard to his left.

Henry also issued ordinances meant to control the behaviour of his troops as they set out into a country peopled by those he viewed as his rightful subjects:

> Meanwhile, among other most honourable ordinances, the king had wisely instructed the army under penalty of death that no more arson should be committed (as had been done at the beginning), that the churches and other sacred buildings should be left untouched along with their property, and that no one should lay a hand on a woman, a priest, or a servant of the church – unless they happened to be armed, or were committing violence or assault.[11]

We do not have copies of the exact ordinances as they were sent to the captains of the army to be read aloud to their men, but surviving texts from some of Henry's later campaigns show a remarkable consistency with what the Chaplain reports about the rules of the 1415 campaign.[12] The king apparently took a keen interest in the behaviour of his men, and he insisted on strict, typically deadly punishment for any disciplinary infraction.

It's easy to imagine that Henry's interest in controlling his army was driven by religious concerns above all else. He was a good

Christian king, after all. But these rules and regulations were common, even if they haven't commonly survived. There were military necessities. At Shrewsbury, he and his father had almost lost the battle when the discipline of the right side of their line failed. Only his ability to order his own charge had saved the day. He had likewise seen in Wales how easy it was for forces moving through hostile territory to be whittled down by their adversaries if the columns didn't hang together and stragglers could be picked off. To win the war, discipline had to be maintained.

Unless it didn't have to be. Because this was about military necessity and not high-minded principle, there can be no question that Henry was prepared to set the rules aside if it was to his advantage to do so. In his play *Julius Caesar*, Shakespeare has Mark Antony famously proclaim the need to 'let slip the dogs of war',[13] but we need go no further than the prologue to his *Henry V* to find the threat made clear for the campaign in 1415:

> Then should the warlike Harry, like himself,
> Assume the port of Mars; and at his heels,
> Leash'd in like hounds, should famine, sword and fire
> Crouch for employment.[14]

The hounds of destruction might have been leashed by Henry's ordinances, but they were also there, ready to employed. They were always hungry.

They would be fed.

THE SIEGE BEGINS

Henry's initial target was on high alert. Local leaders may not have had the ability to push the English off the shoreline, but Harfleur was a walled town. Fortifications are force multipliers, and the three days that it had taken the English to land had brought several hundred additional reinforcements to further man its walls. It had also given the city's defenders time to take steps to make an English siege difficult indeed.

Though the walls are long since gone, the situation Henry faced is clear even today. Harfleur sits in a valley astride the River Lézarde, surrounding what was then a decent port off the mouth of the Seine; this port was no doubt what made the city such a tempting target for the English. Modern drainage and canal work have made the river running south of Harfleur a straight shot through dry ground, but in 1415 it would have cut a winding course through muddy, tidal marshes. To deter an English attack from this direction by ship, the waters were staked and the channel cut off by chains. The ground north of the town was far drier on either side of the meandering Lézarde. As soon as they were aware that the English were coming, the townspeople had closed the river's control gates on the north side of the town, forcing its waters to back up into the valley to the north. Ultimately, this makeshift lake spilled out around the city's western walls, filling the deep ditches in front of them. The city's weakest points – as was often the case – were its three gates. These were protected by newly built timber barbicans: fortifications that pushed the defence-works further out from the existing walls and put potential besiegers under fire from multiple directions at once. The people of Harfleur had done what they could.

Henry established his initial headquarters at the priory of Graville, high on a hillside overlooking Harfleur. By the time he and his commanders were looking down upon the city, the *Gesta* tells us, the low-lying plains were covered in water up to a man's thighs. The water was far deeper in the ditches before the walls. The duke of Clarence had to take his men on a long night march north of the town to get them to the other side of the valley, arriving by dawn on 19 August, at which point the English had the city surrounded. How many people were trapped inside, is unknown. There were probably at least 6,000 people living there when the English had first landed, though many would have subsequently fled.

Henry called on the ones who were left to surrender. When they refused, he ordered the dozen or so artillery pieces deployed around the town to open fire. A French source would later claim that the gunpowder weapons that unloaded upon the city were of 'monstrous size, spewing out great boulders amid clouds of thick smoke and a noise like the fires of Hell'.[15] We don't think the calibre of the English artillery was extraordinary. The guns had been brought by ship, then hauled up and over the hills from the landing beaches.

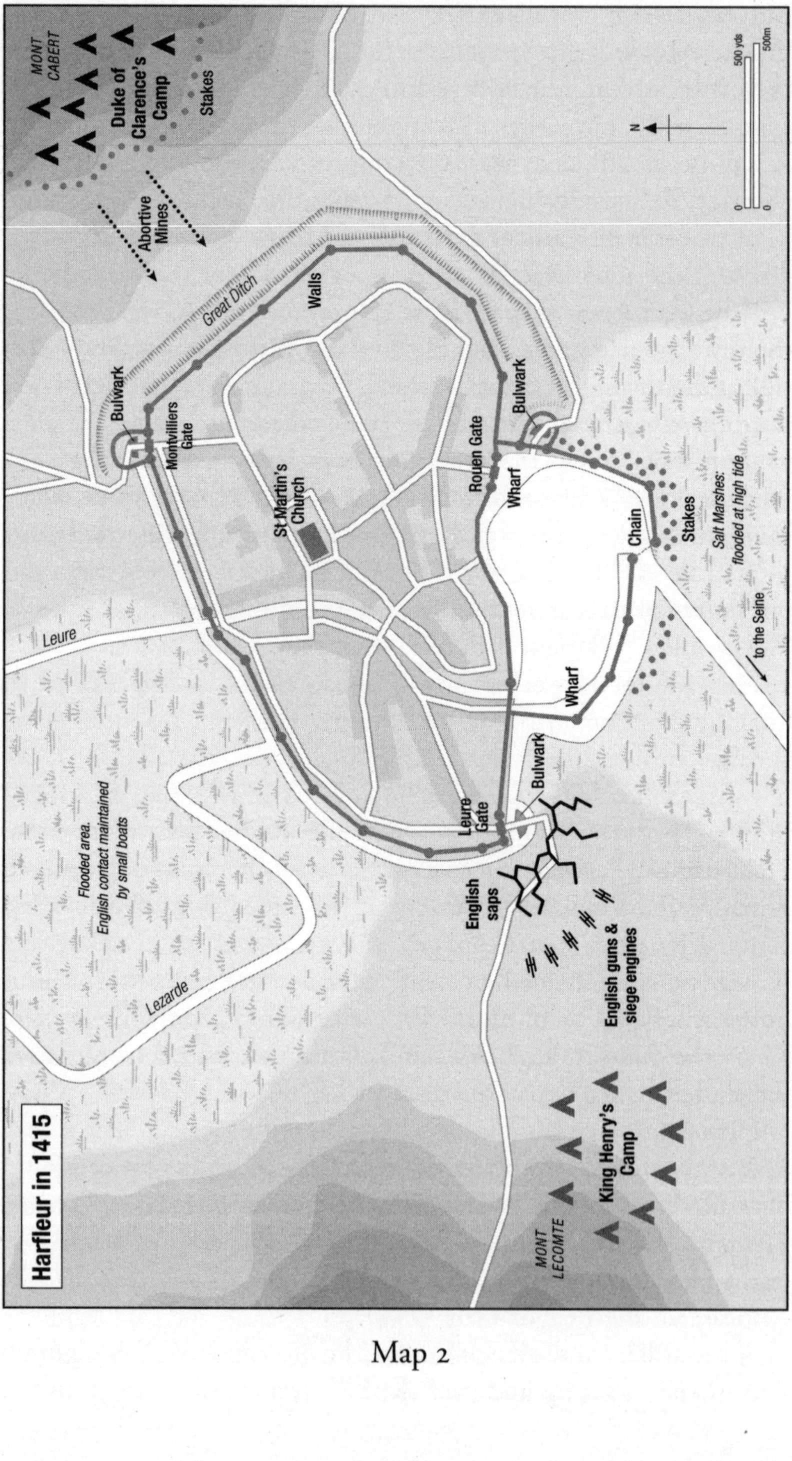
Harfleur in 1415
MONT CABERT
Duke of Clarence's Camp
Stakes
Abortive Mines
Great Ditch
Walls
Bulwark
Montvilliers Gate
St Martin's Church
Rouen Gate
Bulwark
Wharf
Chain
Stakes
Salt Marshes: flooded at high tide
to the Seine
Leure
Wharf
Bulwark
Leure Gate
English saps
English guns & siege engines
Flooded area. English contact maintained by small boats
Lezarde
King Henry's Camp
MONT LECOMTE
N
0 500 yds
0 500m

Map 2

But no matter how large these guns really were, to the people inside, the boom of their ignition and the thundering crash of the projectiles striking the walls was surely terrifying. And the English split their artillery corps into shifts so that they could keep up a steady bombardment. The air was quickly filled with the throat-choking, eye-stinging black clouds belched out from the cannon.

The people of Harfleur held out.

Day after pounding day.

When breaches were made in the day, the defenders repaired them at night. When tunnels were dug to undermine the city's walls, the defenders countermined them. When bridging works were thrown over the ditches, the defenders burned them. When cannon shot came over the walls, the defenders covered the streets with sand to soften the impact and prevent ricochets. The people of Harfleur might have been few compared to the thousands attacking them, but their defence was remarkable.

Henry hadn't planned to be so bogged down. He didn't need 12,000 men to besiege the city, which meant that most of them were useless mouths to feed. And because he was fearful of splitting his force up, until the city fell his army was literally eating down the time he could keep it in the field.

On 3 September, two letters were sent from the English lines at Harfleur to Bordeaux in Gascony, requesting help. The first, from Henry himself, requested that the English officials there send 'as quickly as possible such a quantity of wine and other victuals as you can provide from your area'.[16] The second was from the archdeacon of Médoc, who claimed a close proximity to Henry: 'As you have heard tell, I am one of his doctors [of law] ordered to go wherever he goes with his household and retinue.' It's an interesting letter, which begins by repeating the king's call for a resupply. While 'the fields are providing an adequate supply of corn, this cannot, however, meet the future requirements of the great army which is with him, and which increases every day'. The clergyman reports further on the situation:

> Please know that the town of Harfleur, with the aid of the Holy Spirit, will be in the king's hands before 8 days at most. For now it is well and truly breached on the landward side and on two

> flanks, and everything destroyed inside. Our king cut off the water supply before Montivilliers, which they had retained so that it could not run into the sea. He has had made great engines and cunning instruments for the protection of his people, and in order to take the town. And when he has taken it, I have heard it is not his intention to enter the town but to stay in the field. In a short while after the capture of the town, he intends to go to Montivilliers, and thence to Dieppe, afterwards to Rouen, and then to Paris.[17]

How accurate is the archdeacon's report? It certainly does not describe what eventually happened. It would be another 20 days before Harfleur fell. Afterwards, the English did indeed march towards Montivilliers and Dieppe – though they garrisoned Harfleur first. They did *not* march towards Rouen, much less Paris.

That doesn't mean such a plan wasn't being discussed. The French appear to have thought it was in the works. One of the main reasons that a relief army wasn't immediately forthcoming for Harfleur is that the French commanders were working to secure Rouen and other, more highly valued potential targets. Losing Harfleur would be unfortunate. Losing the capital of Normandy would be ruinous.

This anxiety may be exactly what Henry wanted. If French forces intercepted the letter from the archdeacon, it would reinforce the threat that was keeping reinforcements away from Harfleur and away from Henry's planned route to Calais, following in the footsteps of Edward III.

I think this likely, as I can't imagine Henry thinking he seriously had a shot at mighty Rouen and mightier Paris when he was bogged down trying to defeat the small garrison and ramshackle defences of Harfleur. Henry was no fool.

SHIT AND THE FALL OF HARFLEUR

Henry was concerned about his dwindling food supplies, but his biggest problem was shit.

His horses and men needed fresh water, and plenty of it, to survive. The primary source for this was the Lézarde. The flooding of the river beyond its natural channels, however, meant that it had swept over grazing lands and waste pits, picking up contaminants as it went. The army only added to the problem. There were now some 12,000 men encamped around Harfleur. Trench latrines would have been dug during the initial encampment, but as the days turned to weeks these would have over-filled. The countless horses and livestock did their business wherever they pleased, and even if the men were careful in trying to clean this up – which they almost assuredly were not – there was no way to catch it all. Added to this were the carcasses of slaughtered livestock thrown down into the marshes in the hope that the tide would carry them away. An army on the move might not need to worry as much about sanitation, but one that is stuck in place for even a short time will soon find itself in a morass of piss, shit, and fouled water.

And that means dysentery.

Gastroenteric disease tore through the English and French like fire through dry grass, striking down besiegers and besieged alike. Bloody diarrhoea was a further vector for disease, its victims needing to drink copious amounts of water to replace the fluids they were losing, which only furthered and widened the cycle of torment.

Soon enough, bodies were piling up. By mid-September, Henry had lost the earl of Suffolk, the man he had chosen to lead a third of his army. The leader of another third, the duke of Clarence, was severely ill but hanging on.

Henry was losing far more men than the townspeople were, but he also had far more men to lose. And with his engineers working to divert the Lézarde upstream, he was gaining more and more dry ground from which to attack Harfleur – while its citizens had less and less water on which to survive. When the English king signalled his readiness to engage in an all-out offensive against the city on 18 September, the defenders offered up an agreement to surrender on 22 September if their countrymen didn't relieve the siege. A truce was agreed until then.

A French response wasn't coming. There had been an effort to run the blockade of English ships and reach the town by sea, but it hadn't been successful. France's naval forces were by no means in a state of readiness: the crown had at least a dozen oared ships in Rouen, but they needed repair before they could be safely set upon the water. On land, most of the French focus was on, first, securing Rouen and, second, raising an army of sufficient size to march out and attack the invader. On 10 September, Charles VI had received the *Oriflamme*, the traditional banner that called the French army to war, but the effort of fielding the army was left to his son, the dauphin, who was 18 and only just beginning to come into his own after being a pawn in the power struggles between the dukes of Burgundy and Orléans. As Harfleur suffered, he was gathering forces at Vernon, between Paris and Rouen.

The muster was delayed by one reason above all: soldiers had to be paid, clothed, armed, and fed, and money was a scarce resource. Both sides faced this issue. It's why the English crown wanted those sick men back to England as soon as possible: the sooner they were out of the army, the sooner they were someone else's problem. It's why the French crown wanted its own army called up only once it was needed.

On 22 September, word arrived from Vernon that the dauphin still hadn't raised significant forces to relieve Harfleur. Its citizens promptly surrendered. Henry received them in his tent, making a dramatic and ceremonial show of his authority.

The army stripped the town of what few transportable goods it had, but there wasn't much. This wasn't the prize that Caen had been for Edward III, and its taking had been far costlier. Dysentery had taken roughly 2,000 English lives since they had landed in France, with another 5,000 or so more alive but too wasted by disease to keep fighting.

If the taking of Harfleur wasn't a second Caen, Henry could still make it something like a second Calais: a permanent military garrison on the shores of France that would serve as a lingering threat to that kingdom. Not only could Harfleur be a launching point for future attacks, but its position near the mouth of the Seine directly threatened that vital artery of French trade and communications. To accomplish this, Henry expelled from town those who couldn't help the English rebuild what they had destroyed. Some 2,000 women, children, and other citizens trudged out onto the roads, carrying what little goods they could. They were eventually met in Lillebonne by Boucicaut: the young man from the battle of Rosebeke was now a marshal of France. He had them transported to safety in Rouen. Meanwhile, Henry set the earl of Dorset in command of Harfleur, with an initial garrison of 300 men-at-arms and 900 archers – and a plea for English settlers to repopulate the ruined city. This message would be sent home with the bodies of the high-born who'd died – commoners had been buried in mass graves – and about 5,000 still-living men who were too ill to be of any help in France.

The only question was whether the king would go with them.

7

Edward's Footsteps, 23 September–15 October

As we've seen, there were those who believed Henry's intention had been to march on Rouen and then Paris.[1] I don't think it was. But *if* it was, such a notion was one more casualty of the dysentery. Between the deaths, the illness, and now the need to garrison Harfleur, Henry had lost more than half of the 12,000 men he had brought from England. An attempt on one of the great cities of France would prove the English king as mad as his French rival.

As he figured on his next moves, Henry sent out a letter challenging the dauphin to personal combat on 26 September. He would have challenged the French king himself, Henry writes, but 'it had pleased God to visit infirmity' upon him – a none too subtle dig at the condition of his rival. Henry insists that the winner of their fight would receive the crown of France after Charles VI's death, and that settling things in this way was both a matter of honour and the proper Christian thing to do:

> Consider well that war results in the deaths of men, the destruction of the countryside, the lamentations of women and children, and so many evils in general that it must bring pain and pity to every good Christian. ... It is better for us, cousin, to settle this war between us ourselves, now and for all days to come, than to allow the misbelievers, by the means of our war, to destroy Christianity, our Holy Mother Church to remain in division, and the people of God to destroy each other.[2]

The 'misbelievers' – *mescreantz* in Henry's French – are Muslims, but he might well have had an eye towards Lollardy and other forces of reform that threatened the status quo of papal dominance. Any and all of them could take advantage of the current schism between the popes of Avignon and Rome, and of course the Hundred Years War in general.

However, if this was truly Henry's driving concern, he could have easily solved the problem without the deaths of thousands by accepting the primacy of the Avignon pope and relinquishing his own claim to the crown of France. But he did neither of these things. Henry wanted peace and unity on his terms. Until then, he was more than happy to sow war and division.

Henry did not expect his offer to be taken seriously. He didn't even expect it to be answered, since the only possible answer would be 'Hell no' – which the English would immediately trumpet as a sign of French weakness.

To the contrary, the offer was if anything a sign of *English* weakness. Henry knew – as the dauphin knew – that the English army in Harfleur wasn't the force it had been when it had first landed. Dysentery continued to scour ranks, meaning that Henry's fighting force got smaller and less powerful by the day. The French army, meanwhile, was gathering strength by the hour. The offer to end things now – one on one – was little more than a public relations ploy, attempting to belittle his enemy while reinforcing his strength to his own men at a time when their morale was as shattered as the ruins in which they slept.

The dauphin wisely ignored the challenge. He knew, as Henry's father had said in declining to duel Louis of Orléans, that 'What a king does, he does for the honour of God and the common good of his realm and of all Christendom, not for mere bombast and greed.'[3]

We can, from the remove of centuries, recognize something of the difficult position in which the young prince of France had found himself. The civil war between the Armagnacs and Burgundians had rocked the kingdom for years – a long sequence of killings, reprisals, and civil unrest instigated by one ruling party against another. There had been attempts at peace, but they had all crumbled quickly. Charles VI's intermittent madness simply left too much power up for grabs. The latest peace had been reached in March, but by no means was the feuding finished. In the end, the dauphin decided to ask the dukes of Burgundy and Orléans to provide men but to personally stay away – there was real fear that their presence would only reignite civil strife among the lords of France. Added to this was a lingering worry that Jean the Fearless was allied with England. This wasn't true, but it was a reasonable suspicion in light of all that had happened. Concern over Burgundy's loyalty was probably the number one thing preventing the crown from moving faster to respond to the English. Charles and the dauphin didn't want to leave the immediate vicinity of Paris for fear that Burgundy would take control of the city in their absence. War requires total focus, but France was, in a manner of speaking, marching to the fight with only one eye on the enemy – and the other looking over its shoulder.

THE PLAN: CALAIS

Henry intended to march to English-held Calais.

I suspect this was his plan all along. If it wasn't, it must have been something he decided quickly after Harfleur fell. By 7 October his men in Calais knew that the king was planning to come their way, which meant that the message had already had time to pass by ship between the two ports.[4]

His advisors, the *Gesta* tells us, didn't think the king's plan a sound one:

> Although a large majority of the royal council advised against such a proposal, as it would be highly dangerous for him in this way to send his small force, daily growing smaller, against the multitude of the French which, constantly growing larger, would surely enclose them on every side like sheep in folds, our king – relying on divine grace and the justice of his cause, piously reflecting that victory consists not in a multitude but with Him for Whom it is not impossible to enclose the many in the hand of the few and Who bestows victory upon whom He wills, whether they be many or few – with God, as is believed, affording him His leadership, did nevertheless decide to make that march.[5]

His advisors were right to worry. They had lost a great many men. The leading modern researcher of the campaign has calculated that the remaining English army now numbered as many as 9,000 men in total.[6] According to the eyewitness of the *Gesta*, though, what remained was even less: just 900 men-at-arms and 5,000 archers. I find the smaller count more plausible for a number of reasons.[7] I favour the smaller number provided by the eyewitness, but even if it was several thousand more men, it would soon be outnumbered by the gathering French forces – if it wasn't already – and though the men who were most debilitated by sickness were being sent home, many of those remaining were not well. All this and it was now October, which meant that the weather was likely to become increasingly unpredictable.

Little wonder that they advised the king to board ship and return to England as soon as possible.

Nevertheless, Henry wouldn't do it. It's important to consider what he might have been thinking, since Henry's intentions for his march – and therefore his mindset going through it – have enormous implications for the battle that eventually came about at Agincourt.

While Harfleur was in English hands, it had been a hard fight. The city was fallen, and not just metaphorically: many of its fortifications were in ruins, and the countryside was in shambles. The entirety of his army could not quarter there. Henry knew he had either to sail them somewhere or march them somewhere.

Sailing them somewhere required a fleet, and it's an open question whether he had enough of one at this point. Henry's ships had been full to bursting on the way over from France, and that fleet had by now been reduced as vessels had returned to trade routes and other duties. What was left dwindled still further through the very pressing need to defend Harfleur: it was a port on the mouth of the Seine, which meant a stout naval presence had to be maintained there. Without one, the French would quickly blockade the city and leave it in grave danger.

Despite this, even if he had the means of transport, sailing men somewhere almost assuredly meant sailing them home. That's where he was sending his sick men, and for good reason. Fewer mouths to feed in the ravaged city of Harfleur was a good thing for its defence. And fewer pockets to fill was a good thing for Henry's treasury, too. But sailing *all* of his men back to England would mean he was concluding his time in France, and he might well have imagined some truth behind those pre-campaign whispers of what would happen if a 'small incursion' was all he managed across the Channel.[8] He had drained the coffers and led thousands to their deaths. He had bet on glory and God. Harfleur and a half-dead army wouldn't refill those coffers, restore England's reputation, or stabilize his crown. He needed more.

If it was politically dangerous and practically difficult to sail his men from Harfleur, that left the other option: marching them somewhere.

The problem here was the undeniable fact that dysentery had left him with a fraction of the force that he would have wanted to confront the French. Henry might talk a big game about how a small number of men could defeat a larger number of men with the aid of God, but when it came to fighting he was experienced enough to know that numbers mattered. But if, say, he marched his men to Calais, he might be able to solve all his problems at once. Supplies were there. Ships were there. And a successful march getting there would be a show of force readily crafted into a propaganda victory. Henry, it could be said, had gone to France, taken a city, and walked the footsteps of the great Edward III.

There's a wide band of scholars who believe that there is more to it than this. They are convinced that Henry V, as it's often put in military history, was 'seeking battle' when he marched towards Calais.[9] It's easy to see why. A fight is what the king got – albeit way off-track – at Agincourt. If we assume that this was what he intended to do all along then intent and outcome fit into a neat and tidy box. More than that, a battle-seeking Henry also fits with what so many people quite frankly *want* to think about this moment in history: the mythologizing of Agincourt and Henry V started so early – and for 600 years has been so pervasive – that many of us are truly and deeply reluctant to imagine this famous king and his most famous victory in anything but the most glowing, positive terms. It's glory in the highest, and that kind of image sits uneasily with the idea that Agincourt happened *despite* Henry's aims.

But like it or not, the idea that Henry wanted a fight all along is tremendously difficult to square with his actions. This is evident from the very moment of his departure from Harfleur. The French army was gathering in Rouen, about 46 miles due east. But instead of making a move towards it, Henry ordered his army due north – marching away from his enemy as fast and as far as the roads and the coast would allow him to do so. If he wanted to fight the French, it must be said, marching away from them wasn't a good start.

And it was no small distance that he marched. By the time they reached Agincourt, Henry had led his army across more than 200 miles of French countryside, and at no point in this long march did he take a position intended to provoke battle against the French who were tracking and pursuing him. Even to the last minute, he was actively manoeuvring to try to avoid the French, to avoid the fight.

None of this is to say that Henry was a coward, or that he was unwilling to fight if it came to it. We know from Agincourt that the precise opposite of these things is true: when he had no choice, when he had his back to the wall, Henry V fought like a lion and won. But being willing to fight and actively wanting to fight are two very different things.

So it was, I think, a march to Calais. Plain and simple. I can't conceive of any scenario in which he wanted to fight along the way.

Because even just marching there was going to be a problem.

The *Gesta* tells us that the English marching from Harfleur were told to bring rations for eight days.[10] By the straightest walking route possible today – which is straighter than the roads ran in 1415 – the distance to Calais was over 150 miles. This meant he would need to average almost 19 miles a day to get there with the supplies he had, and in October he was afforded fewer than 12 hours of sunlight to cover that distance. Keeping the maths simple – and ignoring the substantial time required to make or break camp, for instance – Henry and his men needed to average more than 1.6 miles per hour to reach their destination. By comparison, during the Crécy campaign in 1346, Edward's English forces had averaged a daily marching speed of just 0.8 miles per hour. Only on a few days when they had the very best roads in France to speed them along did they get close to the pace Henry hoped to make with regularity on smaller country roads. One reason he thought this possible was that his army in 1415, unlike Edward's in 1346, was largely mounted. True, they couldn't gallop all the way to Calais, but horses certainly have a greater stamina and faster pace than the average man. So the plan wasn't technically impossible.

Among other things, though, expecting to move at this kind of speed meant that the English needed to leave their guns and other engines of war behind. This tells us that Henry had no intentions of engaging in another siege. Harfleur had been bad enough, and now the year was getting late. Henry wanted to get to Calais, and he wanted to do it as quickly as possible. His triumph wouldn't be Harfleur alone. It would be Harfleur followed by a ride to Calais, his superiority to the French shown in his freedom of movement across their country.

And, yes, he could do it ... so long as he had no deviation or distraction along the way. If what the *Gesta* tells us about his rations is true – and we have absolutely no reason to disbelieve it – then Henry didn't expect any trouble at all. He thought he could make the journey to Calais entirely unmolested.

It was either astonishing hubris or an astonishing miscalculation.

We might look at the French response to this point as a car at the racetrack. The weeks since the English had landed, the French had been getting the vehicle out of the garage, filling up its tyres, and topping off the tank.

The delay meant that the English were able to win an initial race in taking Harfleur. That wasn't nothing, but it also wasn't a disaster. It certainly wasn't the main event. The aim of the dauphin and the many military leaders advising him was to ensure that their response didn't cause a disaster when the real race started – by, for instance, leaving Rouen or even Paris open to the enemy. So they'd gotten themselves up to the starting line, checked and re-checked their gauges, strapped in, and then sat revving their engines in Rouen and Vernon, gathering power.

EDWARD'S FOOTSTEPS

On 8 October, Henry marched out from Harfleur and headed north.

The race was on.

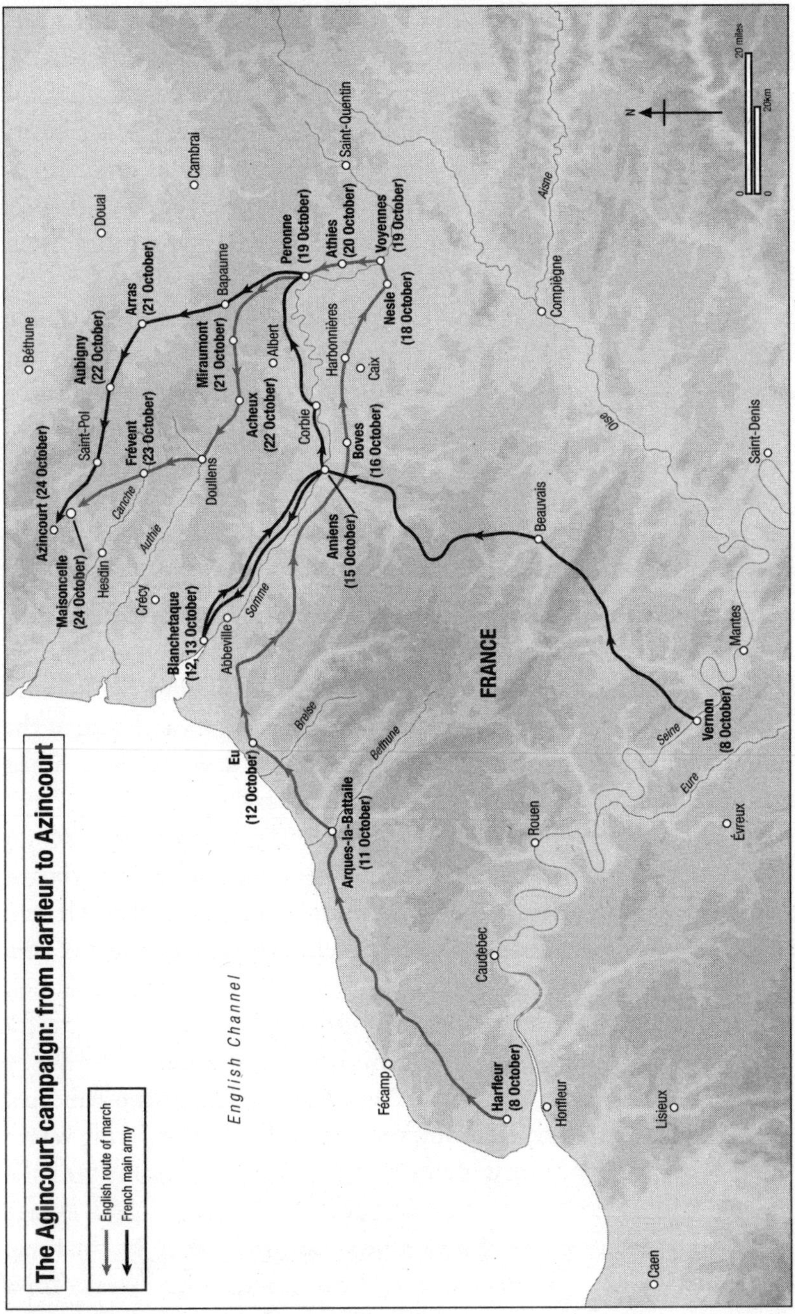
The Agincourt campaign: from Harfleur to Azincourt
English route of march
French main army
English Channel
FRANCE
Harfleur
(8 October)
Fécamp
Honfleur
Lisieux
Caen
Caudebec
Rouen
Évreux
Arques-la-Bataille
(11 October)
Eu
(12 October)
Bresle
Bethune
Seine
Eure
Vernon
(8 October)
Mantes
Beauvais
Saint-Denis
Oise
Compiègne
Aisne
Blanchetaque
(12, 13 October)
Abbeville
Somme
Crécy
Hesdin
Authie
Canche
Maisoncelle
(24 October)
Azincourt (24 October)
Saint-Pol
Frévent
(23 October)
Doullens
Amiens
(15 October)
Boves
(16 October)
Corbie
Acheux
(22 October)
Albert
Miraumont
(21 October)
Harbonnières
Caix
Nesle
(18 October)
Aubigny
(22 October)
Arras
(21 October)
Béthune
Bapaume
Peronne
(19 October)
Athies
(20 October)
Voyennes
(19 October)
Douai
Cambrai
Saint-Quentin
N
0 20 miles
0 20km

Map 3

The dauphin and his men, acting quickly, put the engine of France's military might into gear. The prince himself rode for Rouen to finish organizing the defence there and ensure that the English couldn't unexpectedly double back. Meanwhile, the army gathering at Vernon launched north under the command of the constable of France, Charles d'Albret. With him went the duke of Alençon, Boucicaut, Arthur de Richemont, and many other lords, their banners flying.

As the English and French armies left Harfleur and Vernon, respectively, there were at least 80 miles of road between them. The next days would see that number grow smaller and smaller as the coastline pushed the English march eastwards toward the racing French. The French were determined to get ahead of Henry, cut him off, trap him, and destroy him.

Henry had wisely avoided the problem of crossing the Seine by landing on its northern side, but that wasn't the only problem the English had faced in 1346: Edward, as we know, had been trapped a *second* time by the French at the River Somme. The resulting battle of Blanchetaque had been a remarkable victory for Edward III, and it seems that Henry planned to repeat it by crossing at the ford on his march north. Perhaps he thought it would be a direct way of attaching the legend of that past glory to his throne.

Trouble was, his desire to follow in Edward's footsteps was obvious to all. As early as 6 October, a messenger from Abbeville brought word to Boulogne that Henry was headed to Calais.[11] The French, as soon as they left Vernon, pushed north to reach the Somme first.

THE FIRST DAYS

Henry's initial route was north out of Harfleur, up the valley of the Lézarde. The road ran along the west side of the river. It wasn't the greatest security – the main thing keeping him safe from the French army right now was distance – but it was an advantage nonetheless. Within a couple of miles, the army passed by the town of Montivilliers, whose garrison had no doubt waited weeks for a major attack from the English army that never came. It barely came this day, either. There was only a minor skirmish as the English army marched by, just half a mile away from its rich abbey.

Exactly where the army spent that first night out of Harfleur, the *Gesta* doesn't say. The *London Chronicle* includes an itinerary that goes by Fécamp on the coast, and this would make sense: it's about 20 miles distant from Harfleur, matching Henry's planned daily pace. That said, this itinerary, which was composed around 1443, lays out a frankly impossible route that would pass by Honfleur (on the other side of the Seine) and Barfleur (at the distant tip of the Cotentin peninsula) in the two and a half miles between Harfleur and Montivilliers.[12] The French chronicle of Juvénal des Ursins gives us Fécamp without all that nonsense, but other sources give us Fauville.[13] The fact that no mention is made of a passage by Criquetot-l'Esneval gives an indication of the road Henry actually took: a direct route that crossed the Lézarde just south of Rolleville, then ran by Vergetot, Écrainville, and Maniquerville.

Though he doesn't say where this first camp was located, the author of the *Gesta* is at some pains to make sure his reader knows how very controlled Henry's army was throughout the initial part of the campaign. Henry, it says, issued a blanket order that 'under penalty of death, no one should burn, destroy, or seize anything except food, necessities for the march, and rebels who were found offering resistance.'[14] This wasn't a traditional terrorizing *chevauchée*, in other words, with its wide wake of pillage and destruction. This was an organized march through the lands of Henry's rightful subjects, leaving them in peace.

Perhaps so. Henry's march of eight days certainly left no time for plunder. The army needed to keep moving. On the other hand, the author of the *Gesta* worships Henry. He might well have wanted to hide the darker truth in order to paint Henry as a Christian king. Other sources tell a different story.

The *Gesta* next picks up Henry's march on 11 October, when the army covered 40 miles to arrive at Arques-la-Bataille (Figure 11). This ought to have taken two days if they kept to their pace of 20 miles a day. Instead, it had taken them three.

We don't know where they lost the time, because we don't know the exact location of the English encampments between. All we can say is that they were probably somewhere along the main road between Fécamp and Arques-la-Bataille: this road ran east to Cany-Barville, just south of the D925 today, then over to le Bourg-Dun, where it once again more or less picks up the route of the D925 to Dieppe.

Within a few miles of that major port city, the English army had left the main road – something no one in the army would have wanted to do – in order to make a march cross-country to Arques-la-Bataille, which sat above a marshy valley, just upstream from where three watercourses came together to make their final run to the sea. There was a sequence of bridges here, making this the easiest crossing point, but they were protected by a castle – the ruins of which can still be seen today.

The French knew the English were coming. As Henry approached, cannon fired from atop the castle's walls. The English army moved into battle array. The situation was tense on both sides. The people of Arques-la-Bataille had no doubt heard of the destruction of Harfleur and wished to avoid its fate. Henry and his commanders knew he had no time to spare. And so, the Chaplain tells us, a solution was found:

> And after a short time the king sent to the garrison to ask for free passage, and they, after negotiating for terms and having given hostages, granted the king free passage and a fixed amount of bread and wine with which to refresh the army, in order to ransom their town and neighbourhood from being burnt. We therefore passed through that area by way of the middle of the town, the entrance to which we found strongly barricaded with large trees placed across our route with other obstacles.[15]

This was, in essence, extortion. Henry was promising not to destroy the town if he could have free passage and resupply. If he was magnanimously refusing to let his men terrorize the people in order to show the French what a superior ruler he was – the saintly image that many like to imagine – then this threat would be quite clearly without teeth. The people of Arques-la-Bataille had to believe he meant to destroy them if they didn't give him what he wanted.

Why did he need the resupply? Probably because Henry was aware that, four days into his march, he was already off-pace by at least a day. And he was also seeing, first hand, that the towns of northern France weren't welcoming him with open arms. As his men made their way around the barricades on the roads and bridges at Arques-la-Bataille, Henry and his commanders would have been gravely concerned about what greater obstacles might lie ahead.

The next day, 12 October, started well. Reaching the main road again, they made good time. The crossing of the Yères was made without incident via a bridge near Touffreville-sur-Eu, and the army's 20-mile pace brought them within reach of the town of Eu, which sat above the flat plain where the River La Bresle meandered through marshlands where the tides moved in and out.

Eu was a large town, and a significant number of fighting men had gathered inside its stout walls. They had no interest in letting the English army march by. They made an attack on the English flank, and there was a fierce engagement that left men dead on both sides. Henry, once again knowing he didn't have time to take the city, promised he wouldn't put the surrounding towns and countryside to the torch if his army could safely pass and resupply. The people of Eu accepted.[16]

That night, however, Henry learned that his eight-day plan to reach Calais was in real trouble. Some of the men whom the English had taken prisoner during the town's initial sortie passed along grave news: the army of the constable of France was ahead of them.

The French had already reached the Somme.

FRANCE AND THE WET-GAP CROSSING

Military leaders have long understood the importance of terrain in warfare. In an even fight, superior numbers tend to win. But make the fight uneven by taking a superior *position*, and numbers can become meaningless. There is a reason that Leonidas and the Greeks could famously hold the line against a vastly larger Persian force in 480 BC: it wasn't the strength of their manhood; it was the strength of their position. Terrain is a force multiplier. It's part of the explanation for my principle, about which you'll hear more later, that *a battle is its ground.*

Military manuals past and present devote many pages to discussion of the opportunities and dangers the landscape can present, but for now I want to focus on the one that the French were using at this moment. In modern military jargon, the English were coming up on what is called a 'gap crossing': an obstacle that prevents traditional ground manoeuvres from taking place. Because this particular obstacle – the Somme – is filled with water, it's specifically called a 'wet-gap crossing'. An army on the march typically wants to avoid gap crossings, and wet-gap crossings most of all, because they have to be 'bridged' – in the case of a river, this could be an actual bridge or a ford – and any such crossing point will of necessity be narrower than the surrounding landscape.

This constriction is a choke-point, and its first problem is that it slows the army down. The modern equivalent is evident in rush-hour traffic every day, especially if there's any kind of lane reduction: force the cars into a narrower area, and everything grinds to a halt as traffic backs up.

The second problem is that the army, slowed to a crawl over the narrow bridge, is highly vulnerable to attack. No matter its size, it can only push so many men through the constriction, which means the defending force needs only to destroy that many men at a time to bar passage and stop the entire march dead in its tracks. Alternatively, the defending force could wait, letting the gap do the hard work of dividing the enemy army into smaller units – half on one side, perhaps, and half on the other – that are far easier to engage and defeat in detail.[17]

All of this was in the minds of the leaders on both sides of the Somme in 1415, just as it had been on both sides of that same river in 1346. Back then, the French ahead of the English had broken or barricaded all the bridges of the river in order to deny the crossing so that the French army following Edward could pin him against the river and bring him to ruin. Edward had only managed to escape by making the desperate crossing of the ford at Blanchetaque.

Henry's situation was worse. The French had easily sniffed out his plan to march to the Blanchetaque – as early as 11 October, messengers were reporting as much on the north side of the river[18] – and they were determined to have Edward's footsteps lead the young king to ruin. Tito Livio Frulovisi, in his 1438 *Life of Henry V*, says that the French had lined the banks of the Somme at the fabled ford with 'sharp stakes fixed close together' in order to prevent any crossing.[19] They were ready and waiting.

The *Gesta* reports that this news prompted a great many discussions within the army about whether a battle with the French was about to happen. Some thought it inevitable because the French wouldn't bear the dishonour of not fighting. Perhaps letting slip the veil of sanctity in which he had tried to clothe the king, the Chaplain reports that among other affronts, the English 'had entered their land, remained there for so long, besieged and taken a town, and, at length, with so small a following and so reduced an army, laid waste their country at so great a distance from it.'[20]

Others claimed that a fight was unlikely because most of the French lords wouldn't want to move their forces so far from their own domains for fear that the duke of Burgundy would slip in behind and seize them.

That the Chaplain knew the outcome of the campaign at Agincourt and nevertheless reports these worries among the army might well speak to the general state of panic the English were feeling now that they knew the French army had barred their route to Calais.

Worse, the foresight of the French meant that not only had they taken position on the opposite, north bank of the Somme and burned, broken, or garrisoned every bridge or crossing of that river, but they had also stripped the countryside on the south bank so that the English would be trapped with little hope of resupply.

The ghost of Philippe VI would have been proud. Sixty-nine years after he had pulled his trick on Edward, his countrymen were doing the same to Henry – but they had learned from the one mistake their predecessor had made. What would result would be the same tactics that Bertrand du Guesclin and Olivier de Clisson had mastered: a strategy that caused the invaders to weaken and dissolve through the attrition of disease, desertion, starvation, and raiding strikes before they were crushed entirely.

We can perhaps see how the French planned to conduct that final, crushing engagement through a document found in the British Library in the early 1980s which is a battle plan from the

Agincourt campaign. It presents itself as 'advice' from Boucicaut, submitted to the duke of Alençon, Lord Richemont, and the constable. The plan says that Boucicaut and the constable would take position in the vanguard beside one another: the constable and his men on the right, Boucicaut and his men on the left. Behind the vanguard would be another division – called in the parlance of the time a 'battle' – with Alençon, the count of Eu, 'and the other lords who are not otherwise listed. And if it happens that the English form up in only one battle, these two [French] battles [must fight] together.' On either side of these large bodies of men would be 'two large wings of foot-soldiers', with various lords named to command them. The archers of the French army would be positioned in front of these wings. Around 1,000 mounted men-at-arms would make another battle of the army. It would be positioned behind the second division, 'on the left edge, a little to the rear, and it will be sent to attack the [English] archers and do all it can to break them. And when it charges out to ride down those archers, the battles of foot-men and the wings' will march forward. At the same time, a much smaller unit of 200 mounted men-at-arms and other riders 'will be sent to attack at the rear of the English battle, against their valets and their baggage'.[21]

We have little to compare it to – if written battle plans like this were common, they certainly have not survived in numbers[22] – but it seems a good plan. Boucicaut knew that the English army was heavily reliant both in numbers and in strength on its archers. They had to be disrupted, and the hope would be for the main group of cavalry to do just that. They wouldn't be a solitary charge, however. Boucicaut insists on the coordinated timing of the engagement, and it's probably because they all knew what had happened at Crécy, where the wings of English longbowmen sent the Genoese crossbowmen into a rout that collided with French cavalry and sent that fight into a chaotic death spiral. This time, things would be controlled. The French would have wings of their own, and they would open the attack by launching volleys to suppress ranged attacks from the corresponding English archers. Meanwhile, the infantry on the wings would start to advance, slipping through their own line of archers and trudging forward beneath the missiles. The two main battles in the centre would also advance at this time. Intriguingly, the plan suggests that these main battles would also be on foot. If this is so, it was a testament to Boucicaut's legitimate concern that the many English arrows they would face were liable to send mounts into a panic. Better for the men to be on foot, helms down as they waded forward into the deadly storm. All this would dominate the English perspective on the battlefield – right up to the point that the battle of heavy horse, 1,000 strong, came charging out from behind the French lines to roll over the archers on the English right. And meanwhile the other, smaller battle of cavalry would be sweeping around the English left to take them from behind, baggage and all.

It's a solid plan.

Exactly *when* in the campaign it was supposed to be executed isn't said, but the lords named in the plan – or, more to the point, those *not* named – are an excellent clue. In the final event, the French army at Agincourt would include a number of powerful dukes not mentioned in Boucicaut's advice. Men of such high rank would not be forgotten when it came to battle planning, so the plan must logically pre-date their arrival. One of these 'missing' lords is the duke of Bourbon, who seems to have met up with the French army in Péronne around 19 October, well after the English army had begun its march eastwards up the Somme. The only time prior to this that the French could have reasonably expected an open-field engagement of the kind Boucicaut was planning would be at the Somme. If Henry, paralysed by the closing of Blanchetaque, had hunkered down on the south side of the river, the French would be free to starve him for a few days before moving across at Abbeville. With the English hemmed in by the sea and the river, Henry would be destroyed at the edge of the ford that had saved Edward from destruction. From the French perspective, it would be poetic justice.

Henry must have sensed this danger. Still trying to reconnoitre the situation, he marched to the vicinity of Abbeville on 13 October. The French watched and waited, knowing that every day increased their strength and lessened his own.

Henry's scouts fanned up and down the river just as Edward's had done, desperate to find an opening. All they found were French on the other side of the river, mocking them and daring them to attempt a crossing.

The English didn't have many options. They could try to backtrack to Harfleur, but they had left it more or less in ruins. It was no place for a grand defence, and that was assuming they could even get there. Henry had surely received word that the dauphin had advanced to Rouen, where more forces were presumably being raised. For all he and his commanders knew, that second wave of Frenchmen might be hot on their tails. So a run to the south would seem nearly as suicidal as a run across the Somme to the north. Unable to swim across the English Channel to the west, about the only thing they could do was head east, up the Somme. The constable had gathered the thousands of men in his army in and around Abbeville. If they moved fast enough, the English might be able to get to a crossing that was still open. Unfortunately, each step they took in that direction was a step further into French territory, the very direction from which their enemy was gathering. It must have felt like running into the gaping mouth of Hell in the hope of slipping out between its molars.

And Hell it might have been for the citizens of the countryside, too, according to some of our French sources. The French chronicler Enguerran Monstrelet says that Henry at this point was 'burning and destroying the whole country', while Juvénal des Ursins reports that his army was 'committing countless evil deeds, burning, killing people, capturing and abducting children'.[23] Some of this seems hyperbole – the army had nothing to gain in taking children – but it could have been born out of the real trail of destruction that the invaders made on their way eastwards. Thomas Basin, who grew up in the region in the years afterwards, later wrote that Henry's force was 'ravaging everything on his route'.[24] Whatever Henry's orders might have been, hunger might have overridden them.

The Chaplain describes the English army attempting multiple passages of the Somme east of Abbeville before they neared Amiens on 15 October. One of them was Pont-Rémy, where several French chroniclers suggest that at least some fighting took place before the English gave up and moved on.[25] The English sent units hither and yon, trying to find some way forward as the main bulk of the army made its way along high ground.[26] The next day would be 16 October, the day that Henry had expected to reach Calais. His supplies were running out.

The French army shadowed Henry's movements on the opposite bank. They were better fed and in far better spirits. The constable himself was in Amiens, receiving gifts of wine.[27]

8

Days of Desperation, 16–23 October

Still trudging up the Somme, the English ran into the town of Boves on 16 October. It wasn't a large place. There were no walls, but there was a castle, watching over a bridge across the River Avre, a tributary of the much larger Somme.

Once more, Henry cut the kind of deal he had made with the people of Arques-la-Bataille and Eu. He would leave the town standing if it let him pass through and gave his men something to eat and drink. This was the day that the English rations were scheduled to run out, so filling the stomachs of his tired men while also giving him easy passage over the small river would be an enormous stroke of good luck. To his relief, they agreed.

Word was spreading about the desperate condition of the English, however. As the Religieux says: 'I know by accurate information that they were so pressed by lack of food that instead of ransoming the inhabitants of the towns and countryside for money they asked them for victuals.'[1]

The next day, the English were passing close to Corbie – still heading east, looking for a way across the Somme – when a French force made a sortie against them. The town was on the north bank, walled, and strongly garrisoned. There was little chance that Henry had any hope of crossing at Corbie, so this has every appearance of being an attack of opportunity that the French were making on their weary enemy as it passed by.

Where the attack took place depends on where the English were. And to answer that question we need to look closely at something that has been underpinning almost everything that has been discussed so far:

Roads.

ROADS AND STAKES

Any hiker knows how much easier it is to follow a trail than to bushwhack across the countryside. This is obviously true when a person is crossing broken or forested terrain, but it's also true across relatively open ground. Trails allow a hiker to move faster, with less effort, and with greater safety – following a trail means they are less likely to turn an ankle on something hidden in the underbrush. Trails are a good thing.

Multiply a single hiker by thousands, and you begin to see how essential it was for armies to follow not just trails, but *roads* whenever possible. This is why, whenever I'm asked to search for a battle or reconstruct a campaign, I immediately look for the roads. More often than not, these are the routes by which the armies moved across the landscape. They were the routes of supply and communication, the lines of attack and retreat. It's not that men and horses *can't* move across the countryside, but they didn't want to if they could in any way help it.

In the Middle Ages, some of the best roads remained those built by the Romans in centuries past. These had been built to last: paved and drained, made straight and made for speed. It was just such a road that Henry hoped to reach and follow. One of several ancient routes that went by the name Chaussée Brunehaut in his time, it was a well-used Roman road that ran from Montreuil to Amiens and from there eastwards to where it crossed the Somme just south of Péronne. Today, it underlies the D1029. It was wide, straight as an arrow, and in good repair. If the English reached it, their run eastwards would be sped along considerably, and that could make the difference between being trapped by the French or at last getting around them and back on track to Calais.

The French knew this even better than the English did. The road ran across their lands, after all. I suspect this is exactly why they made a sortie out of Corbie to try to keep the English from using that veritable highway and force them onto slower routes.

The road out of Corbie meets the Chaussée Brunehaut at the town of Villers-Bretonneux, just over three miles from the Somme. Here, I think, the engagement must have happened. Tito Livio Frulovisi, making no effort to restrain his bias, says that 'many cavalry and infantry ran together into the English with a terrific sound and a great impetuosity, as is the custom of the French.'[2] Despite this, the attackers were, after a hard fight, turned back by the English. The clergyman John Capgrave, writing more than three decades after the campaign, says that the French 'were put to flight by the actions of the archers'.[3]

This is a good time to talk about the archers, which were Henry's greatest strength and his greatest weakness. There were 5,000 of them, and they were a force to be reckoned with at range. When we think of 5,000 arrows launched into the air at once, it's easy to see how people in the Middle Ages could talk of 'storms' of the deadly projectiles. But medieval warfare wasn't a video game. Archers didn't have unlimited ammunition. Records from the Tower Armoury around the time of Edward's Crécy campaign show that a fairly standard allotment of two sheaves – containing a standard 24 arrows each – was assigned to each archer.[4] We suspect that Henry had come to France with even more: the Earl Marshal alone brought 100 bundles of arrows for his men.[5] But those supplies had been significantly depleted by the long siege of Harfleur. Worse, the English chronicler known as Pseudo-Elmham emphasizes, because the English intended to march quickly to stay ahead of the French, Henry made the decision that, 'in order to secure an easier journey, the wagons should be left behind and the loads of victuals and other things which were to be brought with them should be carried on the backs of the horses'.[6] There would have been a few carts brought along – we know from what happened after the battle of Agincourt that the king had brought along his pavilion and other royal baggage that wasn't going to fit on the back of a horse – but they cannot have been many.[7] This greatly limited the arrows each archer could expend. The little fighting they had seen on the march so far had dwindled the stock further, costing them desperately needed ammunition. It might be common to imagine the English longbowman as some kind of pre-modern machine gunner launching shots with impunity, but the truth is that he put each arrow to his bow with the hope it would be the last he would need to loose. An arrow shot was an arrow spent.

So while 5,000 archers could in theory put up 5,000 shots in a single volley, they couldn't do so for any significant amount of time.[8] Even if they still had two sheaves of arrows each at this point – I suspect they did not – and they loosed an arrow at a steady pace of one every five seconds, they would be out of ammunition in exactly four minutes. Sure, they would have put some 240,000 arrows into the air, but the majority of the shots would have missed target or broken harmlessly on the enemy's shields, helms, and armour. Some would have found their mark, weakening the enemy to one degree or another, but the archers from this point forwards would be reduced to unarmoured men fighting with hand weapons, which they had little expertise in using. Archery, in other words, needed to be closely monitored. Every shot had to count.

Henry's other problem with the archers, and the one that he might have just seen come to a close call at Corbie, was that they were gravely susceptible to cavalry charges. The power of a driving horse is enormous – there's a reason that engine output is rated in terms of its horsepower – and it didn't take long for fighters to recognize that the impact a horse can make on a line of men devastates morale just as much as bodies. A cavalry charge was a great way to disorganize, disperse, and destroy an opponent. As with all things in military history, this offensive tactic birthed defensive solutions – a wall of shields and men armed with spears, for instance – that could in turn morph into their own offensive tactics. And so it goes. There had been many reasons that Edward had won at Crécy, but one of them was the soundness of his basic tactics on that field: two wings of protected archers would funnel the enemy into a packed centre that made them ever-easier targets as they tried to reach the heavily armoured, dismounted English knights.

Protected archers, mind you. Edward had put those men in woods and hedges or behind the makeshift wood walls of his wagenburg. This kept them safe from cavalry charges. Whatever had happened at Corbie, we can guess that Henry had no such assistance from the terrain. And looking forward to a march into an increasingly unfamiliar landscape, he had to assume that future attacks might also not be on ground of his choosing. His wings of archers – a far greater proportion of his force than expected – might be overrun. If that happened, he was doomed.

The Chaplain tells us at this point rumours began circulating in the English camp that prisoners – probably men who were seized in the fight that had just taken place – had divulged something of the French plans: 'the enemy command had assigned certain squadrons of cavalry, many hundreds strong and mounted on barded horses, to break the formation and resistance of our archers when they engaged us in battle.' This was exactly what Henry feared. And so he improvised a solution. Edward had used his wagons to help give his bowmen protection. Henry would use makeshift spears:

> The king, therefore, had it proclaimed throughout the army that every archer was to prepare and fashion for himself a stake or staff, either square or round, but six feet long, of sufficient thickness, and sharpened at both ends; and he commanded that whenever the French army drew near to do battle and to break their ranks by such columns of horse, all the archers were to drive their stakes in front of them in line abreast and that some of them should do this further back and in between, one end being driven into the ground pointing down towards themselves, the other end pointing up towards the enemy above waist-height, so that the cavalry, when their charge had brought them close and in sight of the stakes, would either withdraw in great fear or, reckless of their own safety, run the risk of having both horses and riders impaled.[9]

Henry wasn't the first to use stakes in this way. At Nicopolis in 1396, Sultan Bayezid had used stakes to break up a Crusader cavalry charge, resulting in the almost total destruction of his enemy as thousands died on the field or were executed later. Boucicaut had been there and was himself in line to be executed when he was recognized among the men and pulled out for ransom. It's an open question how many English were there that fateful day, but word of what had happened there had travelled fast and wide. Men like Henry, who had cut their teeth in battle, would have heard and taken heed.[10]

Outside Corbie, Henry didn't have time to wait for his men to make their stakes. This would be something they would need to do as best they could on the move. This is probably why other sources, like the eyewitnesses Jean Waurin and Jean Le Fèvre (on the French and English sides, respectively), tell us that the order to fashion stakes was made later, after French heralds contacted Henry on 20 October. This was, I suspect, instead an occasion of re-emphasizing the order already given at Corbie, ensuring that as many as possible were produced as battle became increasingly imminent.

This sets the stage for the other event reported to have happened at Corbie. As the story goes, an Englishman stole a copper-gilt pyx from a local church. When he was discovered with this war booty, Henry had him hanged. The Chaplain, perhaps predictably, judges this in Biblical terms, as a just punishment for 'the wrong done to the Creator'.[11] Henry was a pious man, it's true, but we shouldn't neglect the military reasons for the action. If his men were distracted with looting, the whole army would slow, become disorganized. The king could afford neither. As it happens, Edward – not a man typically associated with piety – had done something similar during his flight north from the Seine in 1346. Though they had specifically been given the order not to do so because the army was moving with all speed, a group of 20 men was discovered having looted and set fire to the abbey of Saint-Lucien. Edward had the men hanged beside the road as a warning to the rest of the men to maintain good order.[12]

The primary aim of the French sortie from Corbie, I've suggested, was to push the English off the fast road of the Chaussée Brunehaut. And though the attack was repulsed in what the English thought a terrific victory, it succeeded in moving the English march southwards, down the road that led through Harbonnières and Lihons. On the night of 18 October, the *Gesta* tells us, they found themselves near the town of Nesle. In giving the French the initiative for this change in direction, I'm going against the historical consensus, which sees instead tactical genius on the part of the English king. Here, for example, is one of the consensus voices on the campaign:

> From Corbie the Somme takes a great loop east to Péronne and then south to the fortress-town of Ham. Henry V seized the opportunity to shake off the French Constable's army. Marching

> cross-country he cut across the loop and regained the Somme near the walled town of Nesle.[13]

This would be all well and good, except that our sources make no mention of this being Henry's choice. And given the worshipful stance so many of the sources take towards Henry, if there had been so much as a whiff that the turn south was a clever English gambit – especially since, in the end, it *worked* – I'm certain they would have mentioned it.

But they did not.

It is more likely, then, that Henry's cross-country march was forced on him. The fast road was blocked. French forces appeared to be closing in from the north, and he knew he was in grave danger if he was attacked at a disadvantage. His march was that of a man on the run, not one out-thinking his enemies.[14]

When his army neared Nesle, Henry offered up his usual deal: he would spare the countryside if he could have free passage and supplies for his hungry men. This time, the people refused. Our sources don't provide a lot of information on the matter, but it's hard not to see in their refusal an awareness of the English army's weakness – as well as, I suspect, an awareness of the French army that was gathering all around. We know that the constable and many of the other leaders had their army on the north side of the Somme. They were, at this point, probably strung out between Corbie and Péronne as they followed their own roads to the east. But other forces were approaching from other directions. The net was closing around the English. Their days must have seemed numbered.

Henry was livid. He promised to set fire to the hamlets and leave them 'utterly destroyed', the *Gesta* says. Thomas Elmham, writing shortly afterwards, says that 'out of anger' he carried out this threat.[15] At the same time, Henry learned that there was an unguarded ford across the Somme nearby. Whether this information came from his scouts or from the people of Nesle who were no doubt eager to see him leave, we don't know. But Henry and his army, confident that they had found a way across the river at last, hurried in that direction as dawn broke on 19 October.[16]

THE CROSSING OF THE SOMME

It is interesting that the clerical author of the *Gesta*, who as usual seems our most reliable voice here, was well aware of the danger that the English were in, and why: to get to the Somme, the king 'crossed a marsh through which ran a stream ... so he was hemmed in, as it were, in the angle between the two'.[17] This stream through a marsh is the River Ingon.

Modern canal work has greatly drained the marshes of both rivers that the English faced in 1415, but using old maps we can reconstruct enough of the pre-modern landscape to set the scene.

The road that Henry had been following doesn't go through Nesle. It runs north of it, through what the Chaplain describes as 'quite small hamlets near the walled town'.[18] So Henry might have been threatening Nesle, but he wasn't *in* Nesle. He was, on our modern maps, probably at Mesnil-Saint-Nicaise. There was a crossroads near here. The first road – the one he was on – continued east and a little south, down into the valley of the Ingon, which it crossed beside the modern hamlet of Rouy-le-Petit. The road then ran south-east to the walled city of Ham, which sat at a major bridge crossing the Somme that the English had little chance of seizing. The second road Henry had in front of him came up from Nesle – which had closed its gates to him – and led to a crossing of the Somme to the north-east at Béthencourt-sur-Somme.

The *Gesta* describes the little-used ford that the English headed to as being only about a 'league' away from Henry's encampment near Nesle. The author was essentially eyeballing it, but he was remarkably accurate in doing so. According to the Carolingian principle, a league was three Roman miles, each of which amounts to 1,000 paces – which gives us a *rough* approximate conversion rate of two and three-quarter miles per league. The true measurement from the crossroads beside Mesnil-Saint-Nicaise to Voyennes, where the Somme could indeed be forded, was just over three miles. This was the place, and it won't be the last time that we'll be able to follow the writer's remembrances across the landscape and find where history happened.

Having crossed the Ingon, the English were indeed hemmed in by the two rivers. Henry was, for all intents and purposes, trapped until he could manage the crossing of the Somme. The men were right to be worried. Ham, sure to be heavily garrisoned, was only six miles upstream on the same side of the river. A sortie from there, slamming the English into the rivers and marshes, would have been disastrous. For that matter, Nesle was still close. Its citizens, too, could launch a sortie. The moment was perilous. It was a desperate gamble.

The *Gesta* says that the English identified two crossing points where the water depths reached 'only a little higher than a horse's belly'.[19] These were reached by causeways that wound their way through the marshes. The French had broken these causeways in multiple places, such that only a single-file line of men could manage to get across.

Henry wasted no time. He sent men winding across as quickly as they could. They worked in teams. Some were assigned to the task of protecting the army from attack. Some hurriedly laboured to fill in the gaps in the causeways with anything they could beg, borrow, or steal – logs, bundles of straw, boards from abandoned farms[20] – in order to widen the passages and get at least three men across at a time. Others were dancing their way along the thread of the passage that was already there, wading through mud and water both, to get across and establish a secure bridgehead on the other side.

It wasn't a moment too soon. The English had barely pushed a hundred men across the Somme when enemy cavalry showed up and tried to slam them back into the water. This was the greatest danger of a wet-gap crossing: it could split the strength of an army while providing the enemy with a ready drowning pool.

With a shout, the English who were already across charged out to meet the French, desperate to buy time for their comrades to join them. It worked. The French were pushed back. The crossing, which the *Gesta* says began around 1pm, took the rest of the day.

That night, the mood in the English camp soared. The Chaplain tells us that many of the men had heard a rumour that they would need to go another eight days of marching upstream before they would get a chance to cross, so the shortcut was a relief. More than that, they believed that the bulk of the French force was gathering near Saint-Quentin at the head waters of the Somme, and that the English army could now cut northwards ahead of them, leaving a real chance that they might complete their march to Calais unmolested: 'we were of the firm hope that the enemy army, the army which was said to be waiting for us at the head of the river, would be disinclined to follow us to do battle.'[21] Saint-Quentin was only 20 miles away from Veronnes along the Somme, so if the rumour of eight days to get there is accurate – and not an echo of the eight days of rations they had set out with from Harfleur – then the English commanders were probably anticipating the need to take a circuitous route. This makes sense when you consider that the army was surely out of food and would now be required to slow down and engage in significant foraging operations if it had any hope of maintaining its strength.

But little of that mattered now.

Henry had wanted to make his crossing at Blanchetaque, to follow in Edward's footsteps to Calais. At Veronnes, he had made a Blanchetaque of his own. He was over the Somme.

THE FRENCH HERALDS

Trouble was, the French weren't at Saint-Quentin on 19 October.

As Henry and his men celebrated their crossing of the Somme, the lords of the army of France had instead mustered at Péronne, roughly 11 miles due north – almost on a direct line between the English and their destination of Calais. The constable was already there with the duke of Alençon, Boucicaut, and the army that had been blocking the Somme. The duke of Bourbon had probably just arrived from Rouen with the dukes of Bar and Nevers and the rest of the men who had still been gathering there when the English left Harfleur. The duke of Orléans wasn't there yet, but he was *en route*. With them were many thousands of men.

They all would have known, within hours, that the English had crossed the river to the south and would no doubt soon be heading their way. It was the perfect time for the French lords to march on their tired adversaries and put them to the sword. As the Religieux, writing only a few years later, puts it, the French were ready to do so:

> for the rumour was already spread around that the enemy, exhausted by hunger and cold, were almost unable to defend

> themselves, and that the French army pressed them so close that if they remained in that position they would bring them low with ease and without shedding of blood.[22]

But this did not happen.

Instead, on 20 October, three heralds met the English army at its camp near Athies. They were sent, they said, from the dukes of Bourbon and Orléans. What exactly was said depends a lot on who was telling the story. According to the *Gesta*, they told Henry that the French 'would do battle with him before he reached Calais, although they did not assign a day or place'.[23] The story told from the French perspective is different. According to a chronicle written by the herald of the duke of Berry – historians call this source the Berry Herald – the heralds' message was that the French would give battle at a very specific place and time: 24 October at Aubigny-en-Artois, some 40 miles away. Furthermore, the Berry Herald claims that Henry 'accepted the challenge, promising to come to the field and to fight on that day, without default'.[24] The challenge, we can imagine, was laden with appeals to honour, manhood, chivalry, and all the rest of the frosting men slather on the dry cake of violence.

That something like this happened – that despite what the Chaplain tells us there *was* an arranged time and place – is about the only way to explain what happened next.

Though the French had the English army penned in, they pulled out of Péronne. The writer of the *Gesta* actually confirms this, when he tells us that on 21 October, after passing that town, 'we found, about a mile away, the roads quite churned up by the French army as it had crossed ahead of us many thousands strong'.[25] This was the trail left by the French lords who, believing they had an agreement to fight at Aubigny, had marched north up the main road to Bapaume and Arras beyond it, to await their enemy on the wide, flat, and open ground of Artois – the perfect place to arrange a battle. To many in the French army, it made no sense, as the Religieux describes it:

> But suddenly, at the order of some leaders whose names I do not know, the French were ordered to change their position and to move off to establish themselves elsewhere. They obeyed, but not

> without regret, for they foresaw that this manoeuvre was to the benefit of the enemy.[26]

One can understand the monk's anger. Why had the leaders done this? Was it, as one major historian has suggested, a retreat from the enemy, with the plan 'to intercept the English army somewhere on the route to Calais where they could fight with advantage' while still 'far enough south to rule out the threat of being attacked in the rear by [its] garrison'?[27] I doubt it. It's hard to imagine a better advantage than they had staying where they were: a walled city with gunpowder artillery standing watch over the road that the tired enemy wanted to take, with no place else for them to go. It was about the most advantageous situation a commander could ask for.

The only sensible reason to leave it was if they'd made a deal with Henry to fight elsewhere. Little else makes sense. But why were the French willing to make that deal? Why not crush the enemy there and then?

The answer, I think, comes from Edmond de Dynter, who was the secretary of the duke of Brabant – a man who died on the battlefield of Agincourt. A few decades later, Edmond chronicled the history of the duchy, in which he notes that while in Louvain his duke received letters from the gathered French lords in Péronne, written on 19 October, asking the duke to 'set out in his own person, because in the following week they intended to fight the English, telling him also that the king of France and the dauphin of Vienne would be there in person'.[28] For the chronicler, it's a throwaway fact to explain how Brabant came rushing to join in the fight at Agincourt, where he lost his life. For us, it's a critical data point that might well explain the unexplainable: the French leaders were leaving Péronne and temporarily letting the English off the hook because they had been told that the king or his son would lead their armies in person. This was what had been 'proclaimed far and wide since August', and it was clearly still expected.[29] Problem was, neither man had arrived yet. Nor had word arrived that they weren't coming. So the French leaders in Péronne were buying more time for them to join the army.

The explanation for *that* returns us to the fractured state of the kingdom.

The French leaders gathered in Péronne were an impressive bunch, but far more noticeable is who was *not* there. When Bourbon had hurried north out of Rouen, the dauphin had not come with him. Neither had the king, who was lucid and had by that point arrived in the Norman capital. The duke of Berry was too old to fight, but everyone would have expected the dukes of Burgundy and Brittany to show up. These men were, instead, dithering – negotiating for terms before doing their duty, angling for position over their rivals, making assurances that they quickly decided not to keep. They were, quite clearly, wasting time as they waited to see which way the wind would finally blow. If it was in favour of England, they wanted to be ready to turn that to their advantage, and to the disadvantage of their enemies.

The festering wounds from countrymen were for them more painful, it seems, than the threats from England.

Those wounds, we can see in hindsight, would be a main cause of ruin at Agincourt.

APPROACHING AGINCOURT

The sources all agree that Henry's men were frightened after the appearance of the heralds on 20 October. The king wore his armour, expecting to fight at any moment. His men did likewise. The weight of the gear only served to heighten their exhaustion. In several accounts, it's at this point that the king ordered his archers to make stakes. I think instead he reminded his men of the urgency in following through with an existing order, which had been interrupted in its execution by the hurried crossing of the Somme.

If Henry had sworn that he would fight the French at Aubigny on 24 October, why was he in armour?

His worry, I think, was that the French wouldn't keep to their word. And such doubts would have seemed to be absolutely warranted when the English marched past Péronne the next day, 21 October. The *Gesta* says that some French cavalry made a sortie from the city and had to be turned back by English riders. The Chaplain suspected they were meant 'to entice us within range of enemy shots' from Péronne's walls.[30] Whether or not this was so, it certainly would have put Henry in a mindset to expect an assault at any moment.

Though the road north had been churned up by the French, the English made good speed upon it. The road led straight through the walled town of Bapaume, though, and the even larger fortified city of Arras beyond that. Both might have held garrisons. Neither, after the sortie he had just fended off from Péronne, seemed like places Henry wanted to be.

So, the English tacked west, taking smaller roads away from Bapaume. On the night of 21 October, both Le Fèvre and the French chronicler Pierre Fenin have them encamped near Miraumont.[31] This makes sense. It enabled Henry to skirt around Bapaume, while also clearing the entanglements of the marshy valley of the River Ancre south of Miraumont.

From Miraumont, the best route to Aubigny was a return to the main road north of Bapaume, which the English could follow until they needed to skirt around Arras. Instead, Henry led them further west and a little south, cutting across the country and putting what was then the massive forest of Hébuterne between him and the French to the north. Riding the country roads along the ridgelines, he reached Acheux-en-Amiénois that night. If French scouts were watching, eyebrows would have been raised, but I don't think there would have been great alarm. There was still a good route to Aubigny ahead of the English and still plenty of time for them to take it.

On 23 October, the English army continued west, dropping down onto the main road between Amiens and Pas-en-Artois in order to make the crossing of the River Authie at Thièvres. After following this north for a bit, they rode across the countryside to reach the main road that ran between Doullens and Lucheux.

If Henry had made a vow upon his honour to go to Aubigny – and the weight of the evidence makes it seem likely – then this was the day he broke it. The road he was now on headed north-east, straight to Aubigny roughly 16 miles away. It was an easy, direct march on a solid road.

But he didn't take it.

Instead, he crossed the River Grouche and continued west. As the writer of the *Chronicle of Normandy* says, referring to the arranged battle on 24 October, 'the English did not keep to their covenant that day, but held on their way more to the left than in their direct course'.[32] Speaking about Henry's promise to go to Aubigny, the Berry Herald says, 'In effect, he did the very opposite, because he passed by a place called Beauquesne so that he should reach Calais as soon as possible.'[33]

On the night of 23 October, Henry's vanguard took control of the crossing of the Canche at Frévent, while the rest of his forces spent the night on higher ground at Bonnières-le-Scallon. Tito Livio Frulovisi tells us that the vanguard found that the French were trying to break the bridge at Frévent. These were driven off by 'a bold and powerful assault'.[34]

By this point, the commanders at Aubigny would be well aware of the new English route. In response, the French army hastily packed up and hurried west to cut Henry off once again. Unlike the English, however, who were being forced to use country roads in order to avoid the towns in the region, the French had no such worries. They would have made fast work of eating up the miles on the main road between Arras and Saint-Pol-sur-Ternoise. With luck, they might be able to catch the English somewhere west of that city, before they reached the Ternoise.

Tito Livio Frulovisi tells that, as he rode from Frévent towards the Ternoise on 24 October, Henry sent the duke of York with the vanguard, which was moving ahead of the main army. It was an unusual move, and one that suggested concerns about an immediate attack. The king was right to think his enemies were closing in: 'One scout, with worried face and with anxious gasping breath, announced to the duke that a great, countless multitude was approaching.'[35]

The question of how many were coming is a difficult one. We simply don't have the muster rolls and other data that have allowed us to get a good sense of the size of the English army at the outset of the campaign. The Chaplain claimed that there were 30 times more French than English at Agincourt – that would be something like 175,000 men – though he later says that, by the enemy's own account, it was closer to 60,000.[36] Looking across the English sources, we find that they are all over the place between those two numbers – and that none of these estimates are plausible.[37]

Fig. 1: In this photo, taken on 8 May 1945, General Hastings Ismay stands behind Winston Churchill in the garden at 10 Downing Street. It was General Ismay whose thoughts, during the final planning for D-Day, turned to Agincourt. (Getty Images)

Fig. 2: The movie poster for the 1944 film *Henry V*, directed by Laurence Olivier, featuring the king delivering Shakespeare's famous Saint Crispin's Day speech upon the battlefield. (Getty Images)

Fig. 3: Just how deep does Agincourt pervade the English consciousness? John Lennon's illustrated schoolbook, holding a poem and artwork that he composed at the age of 12, may hold a clue. (Alamy)

Fig. 4: The king of France, having gone mad, raises his sword to attack his companions as they cross through the forest near Le Mans. From an illustrated 15th-century copy of Jean Froissart. (Getty Images)

Fig. 5: This vintage engraving is a colourized rendition of an illustration of the battle of Shrewsbury (1403) that appears in the late-15th-century manuscript describing the life and exploits of Richard Beauchamp, earl of Warwick. (Getty Images)

Fig. 6: In 1340, Edward III quartered the arms of England with those of France – a visual declaration of the end goal of the Hundred Years War. This new coat of arms appears here upon his tomb at Westminster Abbey. (Livingston)

Fig. 7: A 19th-century etching of Owain Glyndŵr, based on his great seal. (Getty Images)

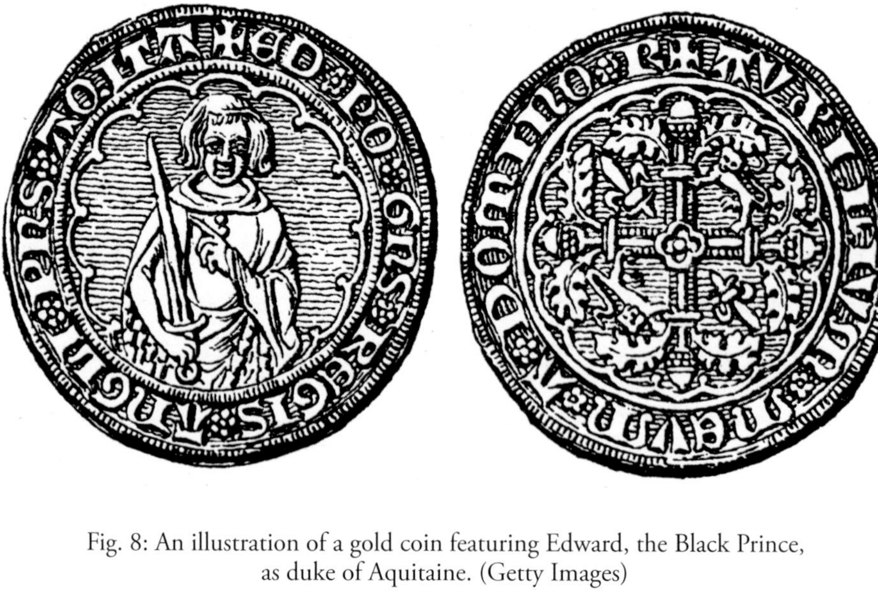

Fig. 8: An illustration of a gold coin featuring Edward, the Black Prince, as duke of Aquitaine. (Getty Images)

Fig. 9: An imaginative illustration of the assassination of Louis of Orléans. Note the fallen duke's severed left hand, which would be so well remembered that a similar wound would be dealt out in vengeance for his murder. (Getty Images)

Fig. 10: Portrait of Henry V. Note that, unlike most royal images, he is portrayed in profile. Was this done to hide the scar of his wound taken at Shrewsbury? (Getty Images)

Fig. 11: The ruins of Château d'Arques-la-Bataille viewed from the south. In 1415, Henry V's army needed to bypass this fortification in order to cross the river valley below. (© Raimond Spekking & Elke Wetzig / CC BY-SA 4.0 (via Wikimedia Commons))

Fig. 12: A close-up of Guillaume de l'Isle's 1704 map of Artois, locating the battle of Agincourt west of the town of Azincourt rather than in its now traditional location east of the town. Elsewhere, this same map is the earliest known to mark the site of the battle of Crécy (1346) and does so in its traditional location. (National Library of France)

Fig. 13: The English crossed the Ternoise near the modern bridge in Blangy. (Livingston)

Fig. 14: A drone image, looking north along the road from Blangy to Ambricourt, from the position where the rival armies at Agincourt would have first come in sight of one another. The English would have been near the lone trees in the foreground, while the French would have been on the unwooded hillsides beyond the wooded valley between them. (Livingston)

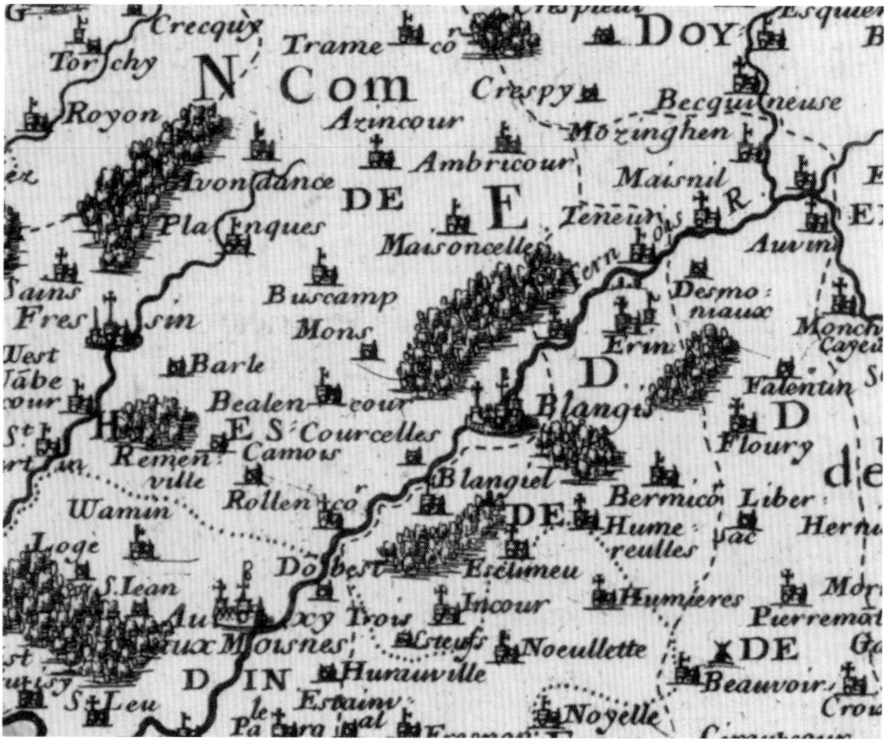

Fig. 15: Executed by Nicolas Sanson in 1656, this map shows the larger stretch of forest that ran south and west of Maisoncelle in the past. (Boston Public Library)

Fig. 16: From the initial contact point, looking north-west. After the French went around the forests in order to get ahead of the English and block their route to Calais, Henry V had his men marched up this road to the town of Maisoncelle, in the trees to the left. Tramecourt is hidden in the woods to the upper right, and straight ahead through the gap between them is the distant town of Azincourt, where the French took their lodgings. It was upon this gap that the English took their position for the battle. (Livingston)

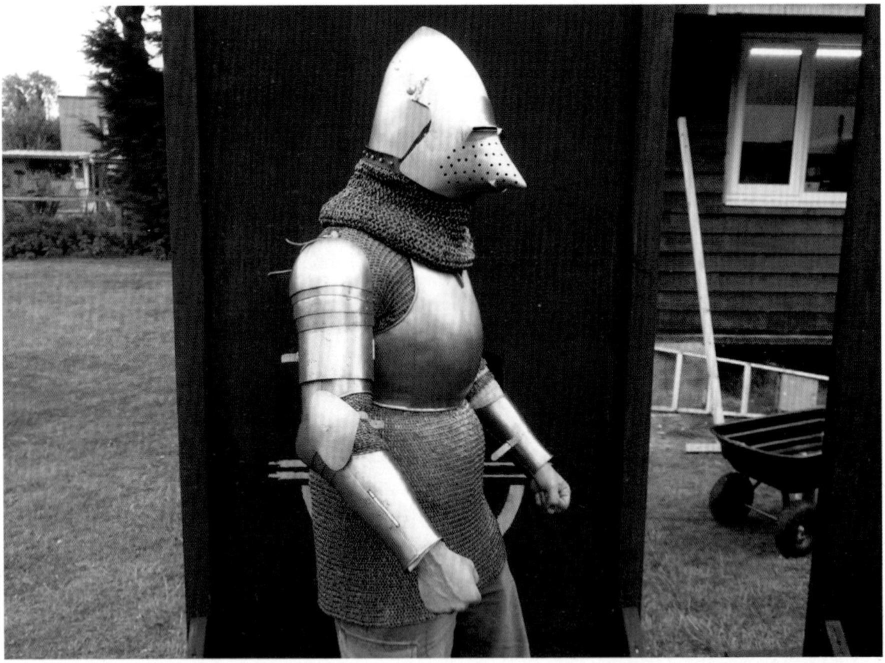

Fig. 17: Replica armour utilized by Tod's Workshop for the 2022 production 'Arrows vs Armour 2'. This is an excellent approximation of the upper-body armour that the French might have worn at Agincourt. Note the 'weak points' at the shoulders and just below the breast plate. Note, too, the high number of straps and buckles. After the battle, these would have been cut in order to strip the valuable armour from corpses. A full list of craftspeople involved in making this armour can be found at https://todtodeschini.com/. (© Tod's Workshops Ltd)

Fig. 18: This early 15th-century illustration of the work of Christine de Pizan depicts a man preparing for battle in the foreground, a process requiring the help of several assistants. (Bridgeman Images)

Fig. 19: The *Calvaire* near Tramecourt, long thought to be associated with a mass grave. Archaeological investigations have found no such evidence. (Livingston)

Fig. 20: Though popularly believed to have belonged to Henry V, this sword – here displayed at Westminster Abbey during the commemorations on the 600th anniversary of Agincourt – in reality belonged to Henry VII. (Getty Images)

Fig. 21: Looking north, from the air above the *Morival*, at the farmland between Azincourt on the left and Tramecourt on the right. On the night of 24 October, the French would have slept throughout the upper half of what is pictured here. The castle of Azincourt was near the small line of woods protruding from the upper left corner, and the *Calvaire* is located in the small, lonely bunch of trees at upper centre. (Livingston)

Fig. 22: A detailed diorama of the battle of Agincourt built for the Royal Armouries in Leeds. (Getty Images)

Fig. 23: The battle of Agincourt in a 15th-century manuscript now held by the Victoria and Albert Museum, London. Note the emphasis on the muddy terrain through which the French are attempting to make their assault. (Getty Images)

Fig. 24: A gouache of the town of Azincourt, painted by Adrien de Montigny between 1605 and 1611 at the behest of Duke Charles de Croÿ (1560–1612). The viewpoint is from south of the town, on the ridgeline north-west of the *Morival*, looking north. (Private Collection)

Fig. 25: A gouache of the town of Maisoncelle, painted by Adrien de Montigny between 1605 and 1611 at the behest of Duke Charles de Croÿ (1560–1612). The viewpoint is from north of the town, on the ridgeline north-west of the *Morival*, looking south: the same position from which the gouache in Figure 24 was made. (Private Collection)

Fig. 26: Looking south-west down the *Morival*, the field known as *L'Anglais* is in the trees at top left, in the buildings edging Maisoncelle. The line of trees in the upper centre marks a depression in the landscape called the *Fosse a Rogne*. (Livingston)

Fig. 27: Key locations pinned to satellite imagery of Agincourt, looking west, with shadows modelled for approximately 9am on 25 October 1415 through Google Earth Pro™. Note that vertical terrain changes are here exaggerated by a three-to-one ratio in order to more strongly emphasize these features. Overlaid atop this reconstruction of the map are the minor and major medieval roads, along with potential English formations at the traditional location and the alternate location argued in this book. (Livingston)

Fig. 28: Looking east, from the air above the *Morival*, at the farmland across which the English took position, just north of Maisoncelle. (Livingston)

Fig. 29: The south side of the woods around Azincourt today, showing the road up from Maisoncelle. The gentle undulation of the terrain would be no insurmountable hindrance to men or horses. (Livingston)

Fig. 30: An illustration made to accompany an early 15th-century copy of Walsingham's chronicle account of the battle of Agincourt. Details to note include the arrow wounds to men and horses, the man at the centre bottom of the image who is bleeding out from the cutting of his artery beneath his armpit, and the two men on horseback in the background whose horns might well be signalling men to charge and retreat. (Alamy)

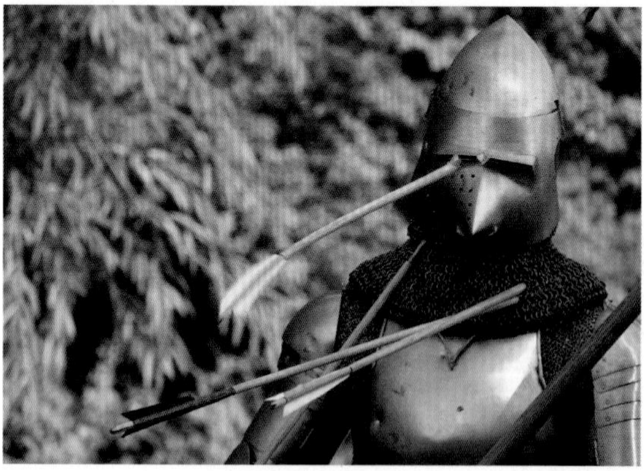

Fig. 31: The replica bascinet being struck by an arrow in the 2022 Tod's Workshop production 'Arrows vs Armour 2'. While the slotted visor has prevented the arrow from penetrating, the impact has caused the shaft to shatter, sending slivers flying. Previous hits have punctured the mail: a hindrance to action even if they, too, failed to penetrate the body. (© Tod's Workshops Ltd)

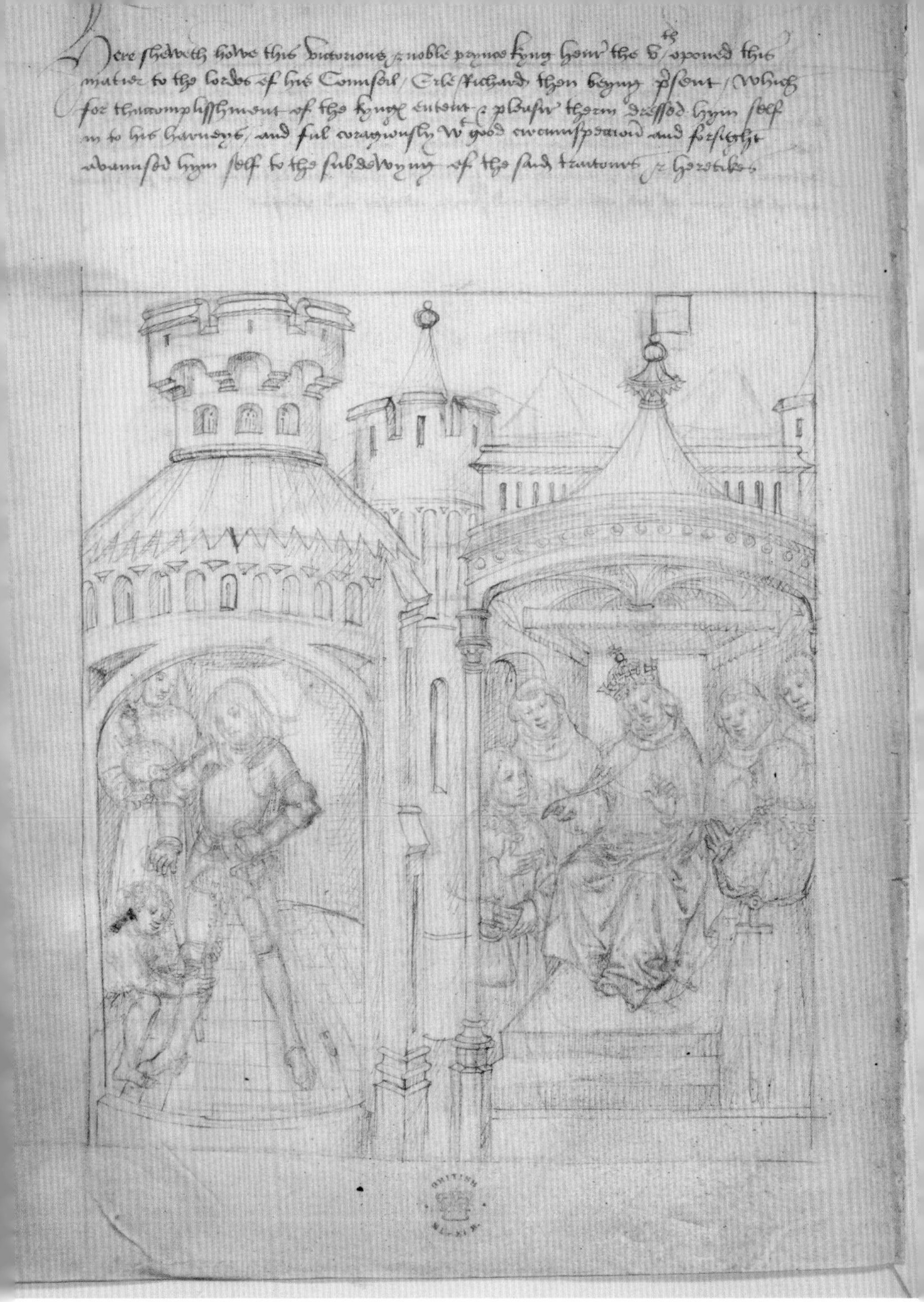

Fig. 32: Richard Beauchamp, earl of Warwick, is dressed for battle in this image from the late-15th-century manuscript describing his life and exploits. Note that he requires two assistants to fit and secure his armour. (Bridgeman Images)

Fig. 33: The assassination of Jean the Fearless in a late-15th-century copy of Monstrelet's chronicle. (Alamy)

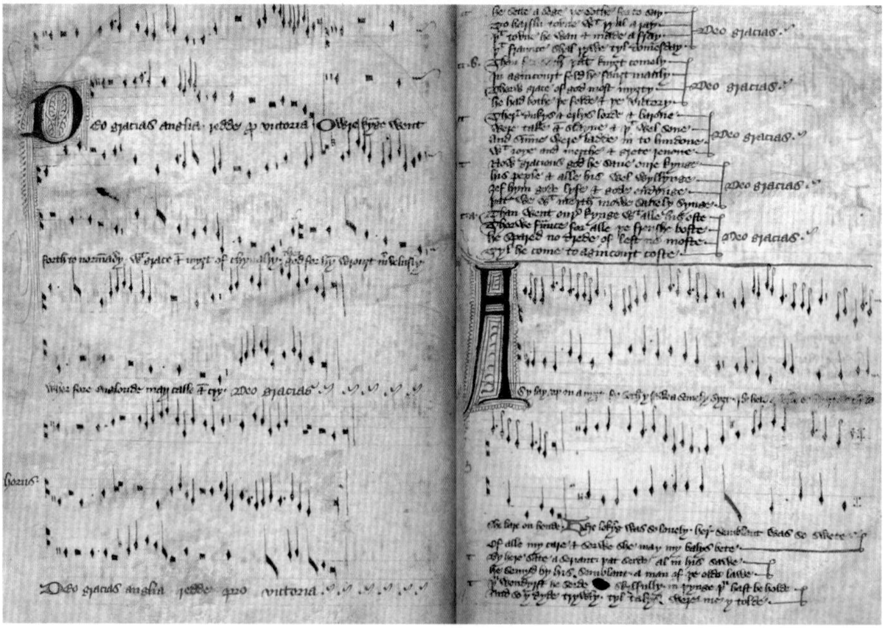

Fig. 34: The Agincourt Carol, one of many songs glorifying Henry V, as it appears in the 15th-century manuscript held by the Bodleian Library, Oxford. (Alamy)

This isn't surprising. The English, having achieved victory, had a vested interest in portraying the enemy numbers as boundless. It made their win all the more incredible.

More realistically, the heart of the French force was closer to the 10,000 men-at-arms who the Berry Herald says fought at the coming battle – plus some.[38] At the most, the French might have added a nearly equal number of *gros valets* – servants and companions, like squires, who could also fight if needed – plus a couple of thousand crossbowmen, archers, and other personnel.[39] That would give them around four times as many men as the English, which is the ratio given by the Religieux, an anonymous contemporary chronicle, and the work of Thomas Basin.[40] Depending on the number of *gros valets* in the army, the ratio of French to English could fall as low as the three to one ratio testified to in Le Fèvre, or even the two to one ratio that many modern historians suggest.[41] Later chapters will discuss the organization of these men. The point to be made for now is that they didn't outnumber the English by 30 to one as the *Gesta* says, or even by six to one as Monstrelet and Waurin claim.[42]

It's common stock to point out how beleaguered the English army was. 24 October was the 16th gruelling day of what was supposed to be a contact-free eight-day march to Calais. The soldiers had marched over 130 miles off-track. The past few days had been wet and cold, and the vast majority of the men were sleeping out in the open: curling up on the driest ground they could find, they would raise their sodden woollen hoods to keep the beating rain off their faces long enough to find a never-restful sleep. Not a few of them were ill, some of them with lingering dysentery carried on from Harfleur. Empty, growling stomachs only added to the torment.[43]

Their suffering, their desperation – all of it serves to make greater their courage, their determination, and the everlasting glory from their victory to come.

The English were indeed suffering.

But so were the French.

Since the English had left Harfleur and the main French army had left Vernon, the two forces had quite remarkably matched their marches mile-for-mile: 235 of them to the point when they finally caught up with each other. They had seen and slept in the same weather. No doubt some of the French too were unwell, though they would have had a far easier time retiring the sick or injured in local monasteries and other sources of care than their foreign counterparts. We assume that they were better fed, too. They had been able to travel through friendly cities, after all, whereas the English had been wisely avoiding them. But the truth here, as it is with so many things, is that we can't know. It would not be typical practice for the people of the cities to offer up their goods to the passing French forces as boundless acts of free generosity. Deals would need to be struck, either by individual men or by rich lords who acquired large quantities of supplies, took what they needed, and then ordered the rest disseminated through their captains who more than likely took their own cuts first. So it was on both sides, as it seems to be in any war. The fullness of a soldier's stomach is most easily measured by his proximity to power.

For centuries, the story of Agincourt has been most often viewed through the lens of the English. It's easy to do this. They were the aggressors in the invasion. And Henry V is a fascinating king.

But telling the story from the English perspective should not relegate the French to the status of background extras in a story of English glory. That's not what happened. The French army wasn't a bunch of rich snobs lounging in hotel rooms who deservedly got thrashed by the plucky, down-to-earth common men of England, no matter what Shakespeare and the movies say.

The truth is that there were rich snobs on both sides. Henry V wasn't sleeping in the cold, by god. When he couldn't commandeer a French house for his comfort, he was sleeping in a beautiful pavilion that had been custom-made for the campaign: work on it had started as far back as February, with orders given to the king's tent-maker authorizing him 'as many workers and other labourers' as he might need for its manufacture.[44] When they had left England for France, the Earl Marshal had brought with him a pavilion for his personal toilet, complete with an iron seat. He even had a tent for the stable of 24 horses he had brought to use on the campaign.[45] In fact, as one historian has rightly observed, although the 'popular image is that the French army was much more lustrous in its aristocratic component' than the English, things were in reality much closer to the opposite: it was the English army that contained 'almost all of the active peers' of its realm, whereas a great many of this same class of men were sitting out on the French side.[46]

24 and 25 October brought about the English crossing of the Ternoise and the battle of Agincourt. I cannot tell the story of the one without the other.

So it's time to zoom in even closer.

It's time to get to Agincourt.

Part Four

Locating Agincourt

O evil day, which all France curses,
When the whole flower of the army was despoiled,
When the joyful rejoicing, the song and the lyre, were lost
And tears, groans, and mourning were brought to all.

Robert Blondel, 1420–22[1]

9

Finding Agincourt

The title of this chapter – 'Finding Agincourt' – presupposes that the battle needs to be found.

This will come as a surprise to anyone who has read one of the many hundreds of books about the battle or visited the modern town of Azincourt, because none of these show the slightest hesitation in telling everyone where it happened: on a flat field between the towns of Azincourt and Tramecourt. It's there on the maps and in the signs about town. There are even cut-outs of English and French fighters strewn about the place to help visitors imagine what happened there.

In previous books, I have referred to the received story of the past as the *Vulgata*. This is the tradition. It's what everyone knows.

Sometimes the *Vulgata* is right, which is fair enough.

In the case of Agincourt, I think much of it is wrong.

More importantly, I think it *matters* that it's wrong. Because I believe, truly and sincerely, that a battle is its ground.[1]

A BATTLE IS ITS GROUND

In a fight, terrain is everything. What people can see and hear, what they can know, where they can stand, what they will fear ... all of it depends upon where they are upon the landscape. It's true for the soldiers. It's true for the commanders. *A battle is its ground.*

This holds for most conflicts today, but it's an absolutely essential truth for pre-modern battles, in which the combatants had no recourse to aerial reconnaissance or detailed mapping information. What the fighters could see is more or less what they knew, so for us to comprehend their actions in the fight, we must try to see what they saw, which absolutely depends upon knowing where they were.

In many cases, unfortunately, we cannot be sure where battles took place, meaning we do not always have a ground to examine. The further back in time we go the more likely this is to be a problem. The 600 years that separate us from Agincourt may be an eyeblink in the geological history of that ground, but it's a very long time in human terms. It means that a lot of information about what happened and where it happened has been lost and might well be beyond recovery.

Though we can attempt to mitigate such problems to one degree or another, even the smallest loss of data can dramatically curtail our ability to speak with confidence about what happened in a given battle, which inevitably has an adverse effect on our understanding of the history of warfare on larger scales.

It should be plainly obvious: *a battle is its ground*, so we should seize any opportunity to identify and confirm battlegrounds where their recovery is even remotely possible.

Strangely, this has not often been a matter of great interest for historians. Judging from the historiography, battlefield locations have been, with a few notable exceptions, largely regarded either as beyond recovery or as already established fact. And, in the latter case, most of our 'known' battlefields are located without any positive confirmation via archaeology: we 'know' where the site is because that is where people believe the site to be. It is, in a word, tradition.

The battle of Crécy is a familiar case in point for my readers. Verified battlefields have revealed a trove of archaeological remains: the detritus of war from an engagement like Crécy should constitute tens of thousands of items.[2] Multiple archaeological surveys of the traditional site of the battle, however, have accumulated exactly *zero*.[3] This is one of the many problems I have with that site, which also does not make tactical or logistical sense – or even match the location of the battle given in our sources. In an essay in *The Battle of Crécy: A Casebook*, I therefore suggested that the battle ought to be re-located to a different site that was identified on the basis of the location data in our sources.[4] I have since refined this position – and the battle reconstruction upon it – in *Crécy: Battle of Five Kings*.[5] My primary fault in these efforts, I have been told, is that if I'm right then a long parade of previous historians would be wrong.

This is not the winning counter-argument I think it's supposed to be. History, at least as I was taught it, acknowledges but does not worship at the altar of previous historians. At a foundational level, historians must interrogate our forebears just as we must interrogate ourselves. Our aim is the refinement of our knowledge about the past – whether that means confirmation or denial of our previously held assumptions is quite beside the point.

As I often say, our aim is not to *be* right, but to *get it* right.

If we interrogate a battle-site location with the result that we re-confirm our assumptions, this is a fine thing. Likewise, if our assumptions are shown to be unfounded, this, too, is a fine thing. In either case, we are able to more closely fit our understandings of the past to what really happened. More than that, we are also afforded the opportunity to engage in the self-reflective work of investigating why the data we are recovering about the past did not fit with our previous assumptions. Does the problem lie within our data or our assumptions? It can turn out, for instance, that once we drill down through the historiography, we discover that the traditional account has been a game of Chinese whispers without evidence from the start. We have been building houses on shifting sands.

And, again, this matters. *A battle is its ground.*

So how do we find that ground? How, in short, do we reconstruct a battle?

ALL-SOURCE ANALYSIS AND THE RECONSTRUCTION TOOLKIT

Agincourt happened. It was an occurrence at a historical place and time. Lacking omniscience, however, we cannot recover the fullness of any dataset about it. This is the basic tragedy of writing history. We begin from a position of loss, and while we may endeavour to fill the gap between ourselves and the Truth (with a capital 'T'), we can never close it. Our work will be, intrinsically and inevitably, deficient. As we aim to minimize that deficiency, we can and should reach for anything and everything we can.

There is a lot we can reach for. Any event in question, occurring at a historical place and time, was subjected to – was *connected* to – the entire range of natural phenomena, to say nothing of the internal and external human forces at play. So one of the first things we have to wrap our heads around is that the departmental silos of modern academia have little to no bearing at all on the reconstitution of past events.

Geological and hydrological forces determined the landscape.[6] Psychological forces determined the mindset. Meteorological forces determined the weather. Sociological forces determined the sides. Narratological forces determined the memorialization of events. And on and on.

True, some of these fields of knowledge may play a lesser or greater part depending on the event. Some might also be irrecoverable. But they were, in the past moment, all present and all associated.

As a result, whenever we approach a conflict, we should try to access every strand of data that we can, whether familiar or unfamiliar. In my methodology, I borrow from the three-letter agencies of the United States government, who call this kind of intelligence gathering 'All-Source Analysis'.[7]

There are literary sources and (rare but exciting) material sources. There are the contextual probabilities of the history of warfare as we understand it. There are secondary sources of experimental archaeology and strategic and tactical modelling, as well as local lore and place-names. At this stage of the game, we must aim to bring every related scrap possible into a single targeting package.

Sometimes it will not be much. If we are very lucky, however, we will find ourselves sifting through a large amount of data. This is the case with Agincourt, which has had a modern army of scholars combing through archives and other resources in search of anything and everything that references the battle. Their hard work has made reams of data available to researchers.

Luckily for us, we stand at an enviable moment in the making of history. Digitized catalogues, combined with networked algorithms, enable the search of thousands of books in seconds.

Satellites and the extraordinary technologies that they enable allow us to spy the ancient marks of roads and buildings that would otherwise lie hidden. Email and virtual communication technologies allow us to connect in real time with our fellow researchers around the world.

Sir Isaac Newton talked of seeing further than others because he stood on the shoulders of giants – he relied on the work that had come before him. Research, properly done, is always this way. And while I'm no Newton, I will say that every day I do in ten seconds what would have taken me hours in the library just 20 years ago. I tip my cap to the giants.

As I sift through my data, I'm always on the lookout for patterns and what we might term multi-source verification: if multiple independent sources tell me the same thing about an event, the probability that this information is true increases.

Something else that helps me sift through my data – something that helps sway probabilities closer to near certainties – is what I've previously called my Reconstruction Toolkit: basic principles that I often apply in conflict analysis. They are, as I'm always keen to point out, principles and not rules. They're tools, and even the best, most handy tools can't be used all the time. But they nevertheless come up so often that any time I go to a job site I make sure I've got them hanging on my belt.

We've already seen the first of these principles: *a battle is its ground.*

Here's another: *follow the roads.*

FOLLOW THE ROADS

Roads can be everything, so I always make sure to seek them out. After all, if the adversaries' avenues of approach to a battle are known, then they are fairly essential to the reconstruction of events: since a *battle is its ground*, we can clearly see that it will help us understand what happened if we can see the terrain as it was approached. We may not be able to walk in the opponents' footsteps in a literal sense, but by no means should this diminish the importance of understanding the limitations and opportunities that the terrain afforded. If nothing else, determining the routes that the adversaries could have taken to the engagement limits the potential fields of conflict.

In the case of Agincourt, there is no question about the main roads in the area. The 1704 map of Guillaume de l'Isle records them, and they precisely fit with what we know of Roman roads and other major arteries of travel in the Middle Ages (Figure 12). On the immediate landscape there was a major road running from Hesdin towards Fruges. Another ran from Saint-Pol to Fruges.

But what of the smaller roads?

Here, we are aided greatly by Napoleon Bonaparte. More to the point, we're aided by the changes he made to the taxation system in France that resulted in a detailed survey of French holdings. This survey recorded in minute detail the dimensions and location of land parcels, buildings, forests, and roads. It also recorded the local names for fields whenever they were known. As this work was done in the early 19th century, the *Cadastre napoléonien*, as they're known, pre-date most of the changes that modern construction equipment wrought upon the landscape. These maps can be a goldmine.

For us right now, what's notable is that the cadastral maps lay out a network of what they call the 'old' roads – that is, the medieval ones. These can be mapped onto the modern landscape using modern satellite imagery. Particularly useful at this stage is the technology of LiDAR – a portmanteau of the words *light* and *radar* – that uses range-detection lasers to create a staggeringly precise elevation map of the earth's surface stripped of vegetation. Revealing the smallest variations in the landscape can spot out stretches where old roads have disappeared under farmland.

Map 4 is the result of putting all this together. Shown as the thicker white lines on the map are the main roads that lay ahead of Henry as he approached Agincourt from the south-east in 1415. The rest, near as we can tell, would have been the smaller, local paths.

We'll get into this in more detail in the next chapter, but at a glance we can see the importance of this mapping work here. The English, we know, were running for Calais. To get there, they needed to outpace the larger French force hunting them, and the best way to do *that* would be to reach the main roads whose wider, more solid paths allowed greater speed. Looking at the web of

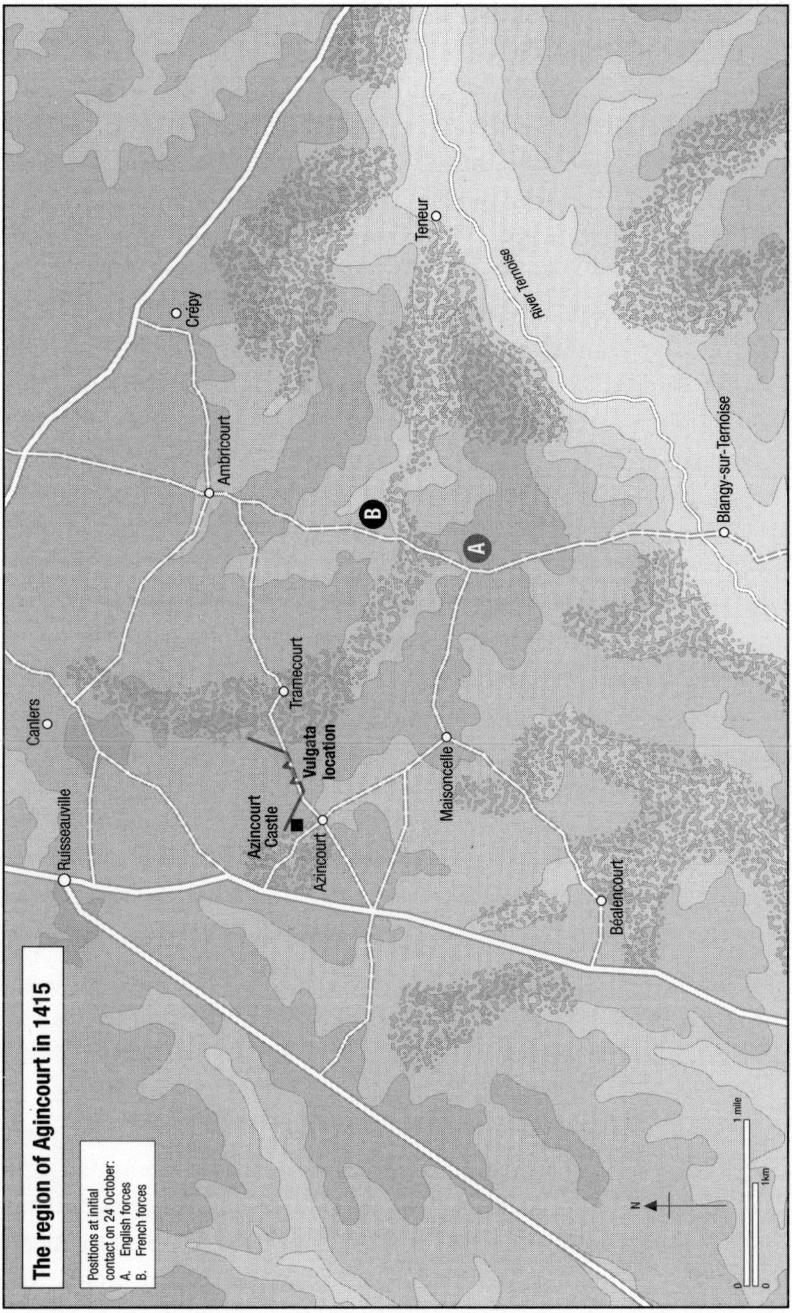
The region of Agincourt in 1415
Positions at initial contact on 24 October:
A. English forces
B. French forces
Ruisseauville
Canlers
Azincourt
Azincourt Castle
Vulgata location
Tramecourt
Maisoncelle
Béalencourt
Ambricourt
Crépy
Teneur
River Ternoise
Blangy-sur-Ternoise
A
B
N
0
1 mile
0
1km

Map 4

roads ahead of their march, we can see that these main roads sat to the English left and right on 24 October – and that both of them converged on the small town of Fruges to the north.

The writer of the *Gesta* states that the English were aware, as they descended into the valley of the Ternoise at Blangy, 'that an enemy force of many thousands was on the other side of the river, about a league away to our right'.[8] This was the mass of the French army, and the location would put them on the main road from Saint-Pol to Fruges – this is the major road coming in from the right in Map 4. The French troops were using it for the same reason the English wanted to: it provided an enormous speed advantage. For the French, it was the way that they intended to manoeuvre around and ahead of the English. Having pursued the English army across France, they were anxious to cut off its advance towards Calais.

Well aware of the French army's location and its aims, Henry's immediate target was the other main road, the one on the English left. The problem *there* was the fact that the road came up from the walled city of Hesdin, which sat about 12 miles down the Ternoise from the crossing that the French had already made at Anvin. Henry didn't have a chance in hell of taking Hesdin on the run, so he had to pick up the road on the other side of the city. Once there, there was still a chance – albeit one that was diminishing fast – that he could make the run to Calais.

FIND THE FORESTS

Roads aren't the only thing shown on Map 4. I've also estimated the reach of the forests, which are noticeably bigger than the woods on the landscape today.

Forests tend to diminish over time. This ought not to be surprising. Human beings use wood for an awful lot of things: building, heating, making room for farms, and so much else. Today, many forests have simply been erased: our hungry saws have done their work until all that is left of the trees is a place-name, a haunting memory on the landscape. So while it's a principle and not a rule – we'll discuss, later on, what might be an exception – our working assumption should be that many of our woods in the area of the battle were bigger in 1415 than what is visible today.

Helping to confirm this are the cadastral maps, which in this area date to 1825. As we would expect, they show woods that are noticeably larger than they are today. These maps get us back two centuries, which is great, but we can be well assured that the woods were *even more* extensive in 1415. An advanced study of deforestation rates in 2009 concluded that in 1850 forests covered 6.3 per cent of usable land in France, compared to an estimated 23.9 per cent coverage in 1400.[9] Local percentages will vary from this regional estimation, but there's nothing on the immediate natural or cultural landscape of Agincourt that would suggest any significant variance to the general rate of deforestation over time. So while we cannot know *exactly* how much more extensive the woods were in 1415 – were they nearly four times larger, as the study suggests? – we can hold the highest measure of confidence that they were more extensive than they were even in 1825. What I've shown on Map 4 is just a rough guess at extrapolating the advance of the woods relative to roads, settlements, slopes, and water availability.

With our reconstruction of the topography as a plan, our many sources as raw material, and our many tools of conflict analysis ready at hand, let's attempt to reconstruct the actions of the opposing forces on 24 October, the day before the battle of Agincourt.

And after that, the battle itself.

10

Reaching Agincourt, 24 October

On 24 October, the English army left Frévent and made for the crossing of the Ternoise at Blangy, almost exactly halfway between the main road crossings at Hesdin and Anvin (Figure 13).

At some point on this day, seven Lancashire archers under the command of Sir Richard Kyghley were captured by the French.[1] One possibility is that they were captured while crossing the Ternoise. This wet-gap crossing, at which point we know the English would have been highly vulnerable, would have been the ideal place either to launch an attack or to station a defensive force to block their movement forward. Just the previous day, the English had needed to force the crossing at Frévent for precisely this reason.

Pseudo-Elmham indeed describes a short fight at Blangy, where the first English riders 'found the men of the enemy in arms, endeavouring in vain to destroy the bridge'. As at Frévent, these were quickly driven off, preserving the crossing for the main army. Pseudo-Elmham reports that the English took prisoners in the action.[2] Another option for the capture of the Englishmen is that they were part of a contingent, ranging out to scout the enemy, which ran afoul of a French unit doing the same work. Small-scale contact of this sort was almost inevitable as the two armies neared each other.

This interplay of reconnaissance surely alerted the French to the fact that the English were attempting a vulnerable crossing of the river at Blangy. The Chaplain tells us that the French had already crossed at this point, so this news would have sent French forces peeling away from the main road as it passed through

Crépy. To make the best speed possible to Blangy, they would have followed the track from Crépy to Ambricourt – we can see this on Map 4 – at which point they would push south-west to pounce on the enemy.

The English were efficient, though, and 'crossed over the river as quickly as possible', the *Gesta* says.[3] The vanguard would have been over first. As the rest of the army surged across behind them, they would have climbed up out of the Ternoise river valley to take control of the high ground in anticipation of trouble. Knowing the placement of the roads, we can walk their route today, up from Blangy onto the higher plain where a battle would soon be fought.

The *Gesta* informs us that when the English reached this high ground, the main bodies of the two armies finally saw each other. The 'grim-looking ranks of the French' – again, coming from the English right – were at this point 'rather more than half a mile away'.[4]

That the forces could have so closely approached one another before coming into visual contact implies physical obstructions at Blangy, and a reconstruction of the topography shows that this was very much the case. Not only were the English down in the valley of the Ternoise, but between the English and French positions there had been substantial woods. With the reconstructed topography in one hand and the knowledge of the roads in the other, we see where the two armies would have been when they finally did come in sight of one another. I have marked these positions on Map 4 as 'A' and 'B'. The Chaplain's estimation in the *Gesta* that they were roughly half a mile from each other at this point is remarkably accurate. The measurement by satellite is just shy of three-quarters of a mile.

Our eyewitness account further states that the French were 'filling a very broad field like a countless swarm of locusts' when they were spotted, 'and there was only a valley, and not so wide at that, between us and them'.[5] This, too, checks out: the road from Ambricourt to Blangy that we would expect the French to follow passes through a broad field and then dips down into a shallow, wooded valley just before it rises up to the English position (Figure 14).

It was at this point, the Chaplain relates, that one of the English lords, Sir Walter Hungerford, said that he wished he had brought 10,000 more archers from England. 'Foolish,' Henry replied, stating that he didn't want one such man more added to his numbers. These were the 'humble few' that God had given him, so they would be sufficient.[6] Though we might well doubt the exact quote, the essential content of such an exchange seems probable. Many in the English army, seeing the greater numbers of the enemy, would have been filled with doubt. A smart leader, which Henry seems very much to have been, would have known he needed to nip such thinking in the bud. It was, of course, the seed from which Shakespeare's 'we few, we happy few' would grow – a speech he imagined the king delivering just before battle the next day.[7]

NO MAN IS A FOOL

If the French had indeed been trying to trap the English along the river, they knew now that this was not going to happen. And though they had the enemy in sight, they clearly had no interest in charging down into the wooded valley that separated them, then climbing back up it in order to engage. That would be foolish, and another of my core principles of battle reconstruction is that *no man is a fool.* There are exceptions – the reason why this is a principle and not a rule – but our default position should never be that a leader was foolish. Instead, until proven wrong, we should assume that they made what they believed to be the best decision possible given the limitations of the knowledge they had at hand. We might recognize in hindsight that these decisions were in error, but that doesn't mean they were indicators of stupidity. Men rarely work against their own best interests as they understand them – and leaving high ground in order to charge uphill toward an enemy on the facing high ground – while having the momentum and organization of this charge blunted by dense woods – is exceedingly unlikely to be in one's best interests.

Still, the armies recognized that they were now within striking distance of one another. The one thing that *would* make an attack through that valley a wise move would be if it meant catching the enemy in column of march. So both sides reformed from columns into lines of battle.

But with the thickly forested valley between them and no one a fool, neither side was interested in making that first move off high ground. The Chaplain describes the two armies locked in position for a time, probably gauging the other's intentions and trying to organize themselves. When it was clear that no fight would take place that day, the French carefully 'withdrew to a field, at the far side of a certain wood which was close at hand to our left between us and them, where lay our road towards Calais.'[8] In other words, the French, moving behind the trees, had shifted their front from one side of the invader to the other. Writing around 1418, the Englishman Thomas Elmham confirms this same basic sequence: the French appeared on the English right after they crossed the Ternoise, and then they 'established themselves at the rear of the woods'.[9]

THE LAST CAMPS

We should not reconstruct the movements of armies based on *our* need to get them into a particular position. Instead, we should reconstruct their movements based on *their* needs, along with what they could actually see and understand of the situation at hand. *A battle is its ground.*

The French army wanted to entrap the English and put them to the sword. The second step absolutely depended on the first: now that they had caught up with the enemy, they had to prevent Henry from reaching faster roads and any chance of escape. And they well knew what Henry knew: with the French forces continuing to stream up the road from Saint-Pol, his only route was the road up from Hesdin. It had to be blocked.

The movement that the *Gesta* describes on 24 October reflects both forces moving their attention north-west towards this remaining road to Calais. After facing off with the English across that little valley south-west of Maisoncelle, the French were not withdrawing out of weakness. Nor were they withdrawing so that they could foolishly die on the traditional field of our imaginations. Instead, they were very wisely moving into a position that would encircle the English and ensure that they were cut off from their only escape route. Henry recognized the manoeuvre for what it was:

> And our king, on the assumption that by so doing they would either circle round the wood, in order that way to make a surprise attack upon him, or else would circle round the somewhat more distant woodlands in the neighbourhood and so surround us on

> every side, immediately moved his lines again, always positioning them so that they faced the enemy.[10]

Looking at the reconstructed topography, we can see how the *Gesta* and the landscape snap into place. The Chaplain says that the French ended up behind the woods that were initially to the English left. Looking back at Map 4, we can see that these woods are those of Maisoncelle, which run south and east of the village. The place-names recorded here on the cadastral maps include several words relating to woods, and a stretch of forest here is very much the defining feature of the area in our earliest maps of the area, including the 1656 map of Nicolas Sanson, now held by the Boston Public Library (Figure 15).[11] The field opposite this wood – the field in which the *Gesta* says the main French encampment was made 'where lay our road towards Calais' – is marked on the cadastral maps as the *Buisson du Grand Camp* [Bush of the Large Field].[12] The road to Calais runs straight across it, just as the Chaplain says it did (Figure 16).

Henry was cut off and trapped. He had nowhere else to go. The French 'occupied the hamlets and scrub close by', the *Gesta* says.[13] Everyone knew there would be a battle in the morning. The Chaplain describes the English holding position until well after nightfall, at which point they could hear the enemy carousing in their encampment. Henry was clearly on high alert, frightened of being surprised.

When it was certain that no attack would be coming, the king 'ordered silence throughout the whole army' and 'moved off in silence to a hamlet nearby, where we had houses, although very few of them, and gardens and orchards in which to rest'.[14] The order to silence is somewhat peculiar. There cannot have been any imagining that the French watch – no matter their confidence in numbers – wasn't keeping close tabs on the English army out of its own fear of surprise. Eyes would have been on them all night in case they decided to attack or flee. The *Gesta*, in fact, goes on to report just this, as the French 'had fires lit and set heavily manned watches across the fields and roadways'.[15] If the call to silence wasn't about being sneaky, what was it for? I suspect, given the situation, that it was primarily about maintaining control over the army. Men ordered to silence cannot give voice to their fears. And as hard a spot as the English were in, they would be in much further distress if the men panicked. Remember the king insisting his men remain in battle order until well after sunset due to his fear of a sudden attack. That anticipation didn't go away. What rest he and his men got would be with one eye open. They had to be alert to hear and respond to shouts of alarm or trumpets of command.

The hamlet that Henry crept up to and made his headquarters for the night – everyone agrees on this point – was Maisoncelle. The French would have been encamped all along the roads ahead of this position: from the *Buisson* through Azincourt to Tramecourt, with others perhaps stretched out behind to Ruisseauville. Those who were camped closest to the English in and around Maisoncelle were now less than half a mile from the enemy.

This proximity between the forces on the night before the battle is cited across a wide range of our sources. Tito Livio Frulovisi notes that the watchmen of the French camp 'were scarcely 250 paces away from the English'.[16] Fenin explains that Henry lodged 'at Maisoncelle', while the French 'came to lodge at Ruisseauville and at Azincourt and in several villages thereabout, then put themselves in the fields, and lodged so near to the host of King Henry that there was only about four bow shots between the two armies'.[17] Monstrelet says much the same: After crossing the Ternoise, the English could see the French:

> coming from all directions in great companies of men at arms to lodge at Ruisseauville and Agincourt... Soon afterwards the constable arrived quite near to Agincourt in which place all the French assembled in a single army. They all bivouacked in the open fields close to their banners save for men of lower status who lodged in the villages close by. The king of England with all his Englishmen lodged in a little village called Maisoncelle three bow shots away from the French.[18]

Pseudo-Elmham reports that 'not more than a quarter of an English mile' separated the watchfires of the two armies,[19] while the eyewitness account of the *Chronicle of Arthur de Richemont* (written sometime between 1458 and the mid-1460s) describes the French as 'lodged near the English in open country less than half a league from the host of the king of England'.[20] The *Chronicle of Normandy* says that 'the two armies were in sight of each other, and encamped near each other that night', failing to give a specific distance.[21] The eyewitness account of Le Fèvre generally follows Monstrelet, but adds 'I was with them and saw what has been described' when he notes how worried the English were when they were desperately brought into battle lines after coming out of the Ternoise valley the day before the battle. Le Fèvre likewise describes how Henry 'had all his battles move off to lodge at Maisoncelle, which is near Agincourt ... very near to the place where his enemies were which was less than a quarter of a league away, so close that you could hear them very clearly and even hear them calling each other by name'.[22]

The sources all agree: the English were camped in Maisoncelle, and the French were close at hand between them and Azincourt, between them and the road.

The English weren't going anywhere.

Regarding the battle the next day, not all of our sources move beyond the general identification of a site near Azincourt. When they do, however, we find a wide variety of triangulation in the place-names. Thus, while the *Chronicle of Ruisseauville* associates the battle with 'a village named Agincourt',[23] the near-contemporary allegorical poem *Le pastoralet* calls it 'the battle of Ruisseauville', which is further north.[24] The *Anonymous Chronicle of the Reign of Charles VI* seemingly splits the difference, stating that it happened 'in a place near Agincourt and Ruisseauville',[25] yet Fenin places it 'between Maisoncelles and Agincourt', which is where we've just seen that the French were camped.[26] The traditional site is between Azincourt and Tramecourt, a location first specified in the 1460s by Le Fèvre: 'The truth was that the French had ordered their battles between two small woods, one close to Agincourt, the other to Tramecourt.'[27] What defines 'close to' in this case is frustratingly unknown. Similarly, Thomas Basin's *History of Charles VII* states that 'This unlucky battle was fought near to the town of Hesdin in the fields of two villages, the one Agincourt, the other Ruisseauville', leaving us wondering what distance constitutes nearness and which field belongs to which village.[28] The sources are at least consistent that the battle happened somewhere near

Azincourt, but they give us little consistency with which we might pin down a specific site. For all we can tell, any location might depend more on the individual context of the witness – direction of travel, relative position on the field, knowledge of village names – than it does on any modern notion of precision.

But we're at least in the ballpark, for sure.

WHAT THEY WORE (AND WHAT HENRY DIDN'T)

One of the most popular legends about the battle of Agincourt is that part of the reason the French lost was that their men-at-arms were, as Le Fèvre and Waurin say, 'weighed down by armour': mail coats to their knees, plates upon their legs (and chests if they were lucky!), and helmets called bascinets upon their heads.[29] This would be top-flight gear, the best armour that money could buy. We have a terrific illustration that gives a sense of what these looked like – minus a rather remarkable bit of head gear – in an illustration made for Christine de Pizan's *Book of the Queen* in the years immediately preceding the battle (Figure 18). A modern replica of the upper body kit is shown in Figure 17.[30]

This kind of gear was hardly unique to the French side, though. The knights and lords of England were wearing pretty much the same thing in 1415. So the story about armour, insofar as it is meant to show a difference between the men-at-arms on either side, isn't true. It will hardly be the last of our traditions about Agincourt that's misleading or simply in error. And the problematic traditions aren't confined to just the written stories.

Take, for instance, what Henry V was wearing and riding at Agincourt.

Tito Livio Frulovisi tells us that on the morning of the battle, the king 'put on a helmet and placed over it an elegant gold crown encrusted with various precious gems and with the insignia of the English and French kingdoms. He then seated himself on a white horse.'[31] Pseudo-Elmham adds that he also had a 'surcoat, with the arms of England and France; from which a celestial splendour gleamed on the one side from three golden flowers, planted in an azure field; on the other, from three golden leopards, sporting in a ruby field', and that his horse wasn't simply white but was, in fact, 'white as snow'.[32] On the French side, Le Fèvre and Waurin label the helm 'a very fine bascinet with a visor' – which makes sense given the period – but they describe his mount as 'a small grey horse' instead of a white one.[33]

So what colour was his horse? Both, probably. Henry had brought 60 grooms to France to take care of the 60 (or more) horses that were brought for his personal use on the campaign.[34] By comparison, several of his major lords had 'only' brought 50. He had lost a few of these mounts at Harfleur, and our records attest that he had lost a further 21 horses on the march from there to Agincourt. Some of these might have been casualties of the fighting they had seen so far, but it is more likely that they had been ridden to death, suffering from a lack of food and adequate rest. Even so, the king still had plenty of choices for his mount on the fateful day – one more nail in the coffin of the idea of a beleaguered king down among his band of brothers.

When it came to the 60 royal mounts, we know from records that the vast majority were what were then called 'lyard' in colour: either a white horse with grey spots or a grey horse with white spots. Odds are, it was one of these that Henry was seen riding on the day of the battle.

It's a popular belief that we might also have a good sense of what the king wore to battle because of the helm, saddle, shield, and sword that have been variously displayed in connection with Henry V at Westminster Abbey. Alas, these 'funeral achievements', as they are often called, don't connect to Agincourt. The helm was made for jousting, not war.[35] The saddle began life around 1400 as a war saddle, but its present status is the result of a complete refurbishment to make it an object of display for (we assume) the funeral.[36] The shield was made for Henry IV; like the saddle, it was repurposed for display and 'is unlikely' to have ever been carried by Henry V in battle.[37] The other item rather famously associated with Henry is a sword that was found in the abbey's holdings in the 19th century (Figure 20). Here's what one rather enthusiastic commentator has to say about it:

> It is the sword carried before the king's standard in his funeral procession and given to the abbey ... the weapon that had been

> held by England's most famous soldier king – perhaps the very weapon that 'did affright the air at Agincourt'.

Later, this same expert goes one step further, suggesting that the weapon 'might have been the very sword he carried into battle at Shrewsbury'.[38] One issue here is that it wasn't a sword that 'did affright the air' in Shakespeare's re-telling of Agincourt. It was 'the very casques' (i.e. helmets).[39] But that's secondary to the fact that the sword wasn't possibly carried at Shrewsbury or Agincourt or even in the funeral procession. The sword is of a far later date. Yes, it's associated with a King Henry – but VII, not V.[40]

So what was Henry V actually wearing? Like the French lords on the other side, he wore a long coat of mail, over the top of which his men strapped custom plates on his arms, legs, and torso. His hands slipped into beautifully articulated gauntlets. The surcoat pulled over his head would have been brightly and richly decorated: England's golden lions on a red field quartered with France's golden fleur-de-lys on a blue field. On his head was probably a helmet of the great bascinet type, fitted over neck armour. His sword, like so much of his gear, was probably worth more than the lives of all but his richest companions.

The vast majority of the men in his army that day were archers, as we know. Monstrelet, followed by Le Fèvre and Waurin, suggests that these were almost entirely unarmoured, but we can guess that many would have had simple helms of iron or hardened leather, while for the most part their primary body protection was a close-fitting padded garment, called a jack or doublet. The luckiest might have had brigandine armour or even basic coats of mail, but these cannot have been many. Their legs were in hose, which the French sources say was 'loose round their knees'. Perhaps this was to help with mobility, though it could also be due to dysentery in their ranks, in which case many of the English could have been literally shitting themselves on the march to battle.[41] Le Fèvre and Waurin tell us that no small number of the archers did not even have shoes.[42] If forced into close combat, some of the archers might have had swords, but for the most part they would have used campaign tools that could double as weapons in a pinch: axes, hatchets, mallets, and the like.[43]

And they had the stakes. Those sharpened poles, the archers knew, might be all that would stand between them and the pounding hooves, piercing lances, flashing swords, and resounding cries of 'Montjoy!' that would accompany the charge of the renowned French cavalry. As one modern historian of the fight has rightly pointed out, whether the stakes were a 'practical hindrance to the French' may not be nearly as important as the role they served as 'a psychological protection to the English'.[44]

For most of the archers, trying to catch fitful sleep in a miserable rain on the night of 24 October, the oblivion of those horsemen might have been all they could think about.

11

Testing the Tradition

To this point, while I've been making little corrections, our story has been close to the traditional account of Agincourt. We have certainly ended up at the same spot on the map. The night before the battle, the English were camped in and around Maisoncelle. The French were perilously close by. No one disagrees on this.

I imagine a great many, though, will disagree with what I see as the positions and actions taken during the battle itself the next day. But in order to see how I'm changing these – indeed, to see *why* I must change them – we need to establish the traditional story of Agincourt.

THE STANDARD AGINCOURT

In *The Face of Battle*, his classic study of military history, John Keegan makes clear how pervasive and unquestioned the standard story of Agincourt is:

> The events of the Agincourt campaign are, for the military historian, gratifyingly straightforward to relate. For, as medieval battles go, it is surprisingly well-documented: the chronology can be fixed with considerable accuracy, the exact location of the culminating battle has never been in dispute, its topography has altered little over five hundred years, and there is less than the usual wild uncertainty over the numbers engaged on either side.[1]

We will, in the next chapters, see that the battle isn't nearly as straightforward as Keegan claims. But for now let's just give the standard story as Keegan and generations before and after him have understood it.

On the morning of 25 October, Henry and his army took up position just north of the village of Maisoncelle. The French lined up just south of Ruisseauville about 1,000 yards away. Between them was a narrow plain, pinched between the lines of trees in which were found the towns of Azincourt and Tramecourt. The English set their lines, with the archers all pounding their protective stakes into the ground. Their hope was to fight on the tactical defensive: hold position and make the enemy come to them. This had worked at Crécy and Poitiers. They hoped it would work here.

It did not. The French refused to charge. They realized the English weren't going anywhere, and the longer they stayed put, the more time hunger and disease had to gnaw at them. Meanwhile the French army was still gathering. So why fight on English terms?

Henry talked with his commanders. They all knew the perilous situation just as clearly as did the French. What little chance they had at survival diminished by the hour. They needed to fight as soon as possible. So the English archers pulled up their protective stakes, and the entire English line moved forward into the narrow plain until they were within bow shot of the enemy – at extreme range, around 300 yards away. The standard interpretation is that they pushed up to where the road runs between the villages of Azincourt and Tramecourt – a road that's lined by cut-outs of English archers today, bows drawn as if ready to loose once again. Back in 1415, the very real archers supposedly pounded their stakes back into the earth along this same stretch of field, re-establishing the English line.

Why here? For one thing, it looks like a narrow space today. And a primary narrative about the battle is that the English used a narrow space to neutralize the numerical advantage of the French. In addition, we have the monument of the *Calvaire* just north of this road on the Tramecourt side of the field (Figure 19). Though the monument itself dates to the late 19th century, it is traditionally believed to mark the location of a mass burial of battle dead, though extensive modern excavations of the site haven't found a shred of evidence to prove the tradition.[2]

At any rate, the French *still* wouldn't charge, so Henry ordered his archers to send a volley of arrows at the enemy. This finally did the trick. The French knights, in all their finery, touched spurs to flanks and urged their horses into a trot. Men on foot charged behind them.

Their cavalry reached the English lines first, but they were repulsed by volleys of arrows. Fleeing, 'many riders and loose horses crashed into the advancing line of dismounted men-at-arms', as Keegan describes it.[3] These struggled through the chaos, trying to reach the enemy. But there had been a heavy rain all night. The chronicler Thomas Walsingham tells us that the ground 'was newly sown with wheat', which by medieval methods of ploughing would have left a series of undulating lines across the landscape. These shallow trenches would have collected the rain water, which is why he says it was 'extremely difficult to stand or advance'.[4] We get something similar from Juvénal des Ursins, who reports that the French 'found the worked ground very soft because of the rain'.[5] The chronicler Pierre Cochon adds a little detail on the mud, saying that the French 'sank into it by at least a foot'.[6] However deep it was, anyone who has walked through sucking mud can well imagine the exhaustion of the men struggling through it.

Adding insult to injury, the English archers now sent volley after volley at them, a veritable storm of arrows in the sky. This slowed the French even further. Many went down, pierced by arrows or the broken shreds of them finding gaps in their armour or eye-slits in their visored helms. Some men still got through, driving into the English line. The English flexed back under the onslaught, but they did not break. Henry was in the thick of the bloody melee. He survived. Some of his men did not. But far, far more French were cut down, falling into heaps, drowning in the mud.

The duke of Brabant had ridden hard all morning to get to the field before the battle was done. He was still on his way when the French trumpets sounded the charge. Frustrated, the duke stopped in a thicket just short of the battlefield. He had outpaced his armour, his surcoat, and everything else that a lord of his stature ought to wear into battle, but he was determined to do what he could to help his countrymen against the invaders from England. He borrowed the armour of one of his chamberlains. His secretary, Edmond de Dynter, explains his jury-rigged livery: 'he took the blazon of one of his trumpeters. With a hole cut in it he wore it as a tunic, and for a flag he took the blazon from another trumpeter and attached it to his lance.' With this improvised gear, he threw himself into the fray. 'But alas, the battle did not last much longer for the French who, through their over-confidence, were captured or killed, and so the victory fell to the English.'[7]

All attempts to dislodge Henry from his position failed. As the French fell back in disarray, the English began collecting prisoners for ransom. But things were not quite finished.

'At some time in the afternoon,' Keegan writes:

> there were detected signs that the French were nerving themselves to charge [again] ... and more or less simultaneously, a body of armed peasants, led by three mounted knights, suddenly appeared at the baggage park, inflicted some loss of life and stole some objects of value, including one of the King's crowns, before being driven off.
>
> Either that incident or the continued menace of the French third line now prompted Henry to order that all the prisoners instantly be killed. The order was not at once obeyed ... [but] Henry was nevertheless adamant; he detailed an esquire and 200 archers to set about the execution, and stopped them only when it became clear that the French third line was packing up and withdrawing from the field. Meantime very many of the French had been killed; some of the English apparently even incinerated wounded prisoners in cottages where they had been taken for shelter.[8]

And, with that, the battle was over. Henry was victorious.

This is 'the narrative of Agincourt handed down to us', as Keegan says. It is, in his estimation, 'a good one; it would in any case be profitless to look for better'.[9] I've got dozens of histories of the battle on my shelves. Allowing for little tweaks, this same story is in pretty much all of them. It's pervasive. It's exactly what I was taught. It's the *Vulgata*.

And it's wrong.

STRESS-TESTING HISTORY

History has a lot in common with engineering.

Whether they are designing a bridge, the wing of an airplane, or a new piece of networking software, any engineer worth their graphing calculator will at some key stage put their work through a stress test. They'll simulate an earthquake under that bridge. They'll flex a wing well beyond its expected limits. They'll overload network software with a relentless pounding of bots intent on taking it down. Engineers stress test to find out how and why their designs fail. Knowing the points of failure is the first step towards making their designs stronger, safer, more reliable.

Historians do the same thing.

The designs in the world of history are the things we think we know, and we can – and *should* – stress test them. Knowing their points of failure is the first step towards making our history more accurate.

So let's stress test the *Vulgata* of Agincourt. And let's start in a fairly simple way, by using the ground and the men. We've been told where the ground is.

Now let's see if the men can fit on it.

The tradition says that the English battle lines ultimately met on the woodland-narrowed field near or on the little road between today's towns of Azincourt and Tramecourt (Figure 21).[10] This space was carefully surveyed by Sir John Woodford in 1818. At that time it was roughly 700 yards wide, and it remains relatively close to these dimensions today.[11] How many men need to fit here?

We've been following the account of Agincourt as told in the *Gesta* for much of the last couple of chapters. It was written around 1417. Early sources are usually (but not always) a good thing. The *Gesta* comes from an eyewitness, which is also usually (but not always) a good thing. Other studies have also found it one of the most reliable accounts for the English perspective.[12] Pertinent to our present purposes here, it also happens to give us the smallest size for the English army when it left Harfleur on 8 October: 900 men-at-arms and 5,000 archers, for a total fighting force of 5,900 men.[13]

For our stress test, this will be the starting point. The smallest number of men we need to fit on the traditional field. If the

Vulgata passes this test, we can look at higher numbers. The leading researcher on the campaign's muster rolls and other source materials suggests that the number of men ought to be significantly higher, for instance: 'a few hundred either side of 9,000 men'.[14] But just as engineers start the stress small before cranking it up, we're going to start small in our stress test, too.

Actually, let's try to make our numbers even smaller if we can.

We know that the English army, by the day of the battle on 25 October, had lost some men to disease, desertion, death, and disorder. Combing through our sources, it looks as if these might be counted in the dozens.[15] Once again, though, for the sake of starting our stress test with the smallest possible number for the English army, let's pretend that a *lot* more were lost and nobody wanted to talk about it. If we estimated, say, a 10–12 per cent loss of men during the march from Harfleur, then at the time of the battle Henry would be left with roughly 800 men-at-arms and 4,500 archers, for a total fighting force of just 5,300 men.

To be clear, I believe this to be very much on the low side, but I want to start our stress test of the *Vulgata* with the smallest number of men in the English army that one could possibly conceive, even if I think it's significantly less than the likely reality.

Multiple sources speak to the thinness of the English formation that day. Tito Livio Frulovisi says that their ranks were 'scarcely four deep'.[16] Some historians have tried to suggest that this only applies to the men-at-arms and not the archers, but the sources make no distinction of this kind.[17] Pseudo-Elmham, in fact, rather explicitly denies it: 'the English army, in all its lines, was fortified sideways by only four ranks of men, one behind the other'.[18] Our 5,300 men, placed four ranks deep on the field, would give us an English line that would have been roughly 1,325 men abreast.

How can we use this for our stress test? Well, the average man in battle occupies area on the ground. How much ground depends on how closely packed the men are, which depends on tactics, technology, and terrain. Shoulder-to-shoulder in a line-up over flat ground, human beings occupy roughly two feet each.[19] But ours is not the business of packing sardines. In the case of Agincourt, what we need is an estimation of the suitable operational area necessary for early-15th-century men-at-arms and archers. This is a matter on which we can and should welcome the insights of experimental archaeology and period re-enactment, which indicates operational difficulties – that is, fighters increasingly in danger of disrupting or outright harming their fellow fighters – at anything less than five feet per man.

As with the total number of men in Henry's army, however, let's cut this down considerably. For the purpose of our stress test, let's assume a mere yard (three linear feet) per man on the line – allowing only a single foot of space between the shoulders of each man. We won't add any spacing between divisions or any room for operational manoeuvrability at all. I truly don't think this could conform to reality, but, again, it leaves us with the smallest numbers of men about as tightly packed as they could possibly be. It's the easiest bar for the *Vulgata* to clear.

At this basis, a line of 1,325 men abreast would be 1,325 yards wide, which is 625 yards wider than the narrow confines of the traditional field of Agincourt as Woodford measured them in 1818.

But of course the English didn't form a straight line. And the formation men take can greatly change the length of their line.

THE ENGLISH FORMATION

For multiple generations the winning formula in English experience had been a strong centre of dismounted men-at-arms who could hold against a direct assault and fight with close combat weapons, complemented by forward-swept wings of longbowmen to either side that would whittle down the strength of that assault with ranged weapons. This was what had been done at Crécy – the model glory – and so many other fights. It was the tactical defensive. As the enemy tried to attack this position, the archers would 'funnel' the enemy, forcing them into each other. Confusion and chaos would reign as the enemy tripped over each other and slowed – making themselves a more thickly massed target for still more arrows. Any who made it through would run headlong into the waiting men-at-arms, who would maul them.

It was a tried-and-true tactic, but its strength was its weakness: those archers, while formidable at range, weren't great in melee combat. And they were extremely susceptible to cavalry attacks, especially along their flank: all it took was one charge into the 'end' of a wing of archers to roll the whole line up. Nearly the same damage could be done if the wing was breached at any point, which opened up the cavalry to sweeping strikes across the formation's backfield.

The solution that Edward implemented at Crécy was two-fold. First, he utilized the existing woods to fix the ends of those wings of archers. There was simply no way to flank his position and roll them up. Secondly, he used wagons to create a field fortification to protect those in the line. Combined, these resolved the weaknesses of his longbowmen and left them with their formidable and deadly strengths.

To a man, Henry and all his commanders knew this was an extremely good way to win a battle. Any position they took, they would want to try to use the terrain to protect their archers. It didn't matter if it was a river, a cliff, or a forest, they had to fix the end of each wing on *something* that would prevent it from being outflanked. That would be in line with the first part of Edward's solution. As to the second ... well, they couldn't build a wagenburg in the way that Edward had done. They didn't have wagons enough to manage it. Henry probably only had as many as were needed to carry his and his lords' fineries. This was why he had ordered his archers to make stakes. It wasn't quite a field fortification, but it was the best he could do to create protection for his archers beyond their own stout courage and arrows.

Even if the English *could* manage all this – fight on a field with protective terrain to either side and provide time enough for their archers to plant all their stakes – their archer-dominated army was still unwieldy by any traditional reckoning. Henry had, by our stress test numbers, a mere 800 men-at-arms to his 4,500 archers. The English army had been organized into three divisions, or 'battles', since its landing at Harfleur. It had carried this organization all the way to Agincourt: a vanguard in front, a centre battle under the command of the king, and a rearguard. At Crécy and so many other fights, this same sort of division had been the rule, too. We can imagine the battles like waves. The vanguard would hit first. Then the central battle would rush in. The rearguard, if needed, would come into the fight last.

Henry didn't have the numbers to do this at Agincourt. Split his men-at-arms into three battles, and each would have about 267 men. Organize them four men deep, and he would have a centre that was only 67 men abreast. Meanwhile, his wings of archers – each with 2,250 men four ranks deep – would be 563 men abreast. The whole thing would be a 'V', and all it would take would be one breach of those thin lines of archers to destroy them all.

Yes, the archers had stakes to help protect their long lines, but these were not a tried-and-true tactic. At best, they were a story of something the Turks had pulled off years ago. Here, they would be a desperate ploy. The simple truth is that Henry must have had – and frankly *should* have had – grave fears that despite his line of stakes those long archer wings could be readily broken by the inevitable cavalry charges. Again, all it took was one gap for his position to be undone.

What needed to happen was clear. Henry had to widen his centre, prepare it to withstand the assault, and shorten the relative length of his wings.

The Chaplain tells us how Henry set about doing this. His three battles would not be lined up one behind the other. Instead, they would deploy laterally: the king would lead the centre battle, the vanguard under the duke of York would be to his right, and the rearguard under Lord Camoys would be on his left. This tripled the width of his centre, but those lines of archers were still too long. To shorten them, Henry took two groups of archers and placed them between his battles of dismounted men-at-arms in what the author of the *Gesta* describes as 'wedges'.[20]

These wedges have caused no end of consternation among military historians. It is clear that the eyewitness was trying to describe something unfamiliar, something new. He was doing his best, but not everyone has agreed on what that was. Various reconstructions have been postulated: from archers in a straight line with the men-at-arms, to archers in triangular formations that protruded from that straight line, to archers lining up in front of the men-at-arms.

The last of these can be rejected pretty much straight off. Lining up the archers in front of the men-at-arms doesn't fit the 'wedges' description of the *Gesta* at all. It potentially fits the description of Monstrelet – he says some of the archers were 'in front of' the English men-at-arms[21] – though I actually think this reference has been misunderstood, as I'll explain below. Setting that aside for now, the idea that Henry would hide himself and his fellow lords behind his archers also doesn't square much with everything we know of Henry or English battle tactics to this point. Indeed, having a complete frontage of archers would be so foreign to everyone's experience at Agincourt that we would expect reports from both sides to highlight it. They do not.

Putting the 'wedges' of archers into a straight, horizontal line of men would make the English line widest at the centre, which would be a good thing. But why describe them as wedges if they were intermingled within the straight line of men-at-arms? And, as we've just seen, Monstrelet does say they were 'in front of' the front line of the English, not in line with them. It's possible that Monstrelet is mistaken and can be ignored, but the eyewitnesses Jean Waurin and Jean Le Fèvre – there on the French and English sides, respectively, but writing accounts that are heavily reliant on Monstrelet's pro-Burgundian account – repeated his claim. So assuming these witnesses are at least trying to be correct – this tends to be my starting position in battle reconstruction – we need to get the archers forward of the men-at-arms without overlapping them, while still widening the English centre. This leads me to the third option: archers were positioned between the three groups of men-at-arms, but their triangular formation was deployed slightly forward – describing them as 'wedges' would be exactly right – and from the air would have looked like teeth. Henry and his commanders were, quite simply, taking their typical large-scale battle plan – a centre mass of men-at-arms between what Waurin and Le Fèvre describe as 'two wings' of archers[22] – and replicating it within itself. Instead of one deep 'V', Henry had constructed three more shallow ones within the larger whole. This widened his centre and shrank his wings.

It may have been an act of desperation on Henry's part – not something he had even remotely planned to do when he had left Harfleur on his planned eight-day march – but it was also brilliant. Henry had used his weakness to multiply his strength.

Assuming this was the formation, how many men were in its various parts? And, more importantly, at what angles were the wings and the wedges made? The answers to these questions will have a direct result on the total width of the English line from the tip of one wing to the tip of the other. Think about the line as a piece of paper, seen on end: the wings and the wedges would be like folds, which can 'accordion' open or shut. The wider those folds and the sharper their angles, the more the paper can get squished together.

If you don't like maths, you might want to skip the next paragraph. But I promised at the start of this book to be as transparent as possible, and that means showing my work.

We have, if you'll recall, 800 men-at-arms and 4,500 archers in our stress test. We're also estimating a very tight three feet of linear space for each man on the line. The 800 men-at-arms are in three battles of about 267 men each, and with four ranks they would be about 67 men abreast: approximately 201 feet when tightly packed. The archers are where things get speculative, but I will here estimate that the wings and wedges of the formation press forward at 45-degree angles. This is the angle utilized by the beautiful model reconstruction of the battle on display at the Royal Armouries in Leeds (Figure 22), and it conveniently makes the English line fairly narrow without pushing the points of the wedges too far out in front of the lines: these points would be potential weak points, as they weren't being fixed on natural obstacles like forest but simply sticking out into the open. It's also the angle that has been suggested by a leading historian based on – among other things – modern archaeological evidence from the battle of Aljubarrota in 1385.[23] We can be certain that stakes would have been concentrated ahead of them. I'm going to suggest 500 archers in the two wedges between those battles. That's 250 men on each side of the triangle. Four deep, this means about 63 men. That would be 189 feet, but remember that these are swept forward 45 degrees. What we need is the base line between these sides of the triangle – that is, how much space it takes in the side-to-side width of the formation. Thanks to Pythagoras, we can figure that the base of these wedges would be about 267 feet each. This leaves the wings, each of which would have 1,750 men (4,500 men minus two groups of 500 men, then split in half). Four deep would mean 438 men abreast or 1,314 feet. Once more, the Pythagorean theorem lets us find the missing number: 929 feet each. All that is left is addition to get us the width of the overall formation: 929 + 201 + 267 + 201 + 267 + 201 + 929 = 2,995 feet in total, assuming absolutely zero unit division or tactical mobility.

This is still 300 yards too wide for the field as surveyed by Woodford in 1818.

But we *can* make it fit. Keeping proportionate unit divisions and formation the same, we can fiddle with the angles of wings and wedges to get the whole thing into a 700-yard space. If those wedges protrude at steep 76-degree angles it will work, though this makes for an awfully 'pointy' triangle. The most balanced fit would have both the wings and the wedges sweeping forward at a 55-degree angle. That's not unreasonable.

Trouble is, we're stress-testing with the bar to clear at the lowest possible numbers all around. Increase just one of our improbably conservative numbers in the stress test and all bets are off. Remember, we're calculating for 4,300 total men on the English side. A more likely number based on the *Gesta* would be a thousand more than this, and the best guess from the evidence of the muster rolls says we would need to double it.

In addition, as we've already discussed, that tree-line at Tramecourt would very likely be pushed out further towards Azincourt in 1415, perhaps considerably more so. The erasure of forest is, in fact, somewhat essential to the *Vulgata* understanding of Agincourt: there's not much of a wood at Azincourt today, but for the 'narrow' landscape battle reconstruction of the *Vulgata* to make any sense then a thick wood *must* have been there in 1415, protecting Henry's left flank. As it happens, this would in turn serve to make the available space narrower and mean we couldn't even fit our low-ball estimation for the English army.

Our sources often speak of the narrow field of battle, how the English line filled it from tree-line to tree-line. As Pseudo-Elmham describes their position: 'Being so arrayed, the providence of the divine favour was manifestly shown, which provided for so small an army so suitable a field, enclosed within hedges and trees, and with closes and hedges on the sides, to protect them from being surrounded by the enemy's attacks'.[24] Seeking such a narrow field between woods, it is no surprise that as scholars we have been drawn to what looks like a narrow field from the eye of the individual scholar standing upon it today. But of course this present egocentrism is of little value to history: whether the field *feels* narrow to us is inconsequential. All that matters is that it be narrow relative to the numbers on the field. And the numbers we have just reviewed indicate that the traditional site has real problems.

Stress-testing on the numbers alone doesn't have the *Vulgata* looking good.

And it gets worse.

THE MISSING TREES AND THE CASTLE

Traditional accounts of the battle consistently place a long stretch of thick trees in and around Azincourt. These trees are typically depicted as roughly matching the extent of the town's trees and hedges today: on the south side of town they begin halfway to Maisoncelle, and from there they run northwards, spreading out on either side of the Rue d'Azincourt, past the castle, the church, and the museum, all the way to the Rue du Moulin, which is about halfway to the next hamlet, Sénécoville.[25] As we've just seen, this wood is necessary to fix the left side of the English flank and establish the narrow ground for the English army.

Looking around the town today – and you should definitely visit it – you'll see the lovely trees shading the roads and the yards of the good folks who live there. It's pleasant, to be sure, but it's not even close to a forest. What's there today couldn't possibly be expected to protect the English flank.

Of course, it doesn't matter what's there now. None of the trees we see standing today date back to 1415. We need to understand the extent and density of the woods back then.

As we've already discussed, a good rule of thumb for trees is to assume there were more of them in the past. We see them taking up more room when we go back to the cadastral maps of the 19th century, and the best scientific estimates are that they would be up to 400 per cent more extensive if we go back to the 15th century.

Applied to the patchy trees in Azincourt, this might bulk them up enough to give us the woods necessary to protect the left side of the English line.

As it happens, this would also make the supposed battleground even narrower, further breaking our stress testing of the numbers. But let's leave that problem aside for now, because there is reason to think that, although our rule of thumb appears to work for the woods in and around Maisoncelle and Tramecourt, it may not work in and around the town of Azincourt in 1415. Strange as it may sound, for this specific spot it looks as if there weren't *more* trees. There were *fewer* of them.

First, if we look back at the cadastral maps, we don't see an increasing line of trees the way we do elsewhere in the region. Nor do we find place-names that point to disappeared woods like those around Maisoncelle.

Second, Azincourt is a crossroads. Roads can pass through woods – they do so at several instances in the immediate surrounds – but more often than not they edge woods rather than bisect them. This makes crossroads more likely to occur in an open space. It's not a lot of evidence, but it's something. And it almost certainly connects to the next clue.

Third, the one building that we can definitively position around the battlefield in 1415 is the castle of Azincourt. Its remains are mostly beneath a farm today, but in 1415 it was a small, stone-towered fortification just north of where the road from Tramecourt comes into town. Castles in the Middle Ages existed to control the landscape. As one simple definition says, 'Castles played an important part in warfare; not only did they provide a passive defensive role in protecting a particular location, but they also played an offensive role, as a heavily defended safe base from which the garrison could control the surrounding countryside.'[26] The castle at Azincourt may not have been a large one, but it nevertheless fulfilled this important function of controlling the landscape. In this case, its specific location suggests that a major aspect of this was the castle's proximity to those many crossroads. Dense forest would impair this critical function.

Fourth, we know that at least four centuries ago the woods weren't anything like what the reconstructions imagine. We have a painting of Azincourt, which was executed by Adrien de Montigny between 1605 and 1611 at the behest of Duke Charles de Croÿ (1560–1612), who had administration of these and many other domains in the region (Figure 24). The viewpoint is from south of the town, on a ridgeline north-west of Maisconelle, looking north: Azincourt's church of Saint-Nicholas is in the left centre of the town, the tower of the castle is to the right, and the Rue d'Azincourt winds between them, stretching out of view on the way to Maisoncelle at the bottom right. The road to Tramecourt – and the traditional location of the battle – appears to be the line of trees through the field at the right bottom of the frame.[27] Not only is the village not in much of a wood, but the modern extension of the town towards Maisoncelle isn't present. Even more eye-opening, the accompanying long stretch of woods – the one that every reconstruction of Agincourt I've ever seen depends upon – *isn't there*. Both the town and the trees end at the road to Tramecourt – the *Rue Henri V* – that is the location of the advanced English position in the *Vulgata*.

The painting confirms what everything else is telling us: there weren't trees where everyone wants them to be. And if the trees weren't there, then the left side of the English line would have been hanging out in the open from the moment Henry advanced from Maisoncelle to the moment he could reach the castle of Azincourt.[28]

For that matter, the castle itself is an embarrassment to the traditional story of the battle of Agincourt, because it plays no part in the fight whatsoever. Remember, the standard location of Henry's advanced English position is the road from Tramecourt to Azincourt. The castle sits just north of this. So the English left wing wouldn't be fixed on trees. It would be fixed on a French castle.

This would be – and I can't believe I'm needing to point this out – moronic.

Moronic from both sides, frankly. Why in God's name would the English think it was a good idea to use a French fortification to protect the most vulnerable part of their position? Why in God's name would the French have let them do so?

Yet when we look across our histories, the castle is consistently and conspicuously absent, as if its only occupants were ghosts. It may show up on a map, but again and again it goes unmentioned in the actual reconstruction of events.[29] It might as well not be there at all.

And it's not just modern historians. The first English source for the battle to mention the castle is the 1459 chronicle of Peter Basset, which says only that on the march to the area Henry had heard that 150,000 French – a patently absurd figure, for what it's worth – had gathered at 'a castle called Agincourt'.[30] Earlier than this, the castle is first acknowledged in the French chronicle of Monstrelet. Curiously, it's not featured as part of a full-throated roar at the extreme stupidity of the French lords who – if the *Vulgata* is correct – had willingly abandoned a fortification on the battlefield that they themselves had chosen, and retreated *away* from both it and the enemy in order to get properly slaughtered where future tradition would require it. Not at all. Instead, the existence of the castle is first referenced after the battle is well and truly done. At that point, Henry summoned French heralds to him. They were there to spread word of what happened. They were also there, we know from our records of Crécy, to help identify the dead. One of these heralds was named Mountjoye:

> Then the king asked him the name of the castle which he could see close by. They answered that it was called Agincourt. 'As all battles,' the king said, 'ought to take their name from the nearest fortress, village or town where they happened, this battle from henceforward and for ever more will be called the battle of Agincourt'.[31]

Interestingly, our eyewitnesses Le Fèvre and Waurin, though largely following Monstrelet, change this slightly. They say that this question wasn't addressed to Mountjoye and the heralds but to 'the other princes in the area where the battle had been', and that it occurred 'when the king saw the site'.[32] That last line underscores the separation between castle and conflict that's implied in this whole story. If the battle was fought literally at the castle's feet, Henry would have been fighting in its shadow as the day passed on. He would have been a poor military leader indeed not to have noticed it! Instead, it appears the castle first came to the king's attention after the action was done and he toured the carnage – 'saw the site'

– which in the end would have included trails of French dead who had been run down in the rout.

In other words, the reference to the castle here only makes sense if we move the main battle away from it.

That means moving away from the traditional site.

THE MUD

There's more.

Remember the mud? Again and again, we're told that the mud on the field was a problem for the French. It even shows up in early attempts to illustrate the battle (Figure 23). Many historians, in fact, tout the mud as a kind of secret weapon that testifies to English brilliance:

> Henry's wisdom in sending out scouts in the middle of the night to test the ground now paid dividends. As the French cavalry discovered to their cost, the heavy rain had turned the newly ploughed fields into a quagmire of thick mud and surface water, slowing down their horses and causing them to slip, stumble and even fall ... The men-at-arms of the vanguard, who had begun their own advance immediately after the cavalry set off, therefore found themselves in increasing difficulty ... [as] the combined weight of heavily armed men-at-arms, charging on armoured horses, had churned up the already wet and muddy ground to such a depth that those on foot now found themselves floundering in mud up to their knees ... Dragged down by the weight of their own armour, their plate-clad feet slipping as they tried to balance on the uneven, treacherous ground, and struggling against the suction of the mud at every step.[33]

To be sure, it *had* rained. So it was indeed muddy. And that is indeed difficult to traverse.[34] But I doubt it was this dire and one-sided in its effects. The source for the 'quagmire' and mud 'up to their knees' is the Religieux, who provides these descriptions not as part of the sequence of attack but rather as a description of the ground on which the French were made to sleep during the 'torrents' of rain on the night before – and thus not something that

Henry's scouts and 'wisdom' had revealed to him alone. When it comes to the battle, in fact, the Religieux doesn't mention mud as a hindrance to the action or a cause of calamity and death.[35] Nor do the *Gesta*, Le Fèvre, or Waurin – eyewitnesses all.

Even if we stick with the tradition of this knee-deep mud bogging down the French attack, we have problems squaring any of this with common sense. Why, if the French were camped close to the English lines at Maisoncelle – and our sources all agree that they were – did they decide in the morning to *retreat through the muck* to take their position north of Agincourt and Tramecourt?

Worse, the traditional story tells us that Henry made his initial line at the south end of the field but then, when the French refused to give attack, he ordered his archers to pull their stakes so he could march them to a new position within bow shot of the enemy. There, his archers reset their stakes, his lines re-established themselves, and he began shooting. If the mud was so impossible for the French, why did the similarly encumbered English men-at-arms not have the same problems? For that matter, why on earth would the French stand around as the English king struggled all that way up to them?

The same leading account of Agincourt I just quoted on the high drama of the mud chalks up the English victory to 'a classic case of being caught by surprise' because the French cavalry wasn't brought to bear against the vulnerable English 'at this crucial moment'.[36]

But was it a moment?

The standard interpretation, if you'll recall, had the English trudging forward at least 700 yards to their new position. To walk this distance along the paved road today takes a solid seven minutes at a good pace of 100 yards a minute, and this is without encumbrance, difficult terrain, or the need to keep cohesion between men, all of which would slow things down considerably. By one historian's very reasonable estimate, it would take at least 23 minutes to cover this much ground in muddy conditions even without carrying stakes.[37] And of course the whole of the sequence would be much longer than this. I've had to pull tent stakes out of sucking mud in the back-country. It's hard as hell. A six-foot stake that had been driven into the earth? It wouldn't just pop out. Here we had thousands of men heaving and pulling at the stakes to get them out, then struggling all that distance through the sinking mud, dragging the stakes towards the enemy. Then, once they got close, they had to drive them into the ground again.

This didn't take a moment. We're looking at something like 30–40 minutes during which the English pulled stakes and then slipped and heaved through sucking mud, utterly vulnerable. And however long it took them to reach their new positions, the archers then needed to take still more time to drive the stakes back into the ground – meaning they now had to turn their backs to the enemy to start hammering them in. This being managed without incident or bother from the watching enemy, many of the archers would have now needed to take time to re-sharpen these same stakes, since the hammering would have beaten the ends of them flat.[38]

It's like that scene from the 1975 film *Monty Python and the Holy Grail*, in which Sir Lancelot charges across an open field to attack Swamp Castle: the same clip of him running is shown five times in a row as the guards passively watch, before quite suddenly he is upon them in a 'surprise' attack.

The only reason I can figure that none of this has been a problem for most historians is that the only thing that mattered in their minds was the actions of the English. What the French were doing was of no consequence: they would patiently wait as long as was necessary for them to fall in their traditional spot. Like the guards at Swamp Castle, they were waiting for their cue to die.

But this doesn't fit *at all* with what our sources say of the French that day. To the contrary, it is said that they were bickering with each other for the right to lead the vanguard against the English. Remember the duke of Brabant, who was so anxious to get at the enemy that he did so without his gear? He's emblematic of them all. Everything we have about the French says that these men had every intention of fighting and winning. Before them was a once-in-a-lifetime chance to kill or capture the king of England. It was glory beyond all reckoning, right at their fingertips. We're supposed to believe that these men sat idly by while the English took their merry time re-setting their stakes? We're supposed to believe they were *surprised*?

It's worse than that. We're asked to believe that they sat idly by while the English did all this in the course of moving from a weaker position to a *stronger* one. After all, the narrower part of the field into which they'd advanced – if it existed, and I don't think it did – would have neutralized the French advantage in numbers.

The French weren't fools. Nothing that they had done to this point had been foolish. Had they been too trustworthy in retreating from Péronne to Aubigny to await Henry's arrival for a planned fight? Yes. But if anything, this failure would have infuriated them and made them more anxious to get even at the soonest opportunity – exactly as we see in the sources.

Start to apply even the slightest bit of stress to it, and the whole story of the *Vulgata* begins to collapse.

SOMETHING MUST GO

Faced with the choice between the assumed location being wrong or the sources being wrong, it seems that most historians have decided that our sources must be the problem. If we throw out the multiple reports of four-ranks-thin lines, for instance, then we can certainly squeeze more men into the traditional location. Ignore the sources, and it turns out we can make pretty much anything work!

And yes, our sources can *absolutely* be wrong. I have already suggested that the *Gesta*, though our best source for understanding so much of the Agincourt campaign, overestimates the number of French at the battle. The repeated claims that the English ranks were scarcely four men deep might likewise be an exaggeration meant to make their victory more astonishing. If we had evidence – objective proof, beyond tradition, beyond the weight of repeated assumption – that the battle of Agincourt really *had* to happen on the traditional field, then we would of necessity need to determine how and why our sources were misled or were misleading us on such basic facts.

But we have no such evidence.

In 2015 – the 600th anniversary of Henry V's famed victory over the French – Tim Sutherland, a leading conflict archaeologist, surveyed the state of modern investigations on this traditional site of the battle of Agincourt. Despite significant fieldwork that had uncovered Roman and other early artefacts, he reported, *nothing* attributable to the fight in 1415 had been found on that narrow field between the French towns of Azincourt and Tramecourt.

In fact, he concluded, 'there is currently no recorded physical evidence of the battle ever having taken place!'[39]

A pervading unease no doubt rests behind the humour of that last statement. The battle *did* take place, of course. Yet the dearth of evidence to support the *Vulgata* location is a problem. We know from other extant battle surveys that even preliminary fieldwork within a search area as limited as the traditional site of Agincourt ought to produce archaeological evidence on the order of thousands if not tens of thousands of objects.[40]

Yet we have *nothing*.

Sutherland posited the obvious explanation for the dearth of evidence: the traditional site of the battle is incorrect. In 2006, he wondered if it could instead be re-situated to a location north of Azincourt near Ruisseauville.[41] He later suggested instead a site to the south-east of Azincourt near Maisoncelle.[42] One might say that a re-examination of the battle-site would be an obvious first step given the negative archaeological results, but historians, so far, have shown profoundly little interest in taking up either of Sutherland's suggestions.

With the further problems outlined here, however, Sutherland's impulse seems a sound one. If stress-testing our traditional story breaks it, then like good engineers we ought to head back to the drawing board. Instead of starting with assumptions, we should try to rebuild the battle of Agincourt from the ground up and see what we get.

In doing this, I see a lot to recommend Sutherland's second alternative location: the one south and west of the traditional field. If it weren't for the *Vulgata* saying otherwise, an unbiased reading of our data points to this spot.

As it happens, Sutherland is not the first to suggest a location in this vicinity.

Just a year earlier, another historian raised an eyebrow at the inconsistency of the mud and suggested that the battle should be shifted south on the field, placing the English position halfway between Maisoncelle and Azincourt, with the initial French line unchanged. This continued the tradition of ignoring the tactical advantage of the castle on the field, but it at least made it so that the French and not the English were forced to charge much of the length of the field, thereby explaining why the mud was reportedly a greater problem for them. Unfortunately, among other issues, this attempted solution leaves the English woefully exposed: situated at the tail end of the theoretical woods of Azincourt, the entirety of their backfield open to anyone who bothered to follow the roads around those trees.[43]

Others have shifted the battle westwards, which might get around several of the problems with the traditional site. Harris Nicolas, in the maps accompanying the second edition to his *History of the Battle of Agincourt* (1832), placed the battle to the west of the villages of Azincourt and Maisoncelle. But the weight of the *Vulgata* meant this was quickly relegated to an 'error', as one leading historian put it: 'Unfortunately, too, either Nicolas, or his printer, placed the village of Agincourt to the right rather than the left of the armies'.[44] Harris wasn't the first to put the battle in the location he did, either. Figure 12 shows the earliest map of any kind to show the location of the battle on the landscape: a 1704 map by Guillaume de l'Isle. De l'Isle also places the battle to the *west* of the town of Azincourt, not to the east as the *Vulgata* has it.[45]

AN ALTERNATIVE AGINCOURT

As Sutherland noted in his 2015 article suggesting a closer look at this second alternative location, the cadastral maps of Maisoncelle offer up additional reasons to favour a fight centred on this area.[46] Most striking at a first glance is a rise in the landscape on the west edge of the village. This spot, close beside the *Bois Roger* – one of our missing woods, which is opposite the *Buisson du Grand Camp* – is labelled *L'Anglais* [The English], which certainly calls attention to itself as being potentially connected to the battle. Indeed, as we will see, there is reason to speculate that it may have been the site where part of the English baggage was raided by French forces in the course of the battle proper. At any rate, between *L'Anglais* and the broad fields that stretch from the *Buisson* up to the hills of Saint-George beside Azincourt – the very fields crossed by the road to Calais and thus the 'field of Agincourt' according to the *Gesta* – is a shallow watershed labelled on the cadastral maps as *Morival*, meaning 'Death Valley' (Figure 26). As it happens, the *Chronicle of Normandy* associates the battle with just such a feature on the landscape: 'They were drawn up in order of battle in a valley near Agincourt,' it explains: 'Such was the commencement of the battle on that day in the valley before mentioned, where the ground was so soft that the French foundered in it.'[47] Nothing of the sort fits the traditional site, which is flat as a proverbial ironing board and has left historians speculating that by 'valley' the chronicler meant the slightest of dips in the plateau. Not only can the *Morival* check the box of our missing valley, but the low ground it offered would have drawn in the rainfall to make for a genuine quagmire: it could be that the on-and-off problem of the mud in our sources reflects which part of the fields is being examined.

Though this area might be framed as an 'alternative site' for the battle – certainly that's the label used in the scholarship – I think it's more apt to describe it as an alternative *reconstruction*. After all, it essentially starts with Henry in the same spot on the morning of the battle. It simply changes how we view the action from that point forward. We'll see this in the next two chapters when we reconstruct the battle anew.

I've made many visits to the modern town of Azincourt, walking the ground on the traditional site of the battle and the larger surrounds, as often as possible with other historians to bounce ideas around on the ground. Most of these visits have been made with an eye towards finding problems with the logic I present in the rest of this book. In other words, I've been looking for convincing reasons to hold on to the *Vulgata*. To this point, I have found none. Each visitation has only furthered my conviction that the battle of Agincourt didn't go the way I always thought it did. At the same time, every instance in which the traditions have fractured under stress-testing has given us the pieces to build a stronger, more coherent reconstruction of this famous fight.

As an initial example of this, a hypothesized English deployment between Azincourt and Tramecourt – using a painfully conservative estimation of the number of men present – strained the traditional site to the breaking point. But this same number of men is an ideal fit for an army that pinned its left flank on the woods beside Maisoncelle and its right flank on the woods of Tramecourt, facing the castle of Azincourt just under a mile distant. Increase the number of men in the English army to something more reasonable, and the position will readily flex to fit them. Spread the French out facing this same formation, keeping the fight to this southern end of the fields, and the actions of both sides, as we'll see, suddenly make sense.[48]

Depending on how one approaches a battle here, it could be described as being between Maisoncelle and Azincourt, Azincourt and Tramecourt, Azincourt and Hesdin, or even – as the dissolution of the battle pushed the French remnants northward up the roads – Azincourt and Ruisseauville. Each of these descriptors, as we have seen, has been given in one primary source or another.

Here, as opposed to the too-narrow flat land between Azincourt and Tramecourt, thousands of men can line up just as our sources tell us they did.

Here, thousands of men could wade into the hell of battle.

Here, thousands of men could die.

Part Five

The Battle

The air thunders with dreadful crashes, clouds rain missiles, the earth absorbs blood, breath flies from bodies, half-dead bodies roll in their own blood, the surface of the earth is covered with the corpses of the dead, this man charges, that one falls, this one attacks, that one dies, this one recovers, that one vomits forth his soul in blood ...

Pseudo-Elmham, *Vita et Gesta Henrici Quinti*, *c.*1446–49[1]

12

The Morning, 25 October

It rained all night.

The *Gesta* actually doesn't tell us this, but an overnight downpour – and its associated mud – makes frequent appearances across many other independent sources, especially on the French side. Probably the Chaplain thought the rain unnecessary to note after they had seen so much of it on the days leading up to the battle. And not having slogged through it himself, he had not experienced the role that the mud would play in the fight itself.

The French sources, however, remembered it keenly.

Even before the battle itself, the rain must have seemed like insult on top of injury for the French after their long chase after the English. The Religieux, we've seen, observes how they had slept in fields that the 'torrents of rain had flooded and converted into a quagmire'.[1] Even accounting for hyperbole, it would have been miserable.

Nevertheless, French confidence must have been high. The long chase, the sodden night, and all the other miseries would be well worth it. Whatever sleep they managed might have been haunted by ghosts of the losses that previous generations had suffered at the hands of this same enemy. All the raiding. All the killing. Crécy. Poitiers. Nájera.

Rare indeed was the French family that hadn't suffered loss at English hands.

And now this Henry had come. He had killed and rampaged. Probably he had broken faith with the agreement to fight at

Aubigny. They had run him to ground anyway, trapped him among these little northern hamlets. Seeing their haggard enemy in the flesh, these men who had marched the chilled and muddied roads of their homeland were confident that the dawn would usher in a day washed in English blood. They would avenge their forefathers.

'It was said', according to the *Gesta*, that the French were so confident in their strength that they were gambling over the right to claim the lives of Henry V and other enemy lords.[2] I doubt they were doing anything of the kind, though it sounds very much like the kind of rumour English commanders would be passing through the ranks to rile up their men. Thomas Walsingham similarly suggests a correlation between such stories and English morale: the French, he reports, made it known:

> that they wished no one to be spared except certain named lords and the king himself. They announced that the rest would be killed or have their limbs horribly mutilated. Because of this our men were much excited to rage and took heart, encouraging one another against the event.[3]

To this same end, Le Fèvre and Waurin state that Henry told his men, as the lines were about to engage, 'that the French had boasted that if any English archers were captured they would cut off the three fingers of their right hand so that neither man or horse would ever again be killed by their arrow fire.'[4] From this threat was born, according to popular legend, the offensive gesture of the two-fingered salute of a 'V' sign with the palm inward: this was how the English archers let the French know that they had beaten them and therefore still had the fingers on their shooting (i.e. drawing) hands. A fine story, but there's no evidence of the gesture going back this far. And the reported French threat that we have was to take three fingers, not two, so it doesn't make sense there, either.

We must remember that many rumours and tales spread after the event and the English victory – in the last case, after the power of the English archers was proved. In other words, we have to remember that our sources all have their lenses. The story about gambling for English lives that the Chaplain tells us in the *Gesta*, for instance, not only condemns the French for the sin of pride, but it also associates them with the Romans who cast lots for Christ's clothes at the Crucifixion. The defeated French are thus doubly damned. The victorious English, by contrast, are doubly sanctified. This is good for the Chaplain's story, but less good for reality. On the other hand, whole swathes of his story betray no hint of this kind of manipulation: they are perfectly reasonable and eminently realistic. One of the things we'll be doing in this chapter is locking down the final positions of the English and French lines at the start of the battle, and this will mean sifting through the probabilities of who and what we should believe.

My hope in going into a reconstruction process like this is to have the highest degree of overlap between what our sources are telling us, what the ground is telling us, and what our own comprehension of military tactics and technologies is telling us. If we think of these three data streams as forming a Venn diagram, ideally, they should be a single circle – everything accounted for, nothing straining at the limits of sensibility.

The Agincourt *Vulgata* doesn't do this in the slightest.

So we must look, as nearly as possible, for what does.

RECONNOITRING

During the cold, wet night, both sides attempted to scope the other's strengths and reconnoitre the likely field of battle. Pseudo-Elmham describes these efforts on the English side.[5] Monstrelet likewise testifies to them on the French side, with Richemont moving his men 'almost right up' to the English encampment. The result was a small, isolated skirmish but no general engagement.[6] No one wanted to fight at night, when the confusion of darkness would only add to the chaos of a battle. If the seven captured Lancashire archers weren't taken in a scouting manoeuvre earlier in the day, they were probably caught in this night-time action.

Meanwhile, the priests had been busy. They could do nothing to save the many lives that would surely be lost when the fighting started, but they could do something for their souls. Henry himself, according to Waurin and Le Fèvre, heard mass three times – although possible, probably an embellishment to emphasize his religiosity and the role of divine intervention in his subsequent victory.[7]

As the first glimmer of dawn glowed over the woods to the east, around 6:40am, the rain had probably passed. The humid leavings of the departing wisps of cloud further chilled the early morning air.

If the sun was out, its rays would have picked out the colours of each lord's banner, fluttering its signal of his presence and providing a rally point for his retinue. Between the flags and the glinting of light off metal helmets, the various lines forming up on the battlefield would have looked like shimmering waves upon a burnished, iron sea.

Every minute that passed – from sun up to the first trumpets sounding the attack – brought more and more French troops to the field. Lords streamed in along the roads, rushing to make it to the field in time to snatch some shred of glory or booty or preferably plenty of both.

One of them might have been the king's brother, the duke of Orléans. Just 19 years old, he was instantly the highest ranking man on the field on arrival. The fact that he is not mentioned by Juvénal des Ursins in the debate over whether to fight suggests that he was not yet on the field – another reason, as it happens, that the French would have been willing to accept the delay of a truce on 24 October. The Berry Herald says quite plainly that Orléans and other lords arrived on the morning of the battle, with the English already drawn up: this 'caused much rejoicing in the army, even though they came alone or at least with very few men'. After the duke showed up, he held a parlay with the English and, when it failed, battle ensued.[8] The *Chronicle of Normandy* agrees: the dukes of Orléans and Brabant, as well as the count of Nevers, showed up at the last minute.[9]

THE ENGLISH TAKE POSITION

It was, as Shakespeare would make sure everyone remembered, the feast day of the Saints Crispin and Crispinian, twin brothers who preached Christianity to the Gauls in Soissons – the French city that the Armagnacs had sacked in their campaign against the duke of Burgundy just over a year earlier. An inauspicious day, many would come to think, for the Armagnac-heavy French army.

But the common soldiers weren't thinking of such things.

All they knew was the waiting. As soon as they were up, their commanders would have been ushering the men into battle array only to make them wait, hour after interminable hour, for something to happen – a familiar experience related by warriors across the millennia from ancient times to today. Several of our sources say many of them took earth – another question mark on the mud, perhaps – and put it into their mouths as a sign of their acceptance of death. Priests were busy saying prayers and receiving confessions. Archers would have checked and rechecked their bow strings. Some would have joked, probably the dark, gallows humour endemic among fighting men. Some would have boasted. Some would have hidden their hands, shaking in fear. Death would have whispered on the wind, haunting even the bravest mind.

Grappling with this terror, the English took their places.

But where?

The eyewitness Chaplain tells us in his *Gesta* that for Henry the battlefield was 'at no great distance from his quarters' at Maisoncelle, placing the English directly north of the town.[10] Maisoncelle cannot have been large in 1415, but even a few buildings and hedges would have helped create a backstop for the English line. Henry wisely feared the French cavalry – that is why his archers now had stakes – and the village was an obstacle to any attempt by the French to encircle his position from the west and attack him from the rear. Henry was a capable and experienced commander. He would not have neglected this advantage (Figure 28).

A position in front of Maisoncelle also makes fine use of the terrain. We don't know if there was much of a wood around Azincourt, but we can be certain that the trees were thick around Maisoncelle and Tramecourt. They are there today, there in our cadastral maps, and there in paintings of the villages made at the start of the 17th century.[11] (For Maisoncelle, see Figure 25.) As his forebears had done, Henry would want to use such features to protect his flanks. His left would be covered by the woods immediately west of Maisoncelle, directly in front of the field called *L'Anglais* on the cadastral maps. His right would be covered by the woods south

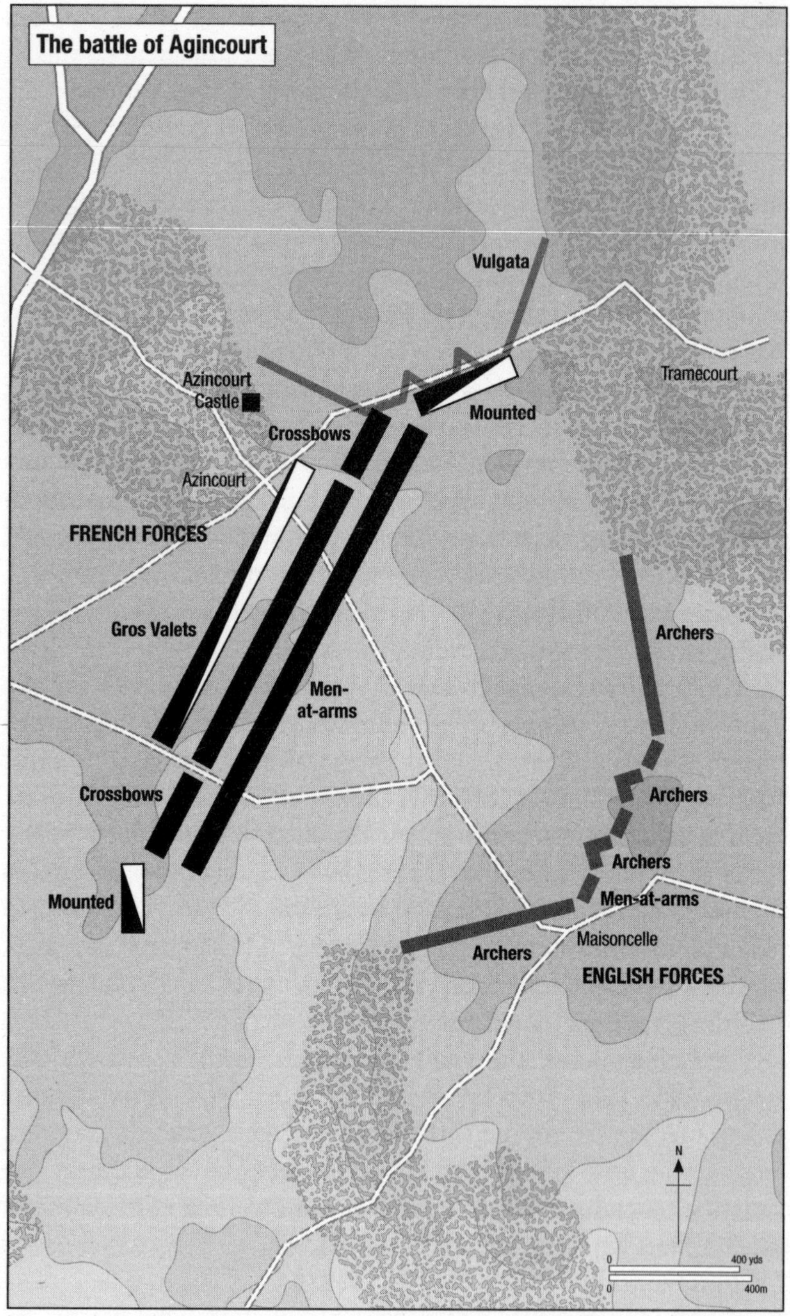
The battle of Agincourt
Vulgata
Azincourt Castle
Tramecourt
Mounted
Crossbows
Azincourt
FRENCH FORCES
Gros Valets
Archers
Men-at-arms
Crossbows
Archers
Archers
Mounted
Men-at-arms
Maisoncelle
Archers
ENGLISH FORCES
N
0
400 yds
0
400m

Map 5

of Tramecourt. Exactly where these points were located would depend on where the trees stood in 1415. Unfortunately, this is something about which we can only guess. As we saw previously, the woods might have been up to 400 per cent more extensive than they are today. I have provided an approximated model of the medieval landscape in Figure 27. The lines of men running between these woods would be largely shaped by the topography of the plateau, which would not be greatly changed from what is visible today.

I introduced the probable English formation in the last chapter. The traditional site failed the stress test that set the wings of English archers at 45-degree angles with a total body of the most conservative number of men within the bounds of reality. The formation I have marked in Figure 27 and on Map 5 uses a more realistic number of men – the *Gesta* numbers – but places them in a slightly more open formation in order to fill the space between the woods.

Behind this line, in or close beside Maisoncelle, Henry had his few wagons rounded up to secure what would have been called a baggage train on the march but was now a tense little encampment. He could not spare many men for its defence, so he would have used the terrain to try to protect it as best he could. It's hard to imagine a more suitable spot for the English baggage than the small area that eventually took the name *L'Anglais*: hemmed in by woods and hamlet both.

Henry had done the best with what he had. He had fixed the ends of his lines against woods, and he had done his best to lengthen his centre and use stakes to protect his archers, but there was no question that he was badly exposed.

This wasn't the ground of his choosing.

The French had him trapped.

THE STAKES

Exactly how did the English use the stakes to protect the archers? The *Gesta*, as you might recall, had this to say about it when the order to build them was given:

> the archers were to drive their stakes in front of them in line abreast and … some of them should do this further back and in

> between, one end being driven into the ground pointing down towards themselves, the other end pointing up towards the enemy above waist-height.[12]

The point, if you'll forgive the pun, is clear: the stakes would be angled towards the French, and they would be driven into the ground in two rows slightly off-set from one another.

Historians have raised eyebrows at what the Chaplain describes. One problem is that in order to have the stakes slanted towards the enemy, each archer would need to have his back to the enemy to drive them into the ground. The other is that, having driven the stakes in, the archers would have been stuck on the wrong side of the barrier they had made.[13]

The second objection is easily solved, since our eyewitness in the *Gesta* does not describe a single 'wall' of stakes. They were in a staggered pattern, and allowing the archers freedom of movement was almost certainly a reason for this. Another reason, almost assuredly, was in order to both deepen and complicate the layout of the defensive barrier. Getting through the stakes almost certainly wasn't a problem for the archers.[14]

As for the first objection, we've already seen in the last chapter that, yes, it's absolutely a problem. The *Vulgata* story that the archers were resetting the stakes within bow shot of the formed-up lines of the French doesn't make sense: having your back to the enemy is a good way to be shot in the back, run down unexpectedly, or simply scattered into disarray by a sudden charge. Henry wasn't a fool, and this would have been completely foolish.

But since historians remain committed to the *Vulgata*, they have instead had to explain that the Chaplain who saw the stakes used that fateful day didn't know what he was talking about. The stakes weren't leaning towards the enemy, it's been argued.[15] They were pointed straight up at the sky. Make the stakes into a more traditional 'palisade' or fence, and the archers wouldn't have to turn their backs on the enemy to drive them into the ground.

There are many problems with this argument, not least of which is that it wouldn't matter a whit to heavy cavalry whether the archers trying to build their defensive line were behind or in front of their stakes. Either way, the labouring, largely unarmoured archers would have been dead meat at such proximity. Besides that, *multiple* sources have the stakes impaling horses in the battle.[16] That's impossible if the stakes were an upright fence. But it would absolutely happen if, as our eyewitness says, they were angled towards the charging enemy.

This won't be the last time that I'm more inclined to trust the contemporary sources over later historians. The Chaplain is right that the stakes were angled towards the French. He is also right that they weren't a solid wall but something more like a chequerboard, close enough together to allow free passage to the archers on foot but not the men on horseback. As for the fact that it doesn't make sense to be setting this line so close to the French ... well, I agree. It didn't happen. Henry's archers set their stakes in their initial position, with plenty of distance between themselves and the enemy. I suspect, but can't prove, that work on the stakes might well have begun in the semi-dark of early morning, as soon as Henry and his commanders had decided on their battle plan. The darkness would have helped provide cover, and the rain would have made it easier to drive the stakes. I only suspect this because it would have been the smart thing to do – and the sources show that Henry V was very smart indeed.

THE AMBUSH

Depending on whether we believe the stories, Henry might have had one more trick up his sleeve to try to give his men a fighting chance.

Juvénal des Ursins says that the English position lay 'between two areas of woodland' – this is what we've seen and what we would expect – but that 'in front of them but a little way off there was another wood where they put a large ambush of archers, and in one of the woodland areas which was on their flank they put a large ambush of their mounted men-at-arms'.[17] Both of these ambushes, he goes on to report, were sprung in the course of the fight. The archers shot the French 'from behind', while the mounted men 'sallied out en masse and came from the rear onto the second battle' of the French, sending them into chaos and flight.[18] These moves left the French vanguard stranded and surrounded.

This would have been a very good plan on the English part. It would be, to some measure, akin to what had happened at Poitiers – which for our purposes can be a reason both for and against believing that it actually happened. On the one hand, it would be more than understandable for the English, in selecting a strategy, to examine a known victory and try to repeat it. On the other hand, it would be more than understandable for Juvénal des Ursins (or his source), wondering what strategy was followed, to examine the same thing and insert it into the later event as an explanation. However, several other sources also note an English ambush plan of some kind. Describing the initial positions, Monstrelet suggests that 'Elsewhere the king of England sent about 200 archers behind his army so that they would not be spotted by the French. They secretly entered a meadow near Tramecourt, quite close to the rearguard of the French, and held themselves there secretly until it was time to shoot.'[19]

This looks really good except – nothing's easy! – that our eyewitnesses Le Fèvre and Waurin actually correct Monstrelet on the point. They deny that such an ambush existed, based on the word of 'a man of honour who was there on that day in the company of the king of England'.[20] It may be for this reason that historians have mostly set it aside.

I can't totally shake it, though. If he could have managed it, an ambush would have been a brilliant move on Henry's part. He faced a more numerous and better fed army that was fighting on its home turf. He had too many archers and not enough men-at-arms, forcing him to create a new formation and use stakes to make up for this problem. For all his trust in God, Henry was a practical man with very real war experience. He didn't turn a blind eye to his weaknesses. He accounted for them.

Monstrelet also reports that there was a contingent of English scouts who, 'in order to frighten the French', set fire to a 'barn and house belonging to the priory of Saint-George of Hesdin' on the morning of the battle, somewhere 'to the rear of the village of Agincourt'.[21] The few historians who have considered this incident at all have placed it north of Azincourt, that is 'the rear' of the town from the perspective of the English. But Monstrelet is a *French* source, and from the French perspective 'the rear' could be *south* of the town. This was the direction of the English lines, which would certainly make it an easier location for their scouts to reach unimpeded. As it happens, the Napoleonic cadastral maps record that the fields on the road to Hesdin south-west of Azincourt – between that town and the little village of Bucamps (its name probably means 'forest-field') – were called the *Les Côtes des Saint-Georges* (The Borders of Saint-George). Would English scouts have headed in this direction? Almost certainly. This was the only possible way out of the French trap: Henry would undoubtedly have sent men in this direction, trying to see if they could squeeze through and race to Calais. The report of Juvénal des Ursins that a group of 'mounted men-at-arms' had been sent to 'one of the woodland areas which was on their flank', separate from the ambush of archers sent to the woods near Tramecourt on the eastern side of the field, strongly implies that these men went to the woods on the western side of the field, in the same direction of the *Côtes des Saint-Georges*. So, if we accept Monstrelet's report of the fire as true and need to fix a location, somewhere in this area would be a reasonable guess: the English 'scouts' of Monstrelet were the 'mounted men-at-arms' of Juvénal des Ursins, and when they recognized that there would be no way for them to get out of the trap, they burned the buildings – either out of spite or in the hope of some small distraction from the fight about to happen.

THE FRENCH FORM UP

The Chaplain, looking out over the thousands of men gathering that morning, describes the French organization as having:

> squadrons of cavalry, many hundreds strong, on each flank of their vanguard, to break the formation and resistance of our archers. And that vanguard was composed of dismounted men drawn from all their nobles and the pick of their forces and, with its forest of spears and the great number of helmets gleaming in between them and of cavalry on the flanks, it was at a rough guess thirty times more than all our men put together.[22]

The Chaplain's claim about their numbers is, as we've already observed, wrong – but it must have *felt* right: the enormity of the

French host must have terrified him and the other exhausted men on the English side. But even if his numbers are off, his description of the French deployment makes good sense.

To understand what he was seeing – and something of the battle to come – we should recall the plan that Boucicaut had put in place for a possible attack on the English near Blanchetaque. In that earlier plan, the French men-at-arms would form into a central vanguard flanked by wings of archers and crossbowmen. Another large battle of men-at-arms would be either behind or beside the vanguard, depending on whether the English presented their battles one behind the other or all in a line (exactly as Henry did at Agincourt). Behind the wings of missile troops would be smaller divisions of infantry. In addition, there would be a battle made of 1,000 heavy horse, which would be on the French left, and a much smaller group of 200 cavalry positioned on the French right. The larger unit would strike the archers, while the smaller would attempt to swing around the English position entirely and attack it from the rear, targeting Henry's baggage and logistical support. Boucicaut's advice was for the vanguard, the wings, and the two groups of cavalry to move forward simultaneously. The French archers and crossbowmen would soften up the English lines as the vanguard charged forward on foot under their covering missiles. The English archers were expected to be in a wing of their own – to some degree mirroring the French set-up – and the larger French cavalry would strike the wing on Henry's right and hopefully blast through it. The smaller French cavalry unit would meanwhile be coming around for its attack from behind.

This earlier plan didn't feature many of the key lords who would fight at Agincourt, so it would have been under continual alteration as the hour of the actual battle approached. This was inevitable given the way that the French army was being forced to come together on the fly, but it was also inevitably 'disruptive', as one historian puts it, 'and hardly conducive to the co-ordination of command in the crucial lead up to the battle'.[23]

This is *absolutely* true.

'Command and control' is a core concept in the modern military. From the individual soldier to the largest unit of manoeuvre, everyone should know who is in command, and the commander should exercise firm control over their subordinate troops: lines of communications must be maintained so commands can flow, communications must be clear so commands are understood, and discipline must be maintained to ensure those commands are followed. If the duke of Orléans, for instance, arrived late to the field, as is generally believed, and then suddenly started throwing his royal weight around, it would cause chaos for the French, who would be left wondering who was in charge and just what the plan was now. And it would contrast sharply with the superior maintenance of command and control within the English army, which had been marching as a single force, with a clear and undisputed commander, for weeks now.

For many in the years afterwards, the loss of command and control was the best explanation for the French defeat. As the Religieux says, 'each of the leaders claimed for himself the honour of leading the vanguard. This led to considerable debate and so that there could be some agreement, they came to the rather unfortunate conclusion that they should all place themselves in the front line.'[24] Juvénal des Ursins similarly says that 'All the lords wanted to be in the first battle, so that each would have as much honour as another, as they could not agree to do anything else.'[25] And Pierre Fenin said that the 'vanguard [was] where they put the majority of their nobles and the flower of their men.'[26]

This 'front-loading' of the French army – and the pride that drove the decision – is common to many discussions of the battle by modern historians. One popular account of the battle calls it 'the greatest dilemma facing their strategists':

> After much argument and many expressions of bad feeling, with every leader of consequence insisting that it was his right to lead the vanguard, they came to a conclusion that was fair but foolish. They would all take their places in the front lines.[27]

It's an appealing idea. It certainly plays into a negative view of French leadership during the battle – and no doubt for some writers a negative view of the French in general. And there are certainly contemporary voices who pointed at squabbles over who got to be where as they sought to allot blame after the defeat.

This would be the same basic problem that had crippled the crown of France for over two decades. The question of who was in charge during the periods of the king's madness had fractured the court, so it's easy enough to imagine the fish rotting from the head, the disorganization trickling down to Agincourt, setting the French leadership bickering among themselves.

Yet the Berry Herald – the source that we would most expect to have a clear sense of who was where since that sort of thing was literally his job – gives us an excellent description of the French deployment.

And very clearly the lords were *not* all up front.

There were, as he describes them, two main battles on the French side. The vanguard had 4,800 men-at-arms, he says, led by the constable and Boucicaut (with 3,000 men), along with the dukes of Bourbon (1,200) and Orléans (600). By his accounting, the second battle had far fewer men – his total comes to 3,000 – but it was hardly devoid of lords: the dukes of Bar (600) and Lorraine (300) were there, in addition to the counts of Eu (300), Marlay (400), Nevers (1,200), Roussy and Braine (200), and Vaudémont (300). Beside these battles were additional wings of men-at-arms, each 600 strong. The right was commanded by Richemont, the viscount of Bellière, and the lord of Combourg. The left had the count of Vendôme and a number of other lords, many of them officers of the royal household. There was also a cavalry force led by Clignet de Brabant.[28]

The Herald doesn't describe where the mounted group was positioned, nor does he make clear whether the wings were beside the vanguard or the second French battle. He also leaves unmentioned where the French crossbowmen and archers were located. For that matter, if there were a significant number of *gros valets* present – and there surely were – then these, too, aren't listed. Probably because they were not men of title, the Herald didn't think them worthy of note. This is a common problem with many of our sources across the period, and it could also have meant that the second line was indeed the same size of the vanguard if all heads were counted.

We can fill in some of the blanks by looking at other accounts of Agincourt, as well as Boucicaut's earlier plan, which it is sensible to imagine was at least somewhat still on the mind of the French command. Boucicaut had suggested that the archers and crossbowmen would be in front of the infantry on the wings, but the *Gesta* states they had to shoot over them.[29] Whether this was an effort to conceal the missile troops or – the disaster of the Genoese crossbowmen at Crécy perhaps looming in their minds – to protect them from the opposing longbowmen is something we can't know.

Several of our sources suggest there were three lines, rather than the two the Berry Herald specifies. This 'missing' third line, almost assuredly, was filled with the French *gros valets*. They were the rearguard, and the Chaplain author of the *Gesta* says they were 'more ready to flee' than fight. This is a description with the benefit of hindsight, but it might have had some truth even in the moment: these were the men with the least experience in battle.

That said, they were still fighting men who could turn the tide.

So while it's not true that *all* of the lords were in the vanguard, there probably weren't any in the third line. This meant there was little effective leadership in the rearguard, which would, in the end, weaken any chance that it could help save the French from disaster. As Pierre Cochon put it in the years after Agincourt, 'all the men of the lower ranks, who were enough to have beaten the English, were pushed to the rear'.[30]

When it comes to Clignet's mounted force, the *Gesta* describes the French cavalry hitting *both* wings of the English archers in the battle,[31] so it seems fair to assume that the horse were split. But this split probably wasn't even. Boucicaut's plan had called for an asymmetrical mounted assault: a large strike on the English right and a smaller one on the rear of the English left. As it would happen, this split fits the likely actual location of Agincourt.

We can see glimmers of Boucicaut's previous plan in the French deployment, and it seems reasonable to assume that their tactics would be similar. The cavalry would be used against the archers, and the vanguard would come at the English dismounted, wading into the fight without horses to spook. They would have sent their mounts to the rear, lining up to face their enemy.

But where?

According to the Religieux, the French began the battle 'about 2,000 paces' away from the English.[32] Thomas Walsingham states that when the day began the two lines separated by 'scarcely 1,000 paces'.[33] Exactly what these distances equate to depends upon the measurement of the 'pace'. By the Roman standard, the pace was the span of ground between a single foot rising and falling, and 1,000 of them totalled up to a Roman mile – about 1,618 yards, by today's reckoning. It's a fair assumption that this is the 'pace' that the Religieux and Walsingham are both using, but it wasn't a standardized measurement the way we're used to them in 2023.

Tito Livio Frulovisi's *Vita Henrici Quinti* places the armies as 'distant from each other for scarcely two or three bow shots'.[34] Alas, a bow shot is not a standardized distance, either. It depends upon the size of the bow and the strength of the man. I consider a typical 15th-century shot at distance to be around 250 yards, giving us a total range of 500–750 yards between the two lines. But bows *could* shoot further. Define a 'bow shot' as 300 yards, and the distance is 600–900 yards.[35] There is a lot of difference between these numbers, not to mention that they need to be tempered by the variance of whatever it means to be 'scarcely' this distance. In any case, this distance isn't an actual measurement on the field. We can't imagine that an archer in the front line of the English army took the longest shot he could, walked forward to where it fell, then loosed another from there and counted that off, too. Instead, this distance was, at best, the approximation from an archer who could judge the rough reach of his first bow shot and then eyeballed the distance past that. The same is true of the paces given by the Religieux and Walsingham. No one truly stepped these distances off. These are guesses from post-battle reports, and they can't all be true.

So who got it closest?

Looking at the actual landscape and measuring the ground with the exactness of geo-positioning satellite technologies, we can see that if the Religieux was using the Roman measurements, his 2,000 paces would reach from Maisoncelle to Ruisseauville. This is a distance of something like 13 bow shots, and it would require that the French had retreated a full Roman mile from any encampment around the French-held castle at Azincourt in order to make their lines. This is highly doubtful. Walsingham's distance cuts this in half, running almost exactly from the northern edge of Maisoncelle to the castle of Azincourt. Frulovisi's 'scarcely two or three bow shots' brings the lines even closer, which makes a lot more sense. At this distance, the English would be 'protected to the rear by the place where they had lodged the night before', as Frulovisi says.[36] The French position would be backed up by a castle. Even better, this fits the locations of the encampments the night before, and it makes tactical sense, too. It also rather precisely matches the eyewitness account of the *Gesta*, which reports that on the morning of the battle the French army 'took up position in front of us in that field [in which they had camped the night before], called the field of Agincourt, across which lay our road towards Calais'.[37]

With their greater numbers, the French could have stretched their lines in a wide arc facing the English position. To the west, they would be on high ground, separated from the English by the shallow watershed of the *Morival* – 'Death Valley'. In the centre, they would be backed by the town, with its castle and surrounds (Figure 29), while to the east, they would be stretched across the traditional battlefield where so many interpreters place the English (Figure 22). Somewhere in the woods of Tramecourt to their left – if we believe the reports of Henry establishing an ambush – a couple of hundred English archers might have been waiting amid the trees.

THE PARLEY AND THE BLAME GAME

Even opposing armies communicate with one another when they are so close, as many of our French sources remind us. The Berry Herald says that the reason no fight happened when the armies met on the afternoon of 24 October is that Henry asked for a truce until the next day.[38] The Religieux goes further, explaining that on 24 October the English 'sent representatives' to the French leaders, 'to offer them reparation for all the damage which they had caused and the restitution of all that they had taken on condition that they would agree to let them return freely to their own country'.[39] Juvénal des Ursins doesn't specify a day or time for such discussions, but agrees that in exchange for safety the English offered 'to quit Harfleur' and return prisoners without ransom.[40] Pierre Fenin, on the other hand, says that this offer was made on the morning of the battle on 25 October, when 'there was a great discussion between the two sides'.[41] The most likely description of the timing comes from the *Chronicle of Ruisseauville*, which tells us that there was an initial meeting 'during the night' of 24 October that established a truce until an official negotiation could take place in the morning. It was in the early morning of 25 October, then, that Henry's representatives met the French and officially 'offered to surrender Harfleur and all the fortresses below Calais and 100,000 crowns' in return for their safe passage to Calais.[42] Le Fèvre and Waurin, who were on opposite sides, agree that the meeting took place on the open ground between the armies. Their account suggests that before a deal was suggested to allow Henry's departure from the field, there was a short negotiation on terms that would end the Hundred Years War entirely:

> On the French side was offered, or so I have heard, that if Henry would renounce the title which he claimed to have to the crown of France, and leave it completely aside, and surrender the town of Harfleur which he had recently captured, the king of France would be content to let him have what he held in Guienne and what he held by ancient conquest in Picardy [i.e. Calais]. The king of England, or his men, replied that if the king of France would let him have the duchy of Guienne and five cities which he named and which belonged to the duchy of Guienne, the county of Ponthieu, a marriage to Catherine, daughter of the king of France, with jewels and garments to the value of 800,000 *ecus*, he would be prepared to renounce the title of the crown of France and to surrender the town of Harfleur.[43]

This going nowhere, talks turned to the English surrendering Harfleur and other restitution in exchange for immediate safe passage to Calais.

The generosity of these terms emphasize what Fenin describes as Henry's 'grave doubts about the engagement'[44] – and they explain why we don't see them mentioned on the English side.

But why weren't these generous terms accepted? Here, we run straight into the problem of bias in our sources – bias that runs so deep we may never know the truth.

The French were mauled at Agincourt. It was a devastating blow. The blame game would have begun even as the last of the mortally wounded were gasping out their final breath. No one wanted to take responsibility. The loss was bad enough, but it would be even worse if there was such an extraordinary offer on the table that had been turned down. Exactly who someone blamed for it all quite naturally resolved itself into a question of who that person *wanted* to blame for it all. The *Chronicle of Ruisseauville* says the constable rejected the English offer.[45] But Juvénal des Ursins says the constable, Boucicaut, and other men 'who had much experience in arms' knew that 'the events of a battle were risky and perilous'. They favoured taking the deal, while the dukes of Bourbon and Alençon, along with other inexperienced lords, accused them of being 'scared'.[46] Is *Ruisseauville*'s account different because its author had an axe to grind with the constable? Perhaps so. I certainly *want* to say that Juvénal des Ursins has the likelier story, but here I have to beware my own lenses: my status as a middle-class American inclines me to believe a story about filthy rich aristocrats getting greedy. However, when I set that instinct aside do I have an unassailable reason for believing Juvénal des Ursins over *Ruisseauville* here?

I do not.

I *am* confident there were pre-battle discussions and offers. The Religieux was quite right to see in them echoes of the battle of Poitiers.[47] In 1356, the Black Prince had so feared the position he had been cornered into that he offered extraordinary terms to King Jean II of France in exchange for safe passage back to his base in Bordeaux. Rather than the single bird in the hand, Jean and his lords wanted the two in the bush. The subsequent battle went completely sideways for the French, and the king himself was captured, leading to the Treaty of Brétigny and all that had followed. Something similar happened here in northern France, the Religieux says: 'having too much confidence in their forces and guided by the poor advice of some of their company they rebutted all proposals for peace.'[48]

It is notable that the sources for these offers are mostly French. The *Gesta* is silent on the matter. This shouldn't surprise us. As with the 21 October agreement to fight at Aubigny, any discussions at Maisoncelle through the night of 24 October and the morning of 25 October wouldn't merit mention in the Chaplain's account because they didn't fit his interests. For him, the need to 'spin' the battle of Agincourt was pressing. It was a victory from beginning to end. Not once had the king wavered in the confidence he had in his men and God's blessing. This was the story that served England. It was the story that served Henry V. The Chaplain wasn't interested in recording anything else. With victory at hand, there was little sense in recording the very real – and very understandable – fear and doubt that Henry had experienced in the hours before the fight. Far better was the story of a heroic king making a divinely sanctioned stand against his enemy.

It was a lie.

The chronicles had deceived in describing Edward III's campaign, hiding the mistakes of the Black Prince at Crécy in 1346. Henry wanted to emulate that glory.

In ways he can't have expected and would surely never admit, he was doing just that.

By mid-morning, it was clear no deal could be made.

It would come down to battle.

THE BAGGAGE HIT

The *Gesta* tells us that after both armies lined up, the French 'astutely kept at a distance' and didn't engage.[49] For all that historians have portrayed the French as ill advised and ill led, they were at least at this point making the right move by not moving. It was probably known that the duke of Brabant could arrive at any moment. On 25 October the duke of Brittany had arrived in Amiens, and he, too, was expected to come to the field.

Henry knew it. The French were, it was suspected, either still gathering strength or patiently letting time and hunger weaken the English. Both were probably true. Every hour that passed brought more men to their lines and further exhausted their enemy. A fight was inevitable, and Henry needed it to happen sooner rather than later.

Probably around 10am – no one was wearing a watch, so it's no surprise we get various times reported from 9 to 11am[50] – Henry summoned his baggage, which had been stationed well behind his position, forward to the immediate rear of his line.

This order is generally glossed over in most accounts of the battle. We're all anxious to get to the battle proper! But it's worth pausing for a moment to look at what this order was and what it meant.

The Chaplain informs us that Henry:

> decided to move against them [i.e. the French], sending for the army baggage in order to have it at the rear of the engagement lest it should fall as booty into the hands of the enemy. (He had previously arranged that this baggage, together with the priests who were to celebrate the divine office and make fervent prayer for him and his men, should await him in the aforesaid hamlet and closes, where he had been the night before, until the fighting was over.)[51]

That this happened seems beyond doubt. Our source for the order is a man who was at the rear of the lines that day. He was a direct participant in the movement he describes. More than that, there's no hint of bias in the order. If anything, we might expect that this particular author, who is elsewhere so focused on making his king look good, would want to *hide* the order.

So let's break the order down.

The baggage was in the hamlet where Henry spent the night – Maisoncelle. We can't now know, but the baggage was probably positioned against the woods on the north-west side of the village, upon the field that would be remembered as *L'Anglais*. Wherever it was positioned in and around Maisoncelle, it was no longer safe there to Henry's thinking. Something had changed in his understanding about the engagement. He needed the baggage moved closer.

In the eyes of some, this passage from the *Gesta* 'makes no sense' if Henry's line was near Maisoncelle, so his line must be moved north in accordance with the traditional location.[52] The trouble is, doing *that* makes no sense of the fact that the *Gesta* very clearly states that the English lines were on a field 'at no great distance from his quarters', which were in Maisoncelle.[53] Choosing to favour one passage over the other looks very much like confirmation bias.

Rather than choose one or the other, I'd prefer if *both* were true. Our Chaplain was an eyewitness, and he was trying to describe what had happened. Let's listen to him.

The English battle line stretched from the woods of Maisoncelle to the woods of Tramecourt. It was no single point on the map. It was over a thousand yards wide. The king stood at its centre. If the baggage was in the centre of Maisoncelle, it was still at least a couple hundred yards from his person. If the baggage was on the western side of the hamlet at *L'Anglais*, then it was more distant still. Our eyewitness could readily describe the English lines as being close at hand – a wing of English archers ran right in front of the hamlet – without being near the king's immediate rear.

The movement of the baggage was unquestionably an act of fear. Now that the fight was upon him, Henry worried that his supplies were in danger. Recognizing the location of the baggage relative to Henry's formation explains this: Henry had archers aplenty, but he was desperately short of men-at-arms. He couldn't spare any to protect the baggage, and in Maisoncelle it would be so far that he couldn't hope to get men there in response if it was attacked.

Henry also knew his history. Just as he had tried to follow the path of Edward III on the campaign, he used the lessons of Crécy here, too. His baggage didn't have wagons enough for a wagenburg – this is the reason his archers had their stakes – but if he pulled the baggage to the centre of his lines then the few wagons he had could at least help protect some of his dismounted men-at-arms, and himself, from a French attack to the rear. He would not have admitted it, but if worse came to worst, having his baggage close at hand might also give him and his highest lords a means of escape.[54]

Why he thought that his baggage – and indeed the rear of his position entirely – was in danger is best explained by the fact that they very much *were*. The *Gesta* tells us that as the baggage was moved forward, it was attacked:

> And at that time French pillagers were watching it from almost every side, intending to make an attack upon it immediately they saw both armies engage; in fact, directly battle was joined they fell upon the tail end of it where, owing to the negligence of the royal servants, the king's own baggage was, seizing on royal treasure of great value, a sword and a crown among other precious objects, as well as all the bedding.[55]

The *Chronicle of Ruisseauville* says that this was done by 'the men of Hesdin'.[56] Juvénal des Ursins also records a connection between the English baggage and Hesdin, where the booty was taken.[57]

Henry's suspicion that something like this might happen could be attributable to any number of factors. Perhaps his scouts had informed him there were eyes keeping greedy watch on his baggage. Perhaps he just had a gut feeling. But we also can't forget Boucicaut's battle plan, which called for a strike on Henry's baggage and rear in order to surround the English and destroy them.

If Henry knew of this plan, then his orders regarding both the stakes and the baggage would make even greater sense.

Did he know?

I wish we could say. It's awfully tempting to imagine that Boucicaut's plan was discovered during the campaign. Henry had taken prisoners at several points along the Somme, and he could have extracted the information from any of them. It was on that march, we can recall, that Henry suddenly gave the order for the stakes to be made as the English became aware of the French cavalry threat. An *en route* capture of the battle plan would also explain how it came to be in the British Library. But the truth is we don't know how it got there.

When it comes to Henry having the plan there's a lot of smoke, but we can't be sure of the fire beneath it.

If Henry was making moves based on Boucicaut's plan, then he would be disappointed. The French didn't stick to the plan entirely. We've already seen some differences in their formation, and the attack on the baggage – despite being there in the plan – doesn't follow it exactly. Boucicaut had imagined a fast-strike cavalry force swinging around the English formation, but the Chaplain describes an attack of opportunity by locals.

Monstrelet, however, suggests the attack was carried out by the French lords Robert de Bourneville and Isambard d'Azincourt, who with their men-at-arms were 'accompanied by 600 peasants'.[58] Fenin gives a similar account.[59] Both sources connect the raid and Henry's order to kill the French prisoners at the end of the battle. The cause-and-effect relationship between the baggage raid and the prisoner killing has been picked up by many modern voices, perhaps because it implies that any moral queasiness we have over Henry's order is remedied by a sense that the French had it coming.[60]

So there is a question not only about *who* hit the baggage, but about *when* it was hit. The *Gesta* says it was at the start of the battle. Other sources – and most historians – say it was at the end.

I favour the Chaplain, who was with the baggage that day. As it happens, the eyewitnesses Le Fèvre and Waurin, revising Monstrelet, interpose a paragraph about the taking of the prisoners between the attack on the baggage and the order to kill the prisoners, completely disconnecting the two events and implying that the baggage strike is described near the end of the battle in their telling because this is when Henry and those fighting on the field learned of it.[61]

That the attack simply wasn't initially known to Henry fits perfectly well with the Chaplain's account. First, we should note that it was only the 'tail end' of the train that was struck. This is probably the part that would be out of view in or beyond Maisoncelle. Second, there were other things commanding the king's attention.

THE ENGLISH ADVANCE

Henry knew if he went on the offensive, his chances of winning were slim to none. If he had to charge out into the open field, the French cavalry would manoeuvre around his flanks. His archers would be crushed. He and his fellow men-at-arms would be surrounded and captured. It would be the end. His chances of surviving if he sat and waited weren't much better: a slow death as his army, exhausted, starving and wracked with dysentery, gradually weakened, until they were finally hopelessly outnumbered by the steady stream of men joining the French host.

If the French refused to give fight, he was doomed.

They had to come to him, and soon.

Boil everything down, and this was it.

And so, the Chaplain tells us, when Henry:

> thought that almost all his baggage had reached his rear, in the name of Jesus (to Whom is bowed every knee, of those in Heaven, on earth, and under the earth) and of the Glorious Virgin and of St George, he advanced towards the enemy, and the enemy, too, advanced towards him.[62]

The battle of Agincourt had begun.

And already we have a problem. What the Chaplain is telling us – that the English advance provoked the joining of collective battle on both sides – violates the *Vulgata*. In the traditional account, the English marched forward, re-established their position, and then had to loose a volley of arrows into the French in order to provoke their charge. As the last chapter discussed, this process would have taken a significant amount of time, and the traditional account asks us to believe that the French stood by, watching it happening and doing nothing.

I obviously don't think that the *Vulgata* is right about this at all.

The Chaplain is.

Historians have tried to find a reason for the *Gesta* to be wrong and the *Vulgata* to be right here. The usual excuse is that the Chaplain was behind the lines and couldn't see what was really going on. That he was behind the lines is correct, but we know he was on horseback and that the men between him and the battle were on foot. We also know that the lines were only four men deep. He wasn't on foot behind some insurmountable wall. He could see everything, probably a lot better than anyone not in the first line. He also had the ability to talk to the men involved at all levels of the fight as soon as the battle was done. This is exactly the point one historian makes when he argues that we should trust the *Gesta*: 'as a royal chaplain, its author was in an exceptionally good position to know the truth'.[63] To assume that this same fellow could have completely missed a 700-yard march, the resetting of lines, the need to provoke the French with an arrow volley, and the long minutes it all had taken – as that very historian actually turns around and does – begs *a lot* of questions.

So instead let's listen to the man who was there. As soon as it was clear the English were advancing, the French set out to meet them.

The *Gesta* is right.

There was no unopposed English advance.

This means other sources are wrong – or at least we're wrong in how we've understood them – because they describe an unopposed English advance. This is a problem, and to solve it we need to follow the *Gesta* further into the action.

Our eyewitness tells us that Clignet's French cavalry, 'posted on the flanks', struck the English first. Their target was the 'archers who were on both sides of our army'.[64] Boucicaut planned to press the attack on the archers at just one side: a mounted charge would hit the English right and roll it back and off the field. Why had Boucicaut planned to hit just one side? It's hard to say, because we don't know if the plan we have was tied to a specific piece of terrain that would have precluded a charge on the left side as well. Assuming that was not the case, it could be that Boucicaut only felt he had cavalry enough to strike one side. Or it could have been that he only had to dislodge one side of the archers to break Henry's formation, so rather than splitting his strength he put everything he had into a hammer blow that would be sure to finish the job. I favour this latter option, but I confess it's only because it's what I would do.

In any case, on the day of the battle, the cavalry hit both sides, 'like two sharp horns', Tito Livio Frulovisi says. And they were stopped in their tracks and scattered, 'forced to retreat in terror'.[65]

I'll come back to how and why Clignet's charge failed in the next chapter, because it is tremendously important. There is a case to be made that the battle of Agincourt, as soon as the cavalry was turned back, went from a likely English defeat to a likely English victory.

First, we need to establish where the English lines were at this crucial point.

The *Gesta* tells us that a scant few of the French cavalry slipped 'through between the archers and woodlands', but they otherwise failed.[66] Under the onslaught of English arrows, the vast majority were either killed or turned back or – and this is the important bit for now! – driven onto the stakes protecting the archers. Tito Livio Frulovisi and many other sources, including our additional eyewitnesses, Waurin and Le Fèvre, confirm this.[67] Horses died on the stakes.

The *Vulgata* claims that this indicates the stakes had been moved forward when the English advanced across the field and then were reset at the forward position. But the Chaplain says nothing of archers pulling or resetting stakes. He doesn't have them changing their lines at all: when Henry 'advanced towards the enemy ... the enemy, too, advanced towards him'.[68] There would be no time for resetting lines or driving stakes. As soon as the English started out, the French were coming. So the stakes cannot have been moved.

This means one of two things. The first is that the English advanced from the line of stakes in order to provoke the French to attack but then fell back to their original position once that attack began. This has a Hollywood appeal: it's a clever 'surprise' tactic of just the sort that shows up repeatedly in films whose stars don't wear helmets in battle. In reality, though, it is dreadfully difficult to pull off. Feigned retreats occur in warfare, but they require practice and precision to ensure that a pretend retreat doesn't turn into a very real one. This might be reason enough to rule it out at Agincourt, though we can also add to it that no source on either side mentions this tactic. And a feigned retreat was uncommon enough – and would be impressive enough – that, had it been used, it would surely have been noted by *someone*.

The second possibility is much more likely: that the English advanced only *part* of their line. The centre moved forward, but the wings of archers – safe behind their stakes – did not. Henry needed to provoke a French attack, and there's no question that advancing his centre would be provocative. It weakened his position. Think back to Crécy, where Edward had been able to use his wide wings of archers to funnel the French knights – wave after wave – into his sturdy centre of dismounted knights. It was a powerful plan, and it was absolutely destroying the French until his son, the future Black Prince, led the vanguard forward, reducing the effectiveness of the longbow onslaught: the further the English advanced, the less threatening the English archers became; the last thing they wanted to do was shoot their own lords. Here at Agincourt, Henry had done his best to replicate Edward's initial plan, but the French had learned their lesson from 1346 and hadn't charged into the teeth of his tactical defence. Only by giving up some of his strength could he hope to provoke the immediate fight he needed.

This basic, common-sense conclusion – that Henry sacrificed a positional advantage to convince the French to do the same – is another strike against the *Vulgata*. In that theoretical engagement, the English forward position would be more advantageous for the English than their initial position one, making it even less likely for the French to take the bait. *No man is a fool.*

But even more important was this: the English centre consisted of England's highest lords, fabulously wealthy men whose capture would make their enemies both rich and the subject of legend. And amid them all was the king himself, dangling like a priceless jewel just outside the reach of the greedy knights of the French vanguard, a prize just too tempting to pass up, no matter the risk. The forward movement of the English banners was like waving a red flag at a bull.

Henry's centre advanced alone.

The archers on his wings remained in position safe behind their stakes. Beginning at their forward-most ends, they began to receive and repel the mounted charge of the French. The archers in the wedges, meanwhile, advanced with the centre. Theirs was a precarious position, though their light armour and mobility meant that they could pull back into the lines of men-at-arms if needed. They weren't just widening the English centre, then, but they were also serving as skirmishers.[69] This would put them 'in front', as the *Chronicle of Ruisseauville* describes, where they were 'always firing on the French'.[70]

The English centre cannot have advanced far, as they would not have wanted to open wide gaps between their wings of archers and their centre. But if the movement succeeded in provoking an almost immediate French advance – as the Chaplain says it did – then they needn't have gone far: the two lines were coming to meet one another. If the lines began 500 yards apart, that would mean each advanced roughly 250 yards. The *Gesta* later tells us that at the point of collision both sides had 'advanced towards one another over roughly the same distance'.[71]

Here, I suspect that the Chaplain, unable to observe the field from a bird's-eye view, may have confused time and distance. He could see both lines move towards each other until they collided. But even accounting for the mud, the French were crossing the land faster: the cavalry reached the forward tips of the English wings long before the English centre would be engaged – they were closer, and horses cover more ground than men. One historian has argued that the French cavalry at Agincourt covered roughly 325 yards in three minutes.[72] The English on foot would have taken roughly 11 minutes to cover the same distance.[73]

The Chaplain is right that the lines more or less set off against each other at the same time, but the exact distances that each side covered before they met would not have been equal. If the English advanced 30 yards, the French horses, their hooves spraying mud, would have gone something like 110 yards – and together they would have covered 140 yards.

Looking at a reconstruction of the landscape and our previous information, about 600 yards initially separated the English centre from the French lines – 'scarcely two or three bow shots', with the French taking an initial position south of Azincourt. The French covered far more of this distance than the English.

Why do I think the French covered more ground? Part of it is the speed. Part of it is that our sources talk again and again about the French struggling through the mud while the English remained 'fresh and unwearied as they had not moved from their advantageous position', as one anonymous French chronicler put it in the 1430s.[74]

And part of it is something that looks like a snag in my notion of a battle positioned further to the south.

THE SNAG AND THE SOLUTION

Okay, so there's one piece of evidence that doesn't appear to fit my locating the battle *south* of the road between the castle of Azincourt and the hamlet of Tramecourt. This evidence comes from Tito Livio Frulovisi, an Italian who had come to England and entered the service of the duke of Gloucester around 1436. Just a couple of years later, he wrote a glowing biography of the duke's brother, Henry V – and, by extension, the duke himself. I've cited it numerous times in this book already. Here, in the standard translation of his text, is what he says about the English advance: 'When within twenty paces of the town of Agincourt they came to the French enemy, with a most sounding of trumpets, they all roused their souls to the fight, they fell upon the enemy and the battle commenced.'[75]

This evidence would no doubt be an important argument against any attempt to shift the battle of Agincourt away from its *Vulgata* reconstruction: assuming that 'the town of Agincourt' here refers more or less to the known location of the castle of Azincourt, and that his 'pace' is something akin to Roman paces (20 of them being just over 32 yards), then Frulovisi provides eminently geo-locatable data and fits the tradition interpretation perfectly.

It doesn't fit my southern location at all.

So, am I totally and irredeemably wrong? It's possible. Despite my best efforts to collect and analyse the evidence for Agincourt I might well be mistaken.

But that would still mean the English marched up to within *30 yards* of a French castle without that fortification playing any role or notice in the battle whatsoever.

This idea boggles the mind. There *must* be another option.

There is.

The standard translation of Tito Livio Frulovisi might be wrong.

Here's the Latin:

> *Et cum ad viginti passus ad oppidum Agincourt ad Gallos hostes devenissent, cum tubicinum clangor maximus ad praelium omnium animos excitat, occurrunt hostes, initur praelium.*[76]

And here's the literal translation:

> And when they had gone about 20 paces towards the town of Agincourt, towards the French host, a great blast of trumpets urges them all to battle. They come together. The battle is begun.

Frulovisi isn't telling us that Henry's army advanced 20 paces *from* Azincourt, but rather that they advanced 20 paces *towards* Azincourt.

This is no small difference.

Instead of being an objection to changing the *Vulgata* account, what Frulovisi is telling us could be one more reason to do so: an advance just 20 paces towards Azincourt would fit perfectly with everything else we've concluded about a more southern battle.

It's *not* a snag.

It's yet another clue.

So why does the standard translation read otherwise? I don't know, but I can say that we must never start with the conclusion. If we *assume* a location 20 paces or so from Azincourt, it's easy enough to make a translation – consciously or not – that matches this assumption.

Regardless, the standard translation is *not* what Tito Livio Frulovisi actually wrote.

What he describes is the battle beginning after an English advance of only about 20 paces from their initial line at Maisoncelle.

We've had the battle of Agincourt in the wrong spot.

13

The Battle, 25 October

A limitation of writing is that it can only describe one thing at a time, and the important actions at Agincourt occurred simultaneously.

Boucicaut's plan called for the dismounted men-at-arms to march on the English simultaneously with the cavalry attacks. On the day of the battle, the French did just this: a unified, combined action that meant that men were marching while horses were charging. The English responded, and all of it was contextualized by thousands of individual men having thousands of individual reactions to what they were seeing, hearing, smelling, feeling.

It's important to emphasize the enormity of the gap that exists between my role as a historian trying to see the 'big picture' of Agincourt and the experience of the men who were there. Their individual stories are often set aside – not always deliberately – but they should not be forgotten. I considered writing this chapter in a second-by-second manner, seen from both sides.[1] Such a splintered story might evoke the chaos and fragmented experience of life and death in the heat of battle, where existence shrinks to a dark tunnel lit by flashes of recognition, steeped in instinct amid the fog of war. But this would be disjointed and confusing – just as individual experiences are – and it would thwart my production of a coherent narrative that describes the totality of what was happening at Agincourt. I mention it only so that you will have it in the back of your mind as you read my favoured point of view: from the English side.

Basing my story on the English perspective isn't driven by nationalism. I'm an American. I don't have a dog in this fight. But the simple fact is that Henry's side is that which has been most typically favoured.[2] It's the point of view most of my readers probably expect, it's the one I've followed to this point, and I think it's the one for which we have the strongest sources.

But I will not neglect the French viewpoint. They didn't come to Agincourt to sacrifice their lives on the altar of Henry V's glory.

They came to win, and they had a coherent plan to do so.

How and why that plan went awry – how it became his glory rather than theirs – is the question I will answer.

SPEECHES AND PRAYERS

We like to imagine that Henry gave a resounding call to arms on the field of Agincourt. Shakespeare portrays this magnificently in the St Crispin's Day speech – the poetry that inspired at least one man planning for the D-Day assault centuries later.

Alas, such a grand soliloquy isn't likely.

Even if he shouted his impassioned plea from horseback, it would not be heard by all the men across the wide front of his army. So whatever words he passed on to his men were no doubt far simpler than Shakespeare has them. They were, more than likely, the same as many other leaders have said in centuries before and after. Keep strength. Keep faith. Maintain order. Trust in God and the man beside you. If you won't stand for the divine, stand for your brother.

His helmet, if Henry wore it yet, would have been opened to allow his voice to carry. Did the men, seeing his face, think on his scar from the wound at Shrewsbury? The story would have been known. For many, it had surely grown in the telling. 'He that outlives this day, and comes safe home', Shakespeare has him say, 'will strip his sleeve and show his scars'.[3] Whether reflecting anything he truly said or not, the sentiment would be powerfully implied in the mere presence of a man with such a scar to show, a man who had indeed lived and come safe home.

Whatever words he spoke, most men would have listened intently. Death felt close now, a shadow in the corner of their vision.

Their lives were in the hands of the king, the men beside them, and the divinity they imagined looking down on the field.

Prayers were said. Some out loud. Some in silence. The priests made invocations to God and the saints. The Chaplain who gave us the *Gesta* was among them.

These actions were repeated on the French side. Speeches were made and prayers were raised. Le Fèvre and Waurin tell a story about a group of 18 Frenchmen, led by Lauvelet de Masinguehem and Gaviot de Bournoville, who 'banded together' and made a pact to 'get as close as possible to the king of England that they should knock the crown right off his head' or die trying. In the battle that followed one of them succeeded, it was said, in landing 'such a heavy blow' on Henry that he knocked one of the jewels out of the crown affixed to his royal helmet. This man, along with all the rest of his sworn companions, did not live to brag about it.[4]

THE BANNERS ADVANCE

With a shout, the English banners were raised to the October sky. Their colours, flapping in the wind rolling over the hills, announced that bloodshed was eminent. No one on either side could have mistaken it.

According to Monstrelet – and followed by the eyewitnesses Waurin and Le Fèvre – Sir Thomas Erpingham, a veteran commander, now rode out in front of the English lines. He steadied his horse, looking from one end of the line to the other. Then he 'threw in the air a baton which he had been holding in his hand' and let out a great cry: 'Now strike!' After this, he hurried back to the lines, dismounted, and took his position on foot beside his banner. 'Then,' the chronicler says, 'the English began suddenly to advance uttering a great cry which much amazed the French.'[5] This response, which rippled across the field, was the order to advance banners.

A number of historians have taken this reference to French amazement as meaning that they were paralysed with awe – which explains why they didn't assault the English during their lengthy advance and resetting of their line.

But our eyewitness doesn't report anything like this, and it doesn't make sense. To the contrary, as the Chaplain says, as soon as they saw that Henry was moving forward – and with every step weakening his position – the French charged out to meet him.

If Tito Livio Frulovisi speaks truly, then the English advanced 'twenty paces' – about 32 yards – in the direction of Azincourt when 'a great blast of trumpets urged them all to battle'.

But those trumpets probably weren't English.

They were French.

Henry's gambit had worked. The enemy was sounding the charge, the provocation and the bait of the king's banner too great to ignore.

We don't know a lot about these kinds of battlefield communication in the Middle Ages. Our sources refer to trumpets, shouts, banners, and other means of communication, but they don't provide much detail about how they worked. About all we can say is that commands were being relayed (see Figure 30).

The English would have quickly perceived that the French were on their way. Provoking such an advance was the entire point of Henry making this bold move. Once he had achieved this aim, there would be no reason for him to continue moving forward, straining the distance between his vulnerable centre and the supporting wings of archers behind him. He would have ordered his men to halt in order to preserve this coverage. We cannot know for certain how far they marched before they recognized that the French were coming and made their stop. Archaeological remains could confirm this, but none have yet been found. It was probably just 40 yards – nothing like the 700 yards in the traditional account of the battle.

Most of the archers in the wings to either side did not move as Henry's men-at-arms and its two 'wedges' of archers went forward. None of our descriptions are detailed enough to know for sure, but it may be that some of the flanking archers, at the point where the wings met the centre, advanced some way alongside in order to prevent too large a gap from opening between the advanced battles and the stationary wings. But even if they did, the vast majority of the archers were still safely behind their stakes on either side, flanking the field.

And the French were coming.

From the Berry Herald's description, the initial onslaught was the French vanguard and two wings of men on either side. But because the field left little room for units to move separately, it may be that these three battles were pushed together to the point that, from the English side, it appeared as the Chaplain describes: a single line of dismounted men-at-arms trudging forward through the mud.

Driving around either side of this massive force came the French cavalry, bearing down on the wings of English archers and their stakes. It is likely that the force that drove across the field on the Tramecourt side was under the command of Clignet de Brabant, who had leadership of the cavalry entire.[6]

But light was showing through the cracks in the French plan already.

Juvénal des Ursins claims that 400 horsemen were assigned to make this attack, but 'they could find only 40'.[7] Monstrelet says there were 120 available out of a planned 800; the eyewitnesses Waurin and Le Fèvre change this to be an intended 1,000 to 1,200 with 800 actually present – though Waurin goes on to say Clignet had a mere 120 with him when he attacked.[8] The *Chronicle of Ruisseauville* is less specific but no less damning: 'It had been ordered that Clignet de Brabant and the lord of Gaucourt and several others come with a very large quantity of good men-at-arms in front of the archers and their fire so that they might break their fire, but without any doubt, only few came.'[9]

Many writing about Agincourt on the French side blamed their failure on Clignet and his failure to bring enough men for the mounted attack. This blame game taints our sources from the losing side just as much as the glory game can taint our sources from the winning side. The allegiance of our chroniclers and the expectations of their patrons should never be far from our minds.[10]

The dismounted men-at-arms were still advancing when the cavalry outpaced them and surged out ahead. Behind their stakes, the archers narrowed their eyes and nocked arrows.

The English longbowmen were veterans. Well-trained, well-disciplined. Determined.

As one man, they drew back their bowstrings.

As one man, they released them.

ARCHERS AND ARMOUR

In 1545, a warship called the *Mary Rose* sank in the Solent, the same water from which Henry V's fleet had sailed for France 130 years earlier. The discovery of the wreck led to extended underwater archaeological work – and the ship's eventual raising in 1982 – that has greatly informed our knowledge of Tudor warfare on both land and sea. Among its stores were 137 longbows, which averaged six feet six inches in height and shot 30-foot arrows (of which more than 3,500 were recovered). The draw-weight of the bows was between 100 and 185 pounds. Modern bows average something more like 60 pounds, which underscores the fact that medieval archery was a hard-won skill. Drawing the bows alone – much less aiming and shooting them in the heat of battle – required significant strength and training. The existence of so many bows on the *Mary Rose* quite obviously implies that this skill was expected of archers in the time of Henry VIII.

Just how well we can extend these draw-weights back roughly a century to the time of Henry V is an open and potentially unanswerable question. No English longbows from the early 1400s appear to have survived. Some have argued that the bows at Agincourt might have had higher draw-weights, but I find this to be unlikely. Loosing a 200-pound bow at an enemy would do significant damage if it hit, but battlefield effectiveness of the longbow came down not to accuracy but to massed volleys. This wasn't sniper work. The archer needed to be able to pull and loose again and again at a potentially high rate of speed. This is an argument for lower draw-weights rather than greater.

A recent experiment utilized a longbow with a draw-weight of 160 pounds of force – probably on the upper end of what was used by Henry's archers in 1415 – against French armour of the type used at Agincourt.[11] The test was highly informative.

The experiment used highly exact replicas of existing medieval artefacts from the period. A test dummy was dressed with a mail hauberk draped and fitted over thick fabric padding. A chest-plate, carefully crafted to match the strength and variable thickness of the metal of period examples, was strapped over it. This plate, notably, had what looks like a metal 'V' on the upper chest and running towards the collar bones. This 'stop-rib', as it's called, brilliantly deflects the chest-impacts of arrows – or the splintered remains of them when they shatter – away from neck and head. Smaller, articulated pieces of armour were strapped over the shoulders and arms. A helmet covered the head: a bascinet with a pointed visor – sometimes called a 'pig-faced' bascinet – that was built on the model of a piece in the renowned Wallace Collection in London (see Figure 17).[12]

The results of the experiment were as striking as they were expected: the plate armour protecting the chest worked as designed. Most of the arrows loosed at it, even from a relatively close range, were deflected harmlessly.[13] The plate couldn't cover everything, however. Full plate armour – what my students like to call the 'walking tank' – didn't exist in 1415. At Agincourt, the typical chest-plate ended at the waist and still left wide gaps at the shoulder joint protected only by mail. So while most of the arrows blasted *off* the plate, they blasted *through* the mail (Figure 31). Shots that struck the shoulder joints, the top of the throat, or the groin were particularly likely to kill. Even those that punctured through the thinner plate on the forearms might kill if they hit an artery – and non-mortal wounds or even arrow strikes that bent plate out of mobility could likewise incapacitate a fighter.

The Chaplain presents it simply: the cavalry was 'forced to fall back under showers of arrows'.[14] Waurin and Le Fèvre, following Monstrelet, similarly attest that the horsemen retreated 'because of the strength of the arrow fire and their fear of it'.[15] We see the same thing in the account of the Religieux – 'But at the first volley of arrows which the archers caused to rain down upon them they turned and fled'[16] – and in that of Walsingham, who explains how 'the leading horses were scattered in that great storm of hail'.[17] Similar sentiments occur across our sources: the cavalry, meant to destroy the archers, were instead driven back by them.

It was far worse than these bare descriptions suggest. Because several things were happening at once.

The horses churning through the mud were large, strong, and well-trained beasts of war. They had some rudimentary armour around their heads, chests, shoulder, and backs, but not everything could be covered. And even armour – struck with enough force in the right spot, at the right angle, at the right time – can fail. When the volleys of arrows came, some found targets. And there was no way to train the horses to ignore the pain of arrows tearing through flesh.

The same was true for the men riding them.

Exactly how many arrows drew blood is impossible to know. But there is no question that many did. And it wasn't a single volley that met the charging cavalry. It was wave after wave. The French were moving as fast as they could, but between the mud and the need to keep their lines in order, the charge at Agincourt wouldn't have been anything like the full gallop that we might see in the movies. It would have taken over two minutes for them to pass between the point where they crossed into the range of the English longbows and reached the line of stakes. As the bowmen could easily put up six shots per minute, each archer could have sent at least 13 arrows flying into a horseman before he was in danger.[18]

Worse, the ratio of English longbowmen to French cavalry wasn't one to one. If we use the largest reported number of cavalry – Waurin and Le Fèvre's 800 men – and the smallest number of archers – the *Gesta*'s 5,000 – then there were more than five archers for every mounted man.

It wasn't 13 arrows per horseman during the charge.

It was at least 65.

How many of these caused damage? The massed cavalry made for an easy target, especially when combining the size of man and beast. And tests of longbows shot against armour show it wasn't just the direct impact of the arrow that could wound or kill. Any arrow that failed to penetrate armour at its initial impact could shatter against it, the head and shaft exploding into deadly slivers spraying up and out. No less than the arrows themselves, these could also kill. This, too, has been shown in the recent experimentation of period arms and armour. One arrow struck the protective metal boxing around the helmet's eye-slit. The armour caused the arrowhead to snap off and fly away as its own projectile. The momentum of the splintered wood behind it, meanwhile, shoved the remainder of the shaft straight through the slit and into what would have been the eye and skull behind it.[19]

There is no question that most arrows would have missed their marks or failed to do more than glance off armour. But the sheer number of shots slamming into so small a force meant they were nevertheless devastating. We can only guess at numbers, but if just one in 400 shots stopped a rider – either by wounding the man or his mount or by breaking his spirit and turning him back – then the initial volley would have dropped 12 or 13 riders out of the 800 who began the charge.

The damage increased with each successive volley. Fewer men to target meant that each man drew more arrows. And as the distance to target decreased, the power behind each shot grew. At the start of the battle, the arrows sent at the French had been launched in a high parabolic arc. Falling, most shattered on the solid metal helmets and plated shoulders of the French. Here and there an arrow might have found a gap in the armour – death by unfortunate statistical probability – but for the most part the first volleys that hit the French were an annoying buzz and pounding clatter. The closer a bow gets to its target, however, the less parabolic an arc it requires. This results in arrow shots that pack more punch while also threatening armoured men more directly through the visors in their helms or the joints at the neck, shoulders, and knees – and even beginning to penetrate weak points in the strongest of helmets and heaviest of armour.[20] Strikes that had no chance of damage at the beginning of the charge might have done so easily by the end. One in 50 shots could have been turning back a rider by the time the charge was on top of the stakes. If, beginning at 260 yards, the longbowmen loosed a volley of 5,000 shots for every 20 yards that an 800-man cavalry covered, the cold maths is brutal:

- Volley 1 (5,000 shots at 260 yards; 0.25 per cent damage): 788 riders still charging.
- Volley 2 (240 yards; 0.25 per cent damage): 776 riders.
- Volley 3 (220 yards; 0.25 per cent damage): 764 riders.
- Volley 4 (200 yards; 0.5 per cent damage): 739 riders.
- Volley 5 (180 yards; 0.5 per cent damage): 714 riders.
- Volley 6 (160 yards; 0.5 per cent damage): 689 riders.
- Volley 7 (140 yards; 0.75 per cent damage): 651 riders.
- Volley 8 (120 yards; 0.75 per cent damage): 613 riders.

- Volley 9 (100 yards; 0.75 per cent damage): 575 riders.
- Volley 10 (80 yards; 1 per cent damage): 525 riders.
- Volley 11 (60 yards; 1 per cent damage): 475 riders.
- Volley 12 (40 yards; 2 per cent damage): 375 riders.
- Volley 13 (20 yards; 2 per cent damage): 275 riders.

This is using the highest reported number of riders, the lowest reported number of archers, an initial volley well short of the 300 yards that many historians assume, and a conservative estimate of the increasing rate of damage. The reality on the day of the battle was almost certainly far worse.

These two or three minutes at Agincourt catapulted the English longbow to a mythic status it still enjoys today. The French cavalry intended to sweep the archers off the field but was instead shredded by them.

The horses were screaming. So were the men.

It's hard to imagine the horror. Men were shot through – arrows ripping into the meat of shoulders and groins, shattering bones and severing arteries. Other men were flung from horses that stumbled or skittered from wounds of their own. The lucky few who made it through to the archers faced grim odds. The stakes could impale the horses whose riders tried to drive through. Riders who attempted to over-leap the deadly line fared no better: it would be a hard jump for a fresh horse under the best of circumstances, but the mud would have made it near impossible. Those who reined in and angled across the front of the stakes – reaching out with their lances to try to knock them down or run through the archers behind them – would have been subject to pummelling, point-blank shots from the longbows. Waurin tells us of the fate of those unhorsed after they reached the English line. They 'fell to the ground amongst the archers, who killed them immediately'.[21] Could riders have weaved their way through the stakes? On dry, unguarded ground, perhaps. But this wasn't some heroic fantasy. It was all the French could do to stay in the saddle. Juvénal des Ursins succinctly describes the horrible reality: 'When the horses felt themselves pierced by arrows, they could no longer be controlled by their riders.'[22]

Every second further snowballed the disaster. Those who hadn't already fallen retreated: 'when they had made their course against the archers they turned back,' the *Chronicle of Ruisseauville* explains, 'because of the arrowfire which their horses could no longer endure.'[23] Still the arrows came. General volleys no more, they were now specifically targeted, as the archers took steady aim at the backs of the men in flight.

THE NEXT WAVE

In the meantime, the first line of dismounted French men-at-arms had been trudging forward through the mud. It would have already been exhausting work, but the cavalry ahead of them had churned the field into a pockmarked morass. As the cavalry dissolved in the hail of arrows, bodies of men and horses littered the ground with grisly obstacles. These corpses did far worse than impede the infantry's progress; the sight of them sapped their morale.

Worse, a great many of the cavalry weren't fallen. They were clinging to the reins of wounded mounts careening away from the English in panic. These huge, maddened beasts bolted away from the flanking wings of punishing archers, funnelled straight into the middle of the field, where they crashed headlong into the advancing line of the vanguard on foot, forcing those in the mud to dodge and scatter to avoid being run down. And each man who darted away pushed and jostled into still more men, sending a shivering wave through the ranks that slowed and disrupted even those men well away from the pain-maddened horses. Le Fèvre says the vanguard suffered 'great disarray' as 'countless numbers of men-at-arms began to fall'.[24]

The dismounted line of French shook and slowed, but the brave men in it still tried to press on, to do their duty and fulfil their mission.

The Chaplain tells us that batteries of crossbows positioned behind and on either side of this advance tried to shoot at the English lines, to soften them up and slow the onslaught of arrows. Here was a lesson learned from Crécy, where the crossbowmen had been sent in first and been viciously mauled by missiles. Instead, the armoured men-at-arms at Agincourt were meant to take the brunt of the attack, giving the crossbows behind the time and space they needed to load and loose in a combined arms assault.

It didn't work. The crossbows loosed, but their bolts 'did injury to very few' before a volley from the answering longbows sent them scrambling back.[25]

Between, the main lines were closing.

According to the Chaplain, the French assault broke into thirds in order to attack the English lines.[26] Here we must recall the English formation, with its three battles of infantry and the two wedges of archers between them. The struggling French, as they finally got close, were shying away from the archers and trying to plunge into the armoured English instead. From above, the French advance might have looked something like a trident trying to shove its points through the paper-thin tissue of Henry's lines.

Why were the French going for the English men-at-arms and not just overrunning the archers? It's often said that this is because there was no honour in killing archers.[27] There was undoubtedly more honour in killing – and certainly more money in capturing – the men of high status. But few men in the mortal immediacy of combat make decisions on such objective terms. For most, decisions are born of the bare instinct of survival. As one historian has said, 'if the knights and esquires of the vanguard had begun the battle with that attitude, it cannot have survived this long'.[28] As the French advanced on the English, they were walking into higher and higher probabilities of harm from the archers that they could not immediately reach with their own close-combat weapons. It wasn't a lack of bravery or a sense of social standing that made the French shy back from the hurtling points. It was natural instinct and common sense.

Pushed together, the French collapsed into a tighter and tighter space.[29] Men tripped and fell in the muck. Here and there someone might have tried to help a friend back to his feet, but there was little hope in the press. Men were stepped over if they were lucky, stepped on if they were not. Boots on backs pressed faces down into the thick soup of the mud. The armour that helped to protect them from the arrows was little more than an anchor now. Many breathed their last drowning in sodden, choking earth.

The English arrows now slowed significantly from the volleys that turned back the French cavalry. Whatever ammunition they'd had when they left Harfleur, it had already been reduced during encounters on their march across northern France. And they had surely spent heavily from the remainder in repelling the charging horses. Each shot had to count now, and the commanders of the archers were no doubt conserving as much as they could from volleys in favour of the devastation of the close-range attacks.

Rather than a constant hail of arrows, we should imagine longer stretches when no shots were loosed and the only sounds were the screams of the wounded as they died, the grunting of the living as they strained forward, and the shouts of the commanders as they tried in vain to keep the line organized. And then, to the horror of the French, a shout rose from the English archers, followed by:

> the terrifying thrum of 5,000 bowstrings singing in unison, the rushing sound of feathered shafts flying up then falling down, a sudden darkening of the light as the arrow-cloud obscured the sun, a deafening clatter of steel on steel, like the heaviest imaginable hail against a tin roof, mingling with a chorus of curses and screams as some of the arrow-tips sank into flesh.[30]

The French pushed on as they could, heads bowed against the driving storm of metal and shattered wood. Waurin and Le Fèvre tell us they didn't 'dare uncover themselves or look up' for fear of having shots penetrate their visors.[31] All a man could see through these narrow slits was the back of the man in front, the mud between, and here and there the shapes of the dead they trampled over. All he could take into his lungs through the tiny breathing holes was his own breath, thickened to choking by fear, the heat of labour, and the scents of blood, piss, and shit both animal and human.

'Many of the French fell,' Walsingham says, 'pierced with arrows, here fifty, there sixty'.[32] Still they pressed on. At first they had faced arrows only from one of the flanking wings; they were now struck from left and right as they came into range and the wedges opened on them. 'Our archers notched their sharp-pointed arrows,' the Chaplain writes, 'and loosed them into the enemy flanks.'[33]

THE MELEE AND THE HEAPS OF DEAD

It's hard for us to imagine the difficulties that each man in the French vanguard had endured to this point. Those still unpierced by arrows were probably bruised despite the thick padding beneath their metal armour. Even those lucky few entirely untouched by the archers would have been exhausted in body and traumatized in mind. 'A truly hellish experience', as one historian describes it – likely too horrific for us to imagine.[34]

But many had made it through. And though their numbers were winnowed, they still outnumbered the English.

This was France's last chance for victory.

The English lines were only four deep. The French could see the standard of the king of England, and Henry himself beside it – a jewelled crown gleaming from atop his helmet. All they needed to do was to reach him. Kill or capture him and it would be over.

The duke of Gloucester, Henry's brother, fought close beside the king. The Chaplain reports that 'he was seriously wounded. And no wonder among so many furiously wielded swords, spears, and axes!'[35] Elmham adds that he was struck 'in the groin', that 'gore flowed down from the sword', and that Henry 'stood over him' to save his life.[36]

Henry himself was indeed in the thick of the fighting. Elmham says that amid the 'great throng of people' fighting, 'the crown of the king was broken off his helmet by an axe'.[37] Later retellings, perhaps inevitably, increase the drama of the moment. It was the duke of Alençon who knocked a jewel from Henry's crown, said some. Others claimed that the king's helmet was cleft in two. In still others, the king was saved by the heroic actions of the Welshman Davy Gam. Like most legends, such stories have a kernel of truth at their root. The Welshman Dafydd ap Llewelyn, an old and reviled enemy of Owain Glyndŵr, had indeed aligned himself with Henry and died on the field at Agincourt. That he gained a new life under Tudor writers should not surprise us: they had a vested interest in showing any connection possible between a 'loyal' Wales and the English crown.

On the day, the outcome hung on a knife's edge. The English position was so thin, so perilously situated, that if it broke and the French gained the English backfield – anywhere along the line – there is little question that all would be doomed.

Both sides knew it.

So the English had to hold along their entire line.

Not a man could give way.

We can see from the reconstruction of the English formation and its placement on the battlefield that the French attack would not be equally weighted across the line. Any attack on Henry's left had to be made through the shallow valley of the *Morival*, an exceedingly difficult prospect. Those attacking Henry's right, however, came across even, flat ground.

What we can reconstruct of the English casualties confirms this lopsidedness. Henry placed his vanguard – his best fighters – on his right, under the veteran command of the duke of York. The duke died in the fighting along with a quarter of his retinue. We aren't certain where Sir Richard Kyghley fell, but evidence suggests he, too, was on the English right. By contrast, the English left was commanded by Thomas, Lord Camoys, who didn't lose a single man. Reconstructing the French losses is more difficult, but it appears that the French facing the English right – led by the count of Vendôme, who was captured – likewise 'suffered very heavy losses'.[38]

The fighting was now desperate on both sides. Everyone knew what was at stake. Many of the French were using axes.[39] Others were using lances that they had cut down for close combat.[40] Many of the English men-at-arms were holding them off with spears. Hollywood may favour the clash of swords, but the tangle of staff weapons was a far more common sight on the medieval battlefield.

Most of the English lives were lost 'in the first fight', as Tito Livio Frulovisi describes the initial impact of the lines.[41] Such was the weight of that charge, that mass of men, that according to the Chaplain the English line staggered backwards 'almost a spear's length'.[42]

The English formation bent. It trembled.

But it didn't break.

And then it began to push back.

The French and English used different weapons, but this wasn't what turned the battle. The English success, both in holding against the French attack, and then in rallying to shove them back, comes down to energy.[43] True, the English were exhausted from their long march across France under deplorable conditions. But when we focus on just this day, the English lines were fresh, on the upswing of their adrenaline rush. The French, after the horrible slog through the mud and the harrowing storm of arrows, were on the other side of that same slope. They were, as various sources report, 'worn out', 'exhausted', 'much worn down', and 'so worn out they could scarcely move'.[44]

Few in the French front line survived the collision. Pushed backwards by the English, pushed forward by their countrymen, they struggled for footing. Slipping. Falling. Pinioned by spears. Stacked up and then smothered in the mud. And whenever one man went down – living or dead – more surged over him.

The uneven landscape of the bodies added to the uneasy footing in the most desperate moments of men's lives.

There was no means for the lords in the French second battle to know the fate of those at the front of the first. All they knew was the noise of the fighting, the plan of attack, and the wavering banner of the king of England, under the assault of their countrymen. They must have thought the weight of their numbers and the strength of their arms could yet turn the tide.

Were they also prodded into the fight by one or both of the supposed ambushes that the English had laid upon the field? Perhaps. But even without those surprises, they had every reason to go forward.

On they came, wading through whatever arrows the English archers had held back, desperate to engage on the front line themselves.

It wasn't foolish given what they knew then.

But it was a disaster given what we know now.

The men of the vanguard no longer had anywhere to go. Retreat was impossible with the next wave of men pushing at their backs. Pinned between enemy and friend, they died. As the Chaplain explains in the *Gesta*:

> so great was the undisciplined violence and pressure of the mass of men behind that the living fell on top of the dead, and others falling on top of the living were killed as well, with the result that, in each of the three places where the strong contingents guarding our standards were, such a great heap grew of the slain and of those lying crushed in between.[45]

Stories of medieval battles often refer to piles of bodies. At Agincourt, the stories were true. And, astonishingly, many of those bodies still breathed – even in the piles, their armour could still potentially save them from being crushed.[46] Among them was the count of Richemont, who survived after being 'pulled from under the dead, a little wounded, being recognized by his coat of arms even though it was all bloody, for two or three had been killed over him'.[47] Waurin and Le Fèvre tell us that the duke of Orléans was also found deep in the piles, when the victors were 'turning over bodies'.[48]

Most were not so lucky. The French poem *Le pastoralet* says the dead were 'sleeping, one on top of the other, in piles, heaps, some lying upwards, some face down', and that many of them 'died lying among the dead without receiving a single blow'.[49] On the English side, John Hardyng claims that those 'slain unsmitten' by the press of bodies were 'thousands more' than those killed by weapons.[50]

These heaps of corpses were now a grisly battleground of their own – a high ground of the dead in a sea of churned mud. The Chaplain describes the English climbing atop them, using the height advantage to butcher 'their enemies down below with swords, axes, and other weapons'.[51]

By now, many of the archers were out of arrows, and those who still had a few arrows left couldn't loose them into the bloody mix of the melee without risking hitting their own. They dropped their bows. Taking anything they had at hand – including even stakes that they pulled and used as clubs – they collapsed in on the enemy and surrounded them, hacking, slashing, and pounding.

Daggers were pressed into groins and necks, digging and sawing at arteries. Blades were pushed into the eye-slits of visors, searching out eyes. Visors were ripped open, exposing faces to mallets raised and brought down again and again.

And everywhere the mud grew deeper, fed by a growing wellstream of blood. Wounded men clawed through it, grimly seeking the safety of an island of flesh on which to stand and fight.

The fighting cannot have lasted long. The *Chronicle of Ruisseauville* says that the whole of the battle lasted a mere half-hour,[52] but this may be referring only to the horrors of the actual melee.

More reasonable for the totality of the fight is the two to three hours found in the *Gesta* and in the account of Tito Livio Frulovisi, who says that no one 'who came into combat during the three hours did so without slaying or being slain himself'.[53]

KILLING THE PRISONERS

The duke of Brabant had stopped the previous night at Lens, which was not far from Aubigny. There, according to Dynter, he was told that the fight would happen 'before mid-day' on 25 October some 36 miles away. After hearing this, 'he had ridden day and night fearing that he would arrive too late'.[54] It was a hard ride. His mount was winded when he made a last-minute stop in a thicket just ahead of the battlefield. He could probably hear the sounds of the trumpets that were sending the first men into the fight. Despite the cold air of the late-October morning, steam rose from his horse's flanks, lathered at the contact points with tack and rider. He had made it, but outpaced the men carrying his battle kit: the finest armour he could afford and a slew of items bearing his coat of arms, including a coat of armour that he would have worn over his body armour, and a flag that would have been carried by his bannerman. These were the dog-tags of their day: the identifiers of who a man was and, if he surrendered on the field, the potential guarantees of his safety by relaying – whether his captor spoke the same language or not – that this was a man of status who ought to be spared in return for a ransom. All of this was still miles away. Brabant could see that the battle was happening now. If he waited for his kit, it might be over before he could help. So the 31-year-old duke improvised. He donned another man's armour. One of his trumpeters had managed to keep up with him, and the duke seized the decorative banner that hung down from his instrument. He tore a hole in it and pulled it over his head as a makeshift coat armour. Then, jumping back into the saddle, he rode out into the fray, following the churned trail of Clignet's cavalry.

We don't know for certain when he arrived on the field, but it was probably near the battle's end.[55] Soon after he got there, he was unhorsed and surrounded. Though he hardly looked the part of a duke with his improvised gear, it was clear he had some connection to wealth. So he was spared.

For the moment.

Across the field, other mercies were beginning to take place as more and more of the French surrendered. The French second battle had only served to crush the first, and then it, too, had been beaten bloody. Those able to retreat slogged their way back towards their initial position, their lives saved only by the archers having no arrows left to plunge into their backs. With the French driven back, the English began to realize they had achieved the impossible.

They had won.

As the threat of death gave way to relief at the prospect of living, thoughts turned to the riches still to be won – the taking of prisoners, the securing of ransoms.

We don't know nearly enough about how this process worked. But Agincourt does give us some clues.

We can assume that those attempting to surrender dropped their arms and fell to their knees. In presenting an imaginative fight between the king of England and the duke of Alençon, Michael Drayton's 1627 poem, *The Battaile of Agincourt*, gives a sense of how chaotic this moment could be. After a dramatic back and forth of blows, 'redoubling thwack on thwack', Henry manages to put the duke on the ground:

> The king thus made the master of the fight,
> The duke calls to him as he there does lie:
> 'Henry, I'll pay my ransom, do me right!
> I am the duke Alençon, it is I!'
> The king to save him put all his might,
> Yet the rude soldiers with their shout and cry,
> Quite drowned his voice, his helmet being shut,
> And that brave duke into small pieces was cut.[56]

Whenever a surrender was accepted without incident, as Le Fèvre and Waurin both note, the prisoners 'had their helmets removed'.[57] This would be a clear sign that they were at the mercy of their captors: a disarmed man without head protection is easy to kill.

The prisoners would have been removed through the battle lines to designated spaces. The Frenchman Ghillebert de Lannoy reports that when he was wounded and taken prisoner in the battle he was 'kept under guard for [a] while' before he was removed to a house – one in Maisoncelle, we assume – with ten to twelve of his wounded countrymen.[58] Such holding areas may not always have been physical. Prisoners were bound by metaphysical boundaries as well: men surrendered upon their honour, and by this they were supposed to be duty-bound. Many of them, no doubt, kept their eyes to the sodden ground for fear of looking into eyes they knew and seeing their failure known.

Only a few men would have stood guard over them during the initial fighting. In those early stages there weren't many men whom Henry could spare for such a task. Every hand was needed in the fight. Could the prisoners slip away, foregoing their honour and re-arming themselves to engage the English once more? Possibly. The Chaplain remarks that 'it was said among the army' that some of the French, 'even of their more nobly born ... that day surrendered themselves more than ten times'.[59] This could suggest that men taken prisoner were re-entering the fray, or it could mean that in the confusion multiple English were claiming a single surrendering man as prisoner – and that the captured man offered himself up to each one of them in hope of staying alive.

As the French lines dissolved, more and more men would have been available for the task of watching the growing numbers of prisoners. Those captured, we must remember, had a worth literally counted in coins: the higher their rank, the larger the sum they would fetch in ransom. For many of the men on campaign, this was the goal they most hoped to achieve. A city like Harfleur was a prize for princes, but a rich man's ransom was something even the lowest-born might hope to claim. Such a reward made warfare the ultimate lottery ticket for the common soldier.

In spite of all these incentives, Henry, as the battle was in its final stages, ordered the prisoners killed. No one disagrees on this point.

It was a mass execution.

We may argue whether it was justified, but we must not let that cover over what happened: helpless men were murdered.

His men balked at the order. It's nice to think they hesitated because they thought the killings immoral. Far more likely, they saw it as voluntarily setting fire to a pile of money. A living man could net 'a large ransom', as Waurin and Le Fèvre point out.[60] Families paid far less for the return of a loved one's corpse.

When the English hesitated, the king ordered an esquire with 200 archers at his command to do the dirty work: 'in cold blood, all those noble Frenchmen were killed and their heads and faces cut, which was an amazing sight to see.'[61]

Among those disarmed prisoners without a helm was the duke of Brabant, whose improvised heraldic surcoat – a trumpeter's banner with a hole cut in it for his head – had saved his life amid the tumult. That simple heraldry was enough to spare him and make him a prisoner, but he had not identified himself as the actual duke of Brabant. Any French who recognized him kept their silence. Their thinking is clear: his ransom as a man of Brabant's court would be far less than his ransom as the duke himself. The silence of his comrades saved him money.

Did he nevertheless cry out his identity when weapons began swinging at exposed heads, as Alençon did in the poem? Almost certainly.

It didn't matter. The killers thought it the act of a desperate man, seizing on any story he could to save his life.

Dynter tells us that when the duke was found in the following days, well away from the main areas of fighting, his only wounds had been to the face and throat.[62] Like so many others, he had been brutally executed.

Why had Henry done all this?

Because he thought he had to.

The Chaplain claims that Henry gave the order as the English searched through the 'heaps' of bodies 'to separate the living from the dead, intending to hold them as prisoners for ransom':

> But then, all at once, because of what wrathfulness on God's part no one knows, a shout went up that the enemy's mounted rearguard (in incomparable number and still fresh) were re-establishing their position and line of battle in order to launch an attack on us, few and weary as we were. And immediately,

> regardless of distinction of person, the prisoners, save for the dukes of Orléans and Bourbon, certain other illustrious men who were in the king's 'battle', and a very few others, were killed by the swords either of their captors or of others following after, lest they should involve us in utter disaster in the fighting that would ensue.[63]

The Chaplain removes blame from Henry by chalking it up to 'God's wrathfulness'. Why did such a tragedy happen? Because God was angry at the French, of course.

Elmham provides a similar account without the theology:

> The French fell before the power of the English. Flight from there was not open to them. They killed them, they captured them and keep them for ransoming but quickly there was a shout that a new battle would begin. Many new battle lines threatened to enter the fray to fight against the weary. There was indeed a great throng of people. The English killed the French they had taken prisoner for the sake of protecting their rear.[64]

We get the same story from our eyewitnesses Waurin and Le Fèvre: the rearguard, along with men who had 'previously been put to flight, regrouped. They had had with them a large number of standards and ensigns and showed signs of wanting to fight, marching forward in battle order.'[65] It looked like the very thing the English had done to start the battle: advance banners. And the English, though for the moment victorious, were in no condition to take on another fight.

Tito Livio Frulovisi sees the same cause. There was the potential of 'another army of the enemy, no less than the first' threatening the English, who 'were exhausted by so long and hard a fight'. Potentially outnumbered by their prisoners, the English couldn't risk a situation where they would fight 'both the prisoners and the enemy', so they killed their captives. He does, however, add a twist:

> Meanwhile, the most prudent king sent heralds to the French of the new army asking whether they would come to fight or would leave the field, informing them that if they did not withdraw, or

> if they came to battle, all of the prisoners and any of them who might be captured, would all be killed by the sword with no mercy. He informed them of this. They, fearing the English and fearing for themselves, departed with great sadness at their shame.[66]

The killing was, if this is true, both a defensive act and an offensive act. If an attack came, Henry needed his own men at the front of the lines, not guarding prisoners behind them. But if he could prevent the attack entirely by frightening off the enemy, that was even better.

There is no question that the remaining third battle on the French side – the rearguard – had yet to engage in the battle. Around the same time as the killing of the prisoners, this force withdrew from the field. None of that is at issue. Only the timing and the rationale are murky.

In the years to come, accusations of cowardice and disloyalty were flung at the men in that rearguard as the French attempted to explain the incomprehensible loss of the battle and to assign blame for it. 'Instead of marching to the aid of their companions who were yielding,' the Religieux complains, 'they heard only their terror. No longer having anyone to lead them, they abandoned in cowardice the field of battle. This ignominious flight brought upon them eternal opprobrium.'[67] Would it really have made any difference to the outcome if they had gone in?

Maybe.

Counter-factual hypotheticals are, as a rule, unprovable. This is especially true for something so inherently unpredictable as battle. That said, the *Gesta* records that the third line was mounted – 'as if more ready to flee than to tarry'.[68] This they eventually did do, as the Chaplain knew. But if they had instead charged the English army, those horses might have snatched victory from the jaws of defeat: the initial French cavalry charge had been destroyed by the English longbows, but at this point it is doubtful that any archer on the field had two good arrows to rub together. The ground was still muddy, it was true, but if the rearguard, rested and fresh, had managed to make an organized charge across the field they might well have punched a hole in the tired English lines and brought ruin upon them.[69]

And Henry V surely knew it.

What he didn't know was that this was exceedingly unlikely. The men of rank had worked hard to be in the vanguard and the second battle – 'a ghastly mistake', as an early anonymous chronicler said.[70] With those first waves destroyed, those who remained on the field were now 'leaderless', as Pierre Fenin puts it: 'there was no control or discipline amongst their men.'[71] The odds are good that these men – younger, untitled, and less experienced – had been expecting only to serve as a pursuing force when the English fled. Shifting them into battle order might well have been a bridge too far.

Without direction and focus, the rearguard must have seen the situation as hopeless. They had just watched the 'flower of French chivalry' march across the muddy field into destruction. They could hear the screams of the wounded and the dying. The glorious banners behind which they had marched to war had been brought low, shredded and torn in the bloody morass. What good would it do for them now to lay down their lives alongside those already fallen? It may have been the honourable thing. Certainly that's what those who later blamed them wanted to argue. But honour, they might have judged, was of little value to a dead man.

If this was indeed their conclusion, it was much the same one that the king of England reached himself. The dishonour of killing the prisoners was nothing compared to his life and the lives of this men. Their position was desperate. Soldiers simply could not be spared for guard duty. It was a terrible calculus, but it had a brutal logic: guard the prisoners and die in the next phase of the battle or kill the prisoners and have a higher likelihood of surviving the next phase. Either way, they would get nothing from the prisoners, so it was better to kill them and increase their own chance of survival.

What Henry perceived as a threat depends on who tells the story. Many sources, as we've seen, say it was the simply the rearguard. But Peter Basset claims that the lord of Rivière Thibouville had 'rallied the enemy to the number of 20,000 men of war ... to give a new battle', thus provoking the executions.[72] The *Chronicle of Ruisseauville* instead says that the order was given because Clignet de Brabant had 'gathered together a large number of men-at-arms to launch another assault on the English'.[73] Dynter says it was indeed the actions of Clignet which prompted the rumour of another attack, but that he was moving back onto the field 'not to fight but to pillage'.[74] The *Chronicle of Normandy* says the killings happened because men of the duke of Anjou showed up.[75] Juvénal des Ursins instead claims there was a rumour that a second French army was coming under the duke of Brittany, expected to arrive at any minute, and that this news rallied the French still on the field.[76] That some of these rumours couldn't be true – Brittany, for instance, was in Amiens at the time – is something we can know that Henry simply could not.

Ghillebert de Lannoy was with perhaps a dozen fellow prisoners – all of them wounded – in a house close to the battlefield when the executions began. He heard that the attack of the duke of Brabant had triggered the action, which doesn't fit the stories that the duke wasn't recognized. Ghillebert's reminiscence is useful, however, for informing us that there was no single means of executing the helpless prisoners. Rather than take the time to kill him and his fellows individually, the English set fire to the house around them. Ghillebert managed to drag himself 'a few feet away from the fire', where he was later found and captured by the English again.[77]

Pierre Fenin, probably writing in the 1430s, suggested a connection between the order to kill the prisoners and the attack on the English baggage train, which made the English fear 'that the French would come upon them to do them harm'. It's not quite an immediate cause-and-effect connection, however, as Fenin is clear that the attack on the baggage occurred closer to the start of the battle rather than its end.[78]

Some modern commentators have nevertheless picked up on the attack on the baggage as an excuse for the killing. When Henry learned of his encampment being hit, the thinking goes, he was enraged at the dishonourable act and took vengeance with a dishonourable act of his own.

Strange logic. It's hard to see the murder of captive men as an equivalent to stealing goods, no matter how precious. If Henry believed this, it doesn't paint him in a very good light. It certainly runs counter to the popular Shakespearean imagery of him as a man of the people rather than a royal who regarded the lower classes as little more than useful meat.

The assault on his baggage train cost him money. He had been robbed, made poorer. We are meant to believe that he would avenge himself against this loss of money by murdering prisoners who were ... worth more money? This is nonsensical. A victim of theft does not throw away the rest of his money to spite the robber.

Worse, the men he was killing had little to do with the attack on the baggage. Remember: the man who was literally there in the rear of the lines – the author of the *Gesta* – doesn't attribute the baggage raid to the French army Henry was fighting.

So what was it that frightened Henry so much?

The English were trapped and forced to fight at Agincourt. Their enemies were in all directions, and French forces had been arriving up to the last minute before the battle began. That rumours would swirl about new armies on the way seems inevitable and, under the circumstances, completely believable.

Whether the immediate threat was the rearguard shifting as they planned their next move in light of the obvious French defeat, or something else entirely, the result was the same. Henry saw a potential threat. He did the maths. He ordered the executions.

And the remaining threat of the rearguard – whether in despair or in fright – withdrew. As they did so, the executions stopped. The prisoners lucky enough to survive would now be subject to ransom.

The battle of Agincourt was over.

VICTORY

It's common for medieval battles to end in rout: when one army breaks and runs, the other pursues – often riding them down on horseback. As the remaining French withdrew at Agincourt, some English did pursue them: as our eyewitnesses, Waurin and Le Fèvre note, 'most of those who were mounted did survive, but those on foot suffered many deaths'.[79]

But the English didn't pursue the French far. Henry was still concerned about keeping his battle line ready. By superior tactics, superb leadership, and not a little dumb luck, Henry had managed to overcome the relatively small numbers of his men-at-arms.

But these would be the men most likely to take to horse in the pursuit. As shown by his order to execute the prisoners, he was well aware that his position was weak. He could not afford to lose even a hundred of his surviving men-at-arms to the chase – however temporary – when there remained a possibility of fresh attack from more French forces.

By late afternoon Henry's confidence that he held the field unchallenged was rising. The French were beaten. No one and nothing more was coming. At last, he probably sent men to scour the French encampment, ransacking whatever had not already been salvaged by the retreating survivors. Many French lords had fallen or been captured in the battle, and their tents and wagons were filled with riches – treasure and desperately needed supplies. The Chaplain notes that the French had 'abandoned to us that field of blood together with their wagons and other baggage-carts, many of these loaded with provisions and missiles, spears, and bows'.[80]

Meanwhile, other men were recovering what they could from the bodies. The *Chronicle of Ruisseauville* tells of the organization involved:

> the king of England had 500 men well armed and sent them amongst the dead, to take off their coats of arms and a great quantity of armour. They had small axes in their hands and other weapons and they cut both the dead and the living in the face so that they might not be recognised, even the English who were dead as well as the others.[81]

While some might have disfigured the fallen out of spite, it cannot have been the majority. Most were stripping the dead of their kit, which included valuable helmets and other gear – all of it slicked and caked with mud and gore. Men who were well armoured had required assistance to get strapped in (Figure 32). No one was now taking time to unclasp, untie, or unbind it all. There was no reason to be neat and tidy. Even with the French beaten, the English were still at intense risk. The sooner this gruesome work was done, the better. To get a helmet off, a blade or hatchet hacked at the strapping under the chin and jaw. And if, as it was pulled free, the helmet somehow got caught up again, then a sharp edge took care of that, too. The same was true of the armour: the scavenging party flipped the dead without ceremony and blades went to work on the straps across their backs and sides. Disfiguration may or may not have been the point, but it was certainly an inevitable consequence.[82] As Juvénal des Ursins notes, servants later struggled to find their lords on the battlefield: 'some were recognizable, but relatively few.'[83]

The coats of arms were one of the only means to identify the fallen, and even they weren't wholly reliable. Edward III, reporting the names of the lords he had killed at the battle of Crécy, was only about 50 per cent accurate.[84] It's a nod to the devastating totality of the English victory that the lists of the dead after Agincourt are more accurate.

How many died?

On 30 October, just five days after the battle, a letter describing the campaign was written in Paris. Received in Venice just over a month later, we have a record of it in the Italian chronicle of Antonio Morosini. Although the French guarding the Somme thought they 'would soon have victory with the aid of God', the letter explains, 'matters had gone from bad to worse. The lords of France had been routed in a battle ... to such a degree that never had such bad fortune or such a great defeat been heard of ... more than 10,000–12,000 had fallen in addition to the barons who had been killed or taken prisoner.'[85] Walsingham provides a rather specific count of 3,069 dead among the knights and squires, though he notes that 'the number of the rank and file was not calculated by the heralds'.[86]

We will never know exactly how many died. Three French dukes were certainly dead (Alençon, Bar, and Brabant), as were nine counts, a viscount, an archbishop, France's constable and her admiral, along with over a thousand knights and many thousands of untitled men whose names we will never recover. Estimates vary widely in the sources.[87]

And then there were the prisoners: two dukes (Bourbon and Orléans), four counts, the marshal Boucicaut, and many others. We have the names of nearly 300 prisoners in existing accounts, but that might be the tip of the iceberg.[88]

One thing is crystal clear.

Agincourt was a massacre.

The English had not gone unscathed, but their losses were minuscule compared to those of the French. The duke of York was dead, as was the earl of Suffolk and a handful of other gentlemen. Most sources claim around 30 total deaths, though over 100 dead can be counted in the fragmentary records.[89] This makes Monstrelet's claim that 600 English died seem reasonable. Waurin and Le Fèvre, who were there, say the reality was closer to 1,600 – though this would have been something like a quarter of the English army, an extremely unlikely number.[90] It was a heavy blow, but nothing like what the French had suffered. The Chaplain says that, after the ransacking of the French encampment, 'we who had gained the victory came back through the masses, the mounds, and the heaps of the slain'.[91]

Henry, never one to miss an opportunity for theatre, returned to Maisoncelle. 'That night,' Tito Livio Frulovisi tells us, 'the most noble royal captive princes served the king at his feast.'[92] It was a declaration of victory, but it was also a pointed political gesture of superiority: unlike the madman who held the throne of France, Henry was a king in force and in bearing on the land itself. It was a comparison that even some of the French would be all too willing to make in the years to come.

Charles was an absent king.

Henry was a present one.

To make the statement as clear as possible, Henry summoned the French heralds into his presence. Both English and French heralds had stood apart from the battle, observing. Monstrelet reports that Henry called upon the herald of the king of France, Mountjoye, to observe that Henry hadn't caused the killing himself but had been forced to do it 'on account of the sins of the French'. He then asked 'to whom the victory should be accorded, to him or to the king of France'. In essence, Henry was attempting to position Agincourt as a trial by battle between their rival claims. Mountjoye, of course, could only reply that the victory belonged to the English king and not his own.[93] It was at this point that Henry asked the French heralds and the captured French lords for the name of the nearby castle. The point of these questions, and the gathering at which they were addressed, was to make public acknowledgement of the

English victory.[94] He wanted everyone to know that he had won: the lords to know their fate, and the heralds to take the word of it to the king of France, the dauphin, and everyone else who still opposed him.

For all that Henry wanted to present Agincourt as a great English victory – and it very much was – he was nevertheless aware that he was still stuck in the middle of France, surrounded by enemies. And while he had beaten the great lords who were there, it would not have taken him long in the aftermath to learn the names of the great lords who were *not* there. If these came against him, as they still very well could, everything might be undone.

In other words, he still needed to get to Calais as swiftly as possible.

His concern is shown in the report from Waurin and Le Fèvre that Henry grew worried that the amount of armour being taken from the field – while worth money and valuable as military gear – would slow down his march. So would the bodies of the English dead.

> He had it proclaimed throughout his army that no one should take more than he was lacking for his own body, and that they were still not out of danger from the French. They had the bodies of the duke of York and earl of Oxford boiled so that they could take their bones back to England. Then the king of England commanded that all the armour which was surplus to requirements and in addition to what his men had carried off with the bodies of some of the English who had been killed in the battle should be put into a house or barn. There they were completely burned and so it was done.[95]

For all that the prayers of the Chaplain and the other men of God on the field no doubt spoke of Heaven and divine glory, the fires consuming the dead must have been the closest thing on earth to Hell.

NIGHTFALL

One of the most famous books to come out of the Middle Ages is Thomas Malory's *Le Morte d'Arthure*. Written around 1470, it canonized the myth of King Arthur as it is known today. Among its most famous scenes is that of Arthur and his son, Mordred, exchanging mortal blows on the field of battle. Afterwards, the king's two surviving men drag him to a little seaside chapel. There, they hear the cries of people upon the battlefield that they had left behind. A dying Arthur commands one of them, Sir Lucan, to find out the cause. Though himself 'grievously wounded in many places', he makes his way there and sees how 'pillagers and robbers were come into the field, to plunder and to rob many a most noble knight of brooches and beads, good rings and rich jewels. And those who were not yet dead, there they slew them for their harness and their riches.'[96]

It's a horrifying scene: shadowy figures scavenging the field, picking through the dead and the dying and despoiling them of anything of value. It's also accurate. Plundering was as awful as it was lucrative.

Fiction, of course. There was no King Arthur. At least not one like that.

But what Malory describes would be the reality of an event like Agincourt.

As the sun set on 25 October 1415, the shadows stretched over the field at Agincourt. The men who had fought and survived, no doubt hoping for unhaunted dreams, fell into exhausted sleep in whatever comfort they could still manage. The blanket of night, hiding the horrors of the field, seemed peaceful at first. But here and there, with the last of the light fading from the sky, the shadows would have come alive.

War breeds scavengers, and in the deepening dark they began their work.

Some were born of desperation, some were born of choice, but they were all unified in their desire to strip everything of value from the dead that the English hadn't already taken. Some might have followed the marching armies – French and English both – for just this purpose. Others might have been drawn in from the surrounding villages with the news of the battle, slipping furtively into the night in the hope that their neighbours wouldn't see them go.

It was foul, gruesome business. Nothing came clean from battle. No one came clean from its aftermath.

Weapons were pulled from wounds, from the grips of dead men's hands. Rings were cut from cold fingers. Purses were shorn from bloodied belts. Sodden leather straps were sliced through so armour could be yanked off bodies. Dying men still living were put out of their misery if they struggled or cried out in the cold. Others were left naked on the ground, shivering out their last breaths.

Birds and beasts, too, slipped out from the shadows. They sought wealth of a different sort, and there was more than enough for all to get their fill.

14

The Days After, 1415–22

As the sun rose on 26 October 1415, the horrors of the night were laid bare. Tito Livio Frulovisi describes it: Henry 'made his way across the middle of the field where he had fought, which was covered with the amazing sight of all the bodies of the fallen, stripped of their belongings'.[1] Le Fèvre says they were 'already stripped naked as the day they were born'.[2] The scavengers had been thorough.

As the English were breaking camp and passing through the battlefield to reach the main roads to Calais, Fenin tells us that living men were still being pulled out from beneath the heaps of the dead.[3] In December 1862, when night fell on the killing ground of the battle of Fredericksburg in the American Civil War, living Union soldiers made bedmates of the dead in hopes of insulating themselves against the merciless bite of cold. No doubt many of the wounded at Agincourt had done the same. Those still alive in the morning either joined the ranks of the prisoners or, if they were too low-born, or their wounds too severe for them to survive transport long enough to be ransomed, they were killed on the spot.

THE DEAD

Thousands of corpses were left on the field. To spare the living world from further nightmares of the dead – and to speed souls to their eternal rest – something had to be done with them. We've seen that at least a couple of the English lords had their flesh boiled off so that their bones could be carried home in more easily transportable coffers. Other English bodies were cremated along with the armour that couldn't be carried.

The French dead were a far bigger problem.

The question of what happened to the battle dead is a mystery.[4] Most were probably laid to rest in mass graves. These would require hallowed ground, for which local monks would have been early to the field once the fighting was done. At Agincourt, however, the dead would have overwhelmed the regional religious spaces even if there had been enough manpower to move them there. The Religieux observes that Henry 'agreed that the bishop of Thérouanne should bless the unhallowed place so that it might serve as cemetery'.[5] The dead would be buried on the field itself. The *Chronicle of Ruisseauville* provides additional detail: 'Louis de Luxembourg, bishop of Thérouanne, blessed the ground and the place where the battles had been, accompanied by the abbot of Blangy and made five graves, and in each grave were buried 1,200 men or more at his costs and expenses, and on each grave was placed a great cross of wood.'[6] These graves might be at the side of the hills of Saint-George just west of Azincourt, along the road to Calais, where we find the place-name *Les Croisettes* [The Crosses]. Similar place-names that seem to bear no relation to battle appear elsewhere, however, so there may be no direct connection. On the other hand, this would be the very spot where de l'Isle's 1704 map places the battle (Figure 12).

At least one additional toponym on our Napoleonic cadastral maps may be of interest here. *La Fosse a Rogne* is today a sunken area below a tree-covered knoll at the base of the *Morival* (Figure 26). It is precisely in line with where we would surmise that any French attempting the left side of Henry's line would have died. The feature's name translates to either 'pit of rage' or 'pit of rotting', and in any case it seems a reasonable location for a mass burial. Such a location is described by Monstrelet, who writes that the main body of the dead – 5,800 men – were buried in a 'square measured out of 25 feet in which were made three ditches as wide as two men', after the ground was blessed by the bishop of Guînes at the command of the bishop of Thérouanne.[7] This description can't be entirely accurate. Even if the men were all a mere five feet tall (which they would not be), only five would fit head-to-toe in a 25-foot ditch.[8] If there were three ditches holding two men abreast, then each 'layer' would contain 30 corpses. 5,800 men would need to be stacked 193 deep. And if the average body in these stacks was eight inches thick,[9] then the three 25-foot ditches would need to be roughly 129 feet deep each – a difficult undertaking even with modern machinery and engineering. If the three ditches were 250 feet long instead – a common enough scribal error – then 5,800 bodies would need only be stacked 19 deep. As it happens, the *Fosse a Rogne* is roughly 250 feet long, though its dimensions would allow as many as a dozen burial ditches side by side instead of just three, which would considerably decrease the depth needed to hold so many corpses. At present, no archaeological survey has taken place in this area.

When it comes to the dead, we must remember that the losses of this event were counted not just in the moment, but across generations. There is simply no way to overstate the effect of the losses at Agincourt on the families of France.[10] Fathers were lost. Sons. Brothers. Husbands.

History books, this one included, too often focus on the scant few men of wealth, privilege, and power. It's a reflection of the sources on which we depend when looking at an event over six centuries in the past. The fates of the great lords are recorded. The fates of the 99 percent of human beings who fought and suffered and bled for them are not.[11] But even if their names are forgotten, we should nevertheless do our best not to forget their fates.

HOME AND WHAT WAS TO COME

The English were still 45 miles from the safety of Calais. Henry kept his men in battle formation, just as he had done before Agincourt, though the king deemed they no longer needed to wear their armour during the march. It's easy to see this as a sense of security at having won the victory at battle, but it was more an acknowledgment of the men's condition. Monstrelet indicates that the army had lost so many horses that 'three-quarters of them were on foot, and were exhausted not just because of the battle but also because of hunger and other discomforts'.[12]

Slowed by their lack of mounts, Henry's men at last reached the walls of Calais on 28 October. Le Fèvre, who was with the English in 1415, describes how those who expected great relief at the end of the journey were quickly disappointed:

> But when such men arrived at Calais where they hoped they could enter to gain refreshment and rest of which they had great need – for most of them had spent eight to ten days without eating bread and of other victuals, meat, butter, eggs, cheese always only the little they could find – they would have given anything to have it, more than you have ever heard of. For there was such a shortage of bread that they did not bother what it cost, but only that they should have some. It is bad enough to think of the poor French prisoners of whom many were wounded and injured being in great distress, for they all wanted to go into Calais. But those of the town refused to let them enter, save for some English lords. They did this so that victuals would not fail and so that the town, which lay on the frontier, would always stay well provided. Thus many of the men at arms and archers who were burdened with the baggage and the prisoners sold their gear and enough of their prisoners to those of the town so that they could get money, and they did not care so long as they could get money and go to England.

Thus did the merchants of Calais, who had shed no blood on the fields of Agincourt, find themselves enriched by the battle as they relieved the desperate soldiers of their spoils.

The experience of the king was different, of course. He entered the town the next day, after several nights in Guînes so that Calais could prepare a hero's welcome of 'great glory and triumph', as Le Fèvre points out.[13] The next month, on 11 November, many of the French who had surrendered at Harfleur and been released on the promise to meet Henry in Calais, came as they said they would. Honour, though often mocked by modern writers, was real to these men. On 16 November, Henry set sail for England with his leaders and his most valuable prisoners.

It was the beginning of an extraordinary few years for Henry. Agincourt had been entirely one-sided. In the words of the chronicler Pierre Cochon, it was 'the ugliest and most wretched event that had happened in France over the last 1,000 years'.[14] There was no question as to who had won and who had lost. It could not have been more decisive. Yet in one sense it had decided nothing. The king of France yet lived. And no great magnates of France responded to the defeat by casting their lot with the foreign king. As King Edward III had discovered after Crécy, it took far more than a victory in battle to gain a kingdom.

In another sense, Agincourt had changed everything.

When Henry left for his campaign, his throne was hardly secure. There had been plots to take his crown at the very hour of his embarkation, and the French rightly wondered if the king would go overseas only to find his throne stolen in his absence – just as his father had done to Richard II. Instead, Henry returned victorious, unquestionably secure in his realm and confident in his prospects abroad.

He made an alliance with Emperor Sigismund in 1416, and in 1417 he brought an enormous invasion force, nearly equal to the one he had brought to Harfleur, onto the shores of Lower Normandy. His first target was Caen – the very city that Edward III had successfully taken at the start of the Crécy campaign in 1346. Once again, it appears he was trying to live up to the model of his illustrious ancestor. By 1419 he had arguably surpassed him: he had taken not just Caen but the great city of Rouen. His armies threatened Paris itself.

All the while, France's internal strife continued to cripple the kingdom. The Armagnac–Burgundian Civil War did not end with Agincourt. Instead, the Burgundians seized on the loss of so many Armagnac princes as a reason to take more power for themselves. By the time Henry attacked Rouen, Jean the Fearless was openly struggling with the dauphin for control of the kingdom of France. This was not the same young man who had been dauphin during the battle of Agincourt. Charles VI's wife, Isabeau, had given birth to 12 children in all: six sons and six daughters. Louis, the dauphin when Henry invaded France in 1415, had died in December of that year. His brother Jean had followed him as dauphin, but he had died in 1417.

So it was yet *another* son of the mad king – this one carrying his father's name, Charles – who met with Jean the Fearless on the bridge at Montereau on 10 September 1419. The meeting was ostensibly meant to secure peace between the two men and present a unified defence of France against England. Instead, one of the dauphin's men took the opportunity to put an axe through the duke of Burgundy's skull (Figure 33).

The assassination nearly ended France.

Philippe the Good, the son of Jean the Fearless, succeeded to his father's title and quickly made a separate peace with the English king. Together, they backed the royal family into a corner.

In May 1420, an agreement was at last struck. The Treaty of Troyes, as it came to be known, arranged Henry's marriage to the French princess Catherine of Valois, who had yet to turn 19. She was the younger sister of Isabella, the child-bride of Richard II in that earlier attempt to bring an end to the Hundred Years War through marriage. More than this, the treaty established Henry as regent of France while Charles VI yet lived, at last putting a theoretical end to the question of who was in charge of the kingdom. The treaty promised that Henry and his sons would be the heirs to the crown when the mad king died. When Catherine gave birth to Henry's first child in December 1421 – a son named after his father – the lad became the heir of both the English and French thrones. The dauphin was disinherited.

It was all done in the name of peace.

It achieved nothing of the sort.

Henry V died unexpectedly in August 1422. His infant son was dutifully crowned Henry VI of England. There was little issue in the transfer of power on the English side. When the mad king died the following October, however, not all the lords of France were anxious to bend the knee to an English baby. Henry VI was crowned in France in 1431, but there were more than a few who rejected him as king. For them, the rightful heir to the throne of France was the dauphin, who ought now to rule as Charles VII.

Of course, he couldn't be crowned. His father had disinherited him, and Reims, the city where French kings were traditionally crowned, was in English hands. It would take decades more fighting – and the intervention of a remarkable young woman named Jeanne d'Arc – to see the tide turn in favour of the French once more and bring King Charles VII at last to his throne.

None of it would have happened had Henry lost at Agincourt.

AGINCOURT IN PERSPECTIVE

Henry won a great victory over France at Agincourt. English history would declare him among the greatest of warrior-kings. Songs were sung about what had happened (Figure 34). But in truth he had beaten a broken kingdom. It was the madness of the king of France, perhaps more than anything else, that led to the victory of the king of England at Agincourt – and his victories in the years afterwards, too. The struggle for power at the highest levels of France left the kingdom's backstabbing lords broken and ultimately beaten before they ever took the field against the English.

This was certainly the belief that circulated in France after 1415. In his chronicle, Monstrelet included a short poem, which also appeared in the register of the parliament of Paris and other places. It reads, in part:

> Leader [king] removed by pitiable fortune,
> Young regent full of his own self-will,
> Blood so divided that no one cared at all for the other,
> Council suspected of bias.
> People destroyed by prodigality,
> Forcing so many men to turn to begging
> That each is in need of help.[15]

The sentiment was widely shared. The letter from Paris to Venice cited earlier, written just five days after Agincourt, deemed the prospects for France to be bleak, explaining 'that the kingdom had fallen into the wrath of God, and that it would soon be destroyed by its divisions, and that if things did not change, the kingdom would be lost'.[16]

The truth that Henry took advantage of a broken nation, that he fought an opponent with one hand tied behind its back, should not diminish his accomplishment. It allows us to see Agincourt in a new light. It was a military victory, to be sure, but it was made possible by political strategies that recognized the fragmented status of the French dukes and leveraged this to maximum English advantage.

In terms of tactics, too, there are changes to how and why we hold Agincourt in such high regard. The popular notion lauds shared sacrifice between Henry and his men, and above all the superiority of the English longbow. To the first point, I can only say that, yes, the king lost a fair number of the 60 horses he brought to France for his personal use, but this doesn't remotely compare – at least not favourably so – to the sacrifices experienced by the vast majority of his men. Henry was a man of the people only insofar as he built his glory upon them. To the second point, there is no questioning the impact of the longbow on the battle. Nevertheless, its positives are exponentially increased by the biggest thing that Henry did not control on that fateful day: the decisions of the French.

For many investigators, there has been no reason to ponder why the French made the decisions they did. It was only necessary that they play their role in Henry's achievements. Even those few who have bothered to question the matter have, in large part, come up empty-handed. As one historian concludes: 'Their choice of battlefield could have been a good one with a different formation; their deployment could have worked well on a different battlefield; but to array their forces in the way they did, on the ground they chose, was little short of idiotic.'[17] But this foolishness hinges on a battle taking place on the *Vulgata* field and in the *Vulgata* fashion.

Shift the battlefield, recognize the desperate nature of both Henry's position and his formation, and the French actions fall into place. Henry didn't beat fools. He beat leaders who were making the best decisions they could based on what they had to work with.

What went wrong?

There's never just one thing. Battles are simply too complicated for that. But if we set aside everything else to focus on Agincourt in a vacuum, we can safely say the French had three especially significant failures, and the English had three corresponding successes.

First, Henry succeeded in provoking the French advance. They ought not to have done so. They knew this, yet the bait of Henry advancing his centre and dangling his own capture before them was too much to ignore. They took the bait, moving straight into the teeth of the English position.

Secondly, the French cavalry utterly failed to dislodge the archers. This was a failure of execution in that they didn't bring enough riders into the assault. It was a failure of technology in that they didn't have armour sufficient to minimize their losses in the face of a withering arrow storm. It was also a success of battlefield ingenuity as Henry's formation and his foresight to protect his most vulnerable men with stakes enabled them to wreak maximum carnage on the enemy from a position of relative safety.

Thirdly, the inability of the rearguard to organize a last-minute charge against the exhausted and arrow-depleted English meant there was no way to wrest the victory out of Henry's hands in the end.

Looking back, we can attribute most of these French failures to pride. They took Henry's bait out of pride. They didn't send enough cavalry forward out of pride. Their leaders were all in the first two battles out of pride. But pride wasn't something innately French.

Agincourt was a clash between two scarred kings. The one absent from the battle, Charles, was scarred in mind. The one present for the battle, Henry, was scarred in body from his wound at Shrewsbury at the age of 16. Henry was also scarred in mind after the trauma of his experience. Thinking himself God's chosen vessel on earth, he was arguably prouder than anyone else on the field.

It is an awful truth that in war that a leader can make all the correct choices and still lose, or stumble through the wrong choices and somehow end up on top. Had Henry advanced and the French not taken the bait, the English king might well have been annihilated and viewed quite differently by history. The same would have been true if his cold decision to execute his prisoners had spurred the rearguard into a spirited charge rather than a dispirited withdrawal. In each and every one of these cases, the plain fact is that Henry made the right calls not because they were *right*, but because they *worked*.

This may not be very satisfying to our human desire for explanation – or, for that matter, a nationalistic desire for exaltation – but it's the truth.

Suggested Reading and Acknowledgements

The traditional understanding of the battle – the Agincourt *Vulgata* – is very much the combined weight of generations of historians, and there is simply no way to account for them all in a popular history of this kind. I have, for the most part, favoured citation of the most recent generation of scholars working on the battle. Those interested in the full historiography of Agincourt can work back down from them, to see the previous giants upon whose shoulders they stand.

For those wanting a quick but well-informed read of the *Vulgata*, I would recommend first and foremost Matthew Bennett's accessible and well-illustrated *Agincourt 1415: Triumph Against the Odds* (Osprey, 1991). Longer but no less readable and entertaining is Juliet Barker's *Agincourt: The King, the Campaign, the Battle* (Little, Brown, 2005). Her examination of the battle manages to be both probing and engaging. Though I take issue with *what* she says at times, not once do I take issue with *how* she says it: she's a truly superb story-teller.

Anyone taking even a passing glance at books about the battle of Agincourt (or my citations in this book) will see one name again and again: Anne Curry. Truly, no one has done more to advance the study of this battle, its associated campaign, and the men who fought in it. Most of her books (and those of her students!) are must-haves for anyone interested in 1415, but I nevertheless must highlight two in particular, which are frequently referenced in these pages: *Agincourt: A New History* (Tempus, 2005), and her still-unsurpassed gathering of the source materials, *Agincourt: Sources and Interpretations* (Boydell, 2000). Even as other books have come and gone, these remain a gold standard in the study of the battle. Her work is of such exemplary quality that when I have disagreed with it I have done so with trepidation.

Among many scholarly examinations of the standard interpretation of the battle, I'm particularly impressed by that of Clifford Rogers: his 'Battle of Agincourt' is found in *The Hundred Years War, Part II: Different Vistas*, a collection of essays edited by Andrew Villalon and Donald Kagay (Brill, 2008).

For the Hundred Years War entire, Jonathan Sumption's multiple volumes of door-stopper-sized history books are an extraordinary trunk onto which more recent research can be grafted. They're fantastic resources, and I'm truly glad to have them in my library ... and often open on my desk.

For a terrific look at the start of the Armagnac–Burgundian Civil War through the eyes of a most remarkable medieval woman, I highly recommend Tracy Adams' book, *Christine de Pizan and the Fight for France* (Penn State University Press, 2014). It has been deemed a 'revisionist' effort in its interpretation of the poet, but I found it insightful, intelligent, and intriguing.

I have been fortunate to work with a number of amazing scholars in my career. Specific to this book, I'm grateful to highlight my many conversations with Kelly DeVries over the years. Not only has he been an immeasurable influence on my work on nearly every aspect of the Hundred Years War – even when we've disagreed! – but he also is responsible for first taking me to the field of Agincourt and then listening with patience and insight as I began questioning the traditional story of what had happened there. I'm equally pleased to acknowledge our comrade-in-arms, Robert ('Bob') Woosnam-Savage, who welcomed me on that same trip and whose questions and observations are always brilliantly insightful. He was also kind enough to make a pass through this manuscript at a late stage and help me improve it on several regards. I'm thankful, as well, to the many scholars who have graciously provided feedback on the pieces of this work that I've shared at conferences over the past few years.

As he has on each of my Osprey volumes, my friend Myke Cole once more helped me by conducting a thorough editorial pass through this book. His questions, comments, and sturdy red pen have taught me much. The book is better thanks to him. So am I.

In the ranks of Osprey itself, I'm grateful to Marcus Cowper for believing I'd have something interesting to say about this amazing battle. I'm thankful to the patient and brilliant Gemma Gardner and the other members of Osprey's editorial staff for helping bring the book along through the trials and tribulations of publishing.

In closing, I want to dedicate this book to my wife, Kayla, whose patience with my need to stare at a nondescript field while talking to myself appears never-ending. This, and so much else, is for you.

Endnotes

INTRODUCTION

1 Rick Atkinson, *The Guns at Last Light: War in Western Europe, 1944–1945* (Henry Holt and Co., 2013), p. 12.
2 *Henry V*, IV.iii.35–36. This and all subsequent quotations of Shakespeare's *Henry V* follow *The Riverside Shakespeare*, second edition (Houghton Mifflin, 1997). On Montgomery's quote and Ismay's reaction, see Atkinson's rich and detailed discussion of the meeting in *The Guns at Last Light*, pp. 1–12.
3 *Henry V*, IV.iii.40–67.

CHAPTER 1: SHREWSBURY AND SCARS, 21 JULY 1403

1 That is, the arrow would be in his line of vision. Whether his brain could have *recognized* such a fast-moving object is not something I care to discover via experimentation. Also, what struck him wasn't a 'bodkin'; see note 10 below.
2 *The Chronica Maiora of Thomas Walsingham, 1376–1422*, trans. David Preest (Boydell, 2005), p. 328.
3 *Henry IV, Part 1*, V.iv.1–14.
4 For a translation, see *Medieval Warfare: A Reader*, ed. Kelly DeVries and Michael Livingston (University of Toronto Press, 2019), pp. 327–29.
5 For statistics, see Piers D. Mitchell, *Medicine in the Crusades: Warfare, Wounds and the Medieval Surgeon* (Cambridge University Press, 2004), p. 163.
6 Translation my own. For the Middle English, see Geoffrey Chaucer, 'The Franklin's Tale', lines 1113–15 in *The Riverside Chaucer*, third edition, ed. Larry D. Benson (Houghton Mifflin, 1987).

7 Quoted in Carol Rawcliffe, *Medicine and Society in Later Medieval England* (Alan Sutton, 1995), p. 76.
8 Their names and work are known to us thanks to their inclusion in John of Woodhouse's account of military expenses, which is preserved in the National Archives in Kew, E 101/25/10. This portion was edited by J.E. Morris, 'Mounted Infantry in Mediaeval Warfare', *Transactions of the Royal Historical Society* 8 (1914), pp. 101–02.
9 On the wound, see Michael Penman, *David II* (Tuckwell, 2004), pp. 138–39.
10 This and all subsequent quotations from Bradmore are my own translation in *Medieval Warfare*, ed. DeVries and Livingston, pp. 284–85. This translation is to be favored over my previous one in the article '"The Depth of Six Inches": Prince Hal's Headwound at the Battle of Shrewsbury', in *Wounds and Wound Repair in Medieval Culture*, ed. Larissa Tracy and Kelly DeVries (Brill, 2015), pp. 215–30. In that older work, I accepted the tradition that Bradmore's Middle English to the arrowhead being 'a bod styll' in Hal's head referred to it being a 'bodkin' arrowhead. In my later re-translation, however, I more correctly interpreted Bradmore to be referring to an arrowhead that 'abod styll' (i.e. still remained) in his head. More globally, Ralph Moffat has subsequently shown that medieval archery had no such thing as a 'bodkin' arrowhead anyway! The term is a modern misreading of our source material, confusing the bodkin type of dagger with arrowheads. See Moffatt, *Medieval Arms and Armour: A Sourcebook, Volume II: 1400–1450* (Boydell, 2023), forthcoming.
11 *Henry IV, Part 2*, V.v.56–58.
12 A collection of sources reporting the young man's change of personality is in Keith Dockray, *Henry V* (Tempus, 2004), p. 96. For a fuller overview of the trauma and its possible connection to this change, see Livingston, 'Depth of Six Inches', pp. 215–30.

CHAPTER 2: ASSASSINATION AND MADNESS, 13 JUNE 1392

1 Translation my own, from Jean Juvénal des Ursins, *Histoire de Charles VI, Roy de France* (A. Desrez, 1841), p. 377.
2 Translation my own, from Enea Silvio Piccolomini, *I Commentarii, Volume II* (Pisa, 1893), Book VI, chapter 4.

PART TWO: A BRIEF HISTORY OF THE HUNDRED YEARS WAR

1 Jean Froissart, *Chronicles*, trans. George Brereton (Penguin, 1978), pp. 189–90.

CHAPTER 3: CRÉCY AND THE MODEL GLORY, 1337–77

1 Nor has our understanding of their motives remained constant. For a new examination of World War II, for instance, see Richard Overy, *Blood and Ruins: The Great Imperial War, 1931–1945* (Allen Lane, 2021).
2 *The Wars of Edward III: Sources and Interpretations*, ed. Clifford J. Rogers (Boydell, 1999), p. 125.
3 Jean le Bel, *The True Chronicles of Jean le Bel, 1290–1360*, trans. Nigel Bryant (Boydell, 2011), p. 173.
4 The battle is traditionally located north of the town of Crécy-en-Ponthieu, but in *Crécy: Battle of Five Kings* (Osprey, 2022) I go through the piles of evidence that point instead to a rise beside the Forest of Crécy roughly four miles south-east. The brief account of the battle given here follows my larger reconstruction of the conflict in that book.
5 Jean le Bel, *Chronicle*, trans. Kelly DeVries, in *The Battle of Crécy: A Casebook*, ed. Livingston and DeVries (Liverpool University Press, 2015), p. 189; translation slightly revised to correct an error in the published version.
6 *Accounts of a Citizen of Valenciennes*, trans. Kelly DeVries, in *The Battle of Crécy: A Casebook*, ed. Livingston and DeVries, p. 211.
7 Quoted and discussed in L.J. Andrew Villalon and Donald J. Kagay, *To Win and Lose a Medieval Battle* (Brill, 2017), pp. 276–77.
8 Villalon and Kagay review the evidence, favouring Froissart, in *To Win and Lose a Medieval Battle*, pp. 299–300.
9 Froissart, *Chronicles*, pp. 178–79. On the lesser numbers, see, for instance, Richard Barber, *Edward, Prince of Wales and Aquitaine: A Biography of the Black Prince* (Allen Lane, 1978), pp. 225–26; and Jonathan Sumption, *The Hundred Years War III: Divided Houses* (University of Pennsylvania Press, 2009), p. 83.

CHAPTER 4: YOUNG KINGS, 1377–99

1 *The Anonimalle Chronicle, 1333 to 1381*, ed. V.H. Galbraith (Manchester University Press, 1927), p. 147.
2 *The Chivalric Biography of Boucicaut, Jean II Le Meingre*, trans. Craig Taylor and Jane H.M. Taylor (Boydell, 2016), p. 36.
3 These numbers are, to be plain, improbable. Pitti's account is translated by Julia Martines in *Two Memoirs of Renaissance Florence: The Diaries of Buonaccorso Pitti and Gregorio Dati*, ed. Gene Brucker (Harper and Row, 1967), p. 38.

4 Exactly what constitutes 'men-at-arms' depends on who is referring to them and when. For an overview within English contexts relevant to Agincourt, see Adrian R. Bell, Anne Curry, Andy King, and David Simpkin, *The Soldier in Later Medieval England* (Oxford University Press, 2013), pp. 95–138.

5 Froissart, *Chronicles*, p. 249.

6 Ibid., p. 250.

7 See, for example, the child's sword on display at the Royal Armouries in Leeds: Robert C. Woosnam-Savage, '"He's Armed Without That's Innocent Within": A Short Note on a Newly Acquired Medieval Sword for a Child', *Arms and Armour* 5.1 (2008), pp. 84–95.

8 *Chivalric Biography of Boucicaut*, trans. Taylor and Taylor, pp. 30–31.

9 For a look at the conditions that led to the Despenser Crusade, see Kelly DeVries, 'The Reasons for the Bishop of Norwich's Attack on Flanders in 1383', in *Fourteenth Century England III*, ed. W.M. Ormrod (Boydell, 2004), pp. 155–65.

10 Jonathan Sumption provides an excellent, detailed account of this important event in *Divided Houses*, pp. 847–53.

CHAPTER 5: CIVIL WARS, 1399–1415

1 Edward Hallett Carr, *What Is History? The George Macaulay Trevelyan Lectures Delivered at the University of Cambridge January–March 1961* (Vintage Books, 1961), p. 16.

2 *Chronique du religieux de Saint-Denys*, ed. L. Bellaguet (Paris, 1839–52), 3.228–32, 266–70, 288–90, and 330.

3 Translation my own, from John Gower, *The Minor Latin Works with In Praise of Peace*, ed. R.F. Yeager and M. Livingston (Medieval Institute Publications, 2005), p. 107.

4 Quoted in Sumption, *Divided Houses*, p. 864.

5 On Owain's claim, see John K. Bollard, 'Owain Glyndŵr, *Princeps Wallie*', in *Owain Glyndŵr: A Casebook*, ed. Livingston and Bollard (Liverpool University Press, 2013), pp. 425–30.

6 Hotspur, 'Battle at Cader Idris', in *Owain Glyndŵr: A Casebook*, ed. Livingston and Bollard, p. 57.

7 For an examination of what is known and not known about this battle – including the question of whether it ever happened at all – see Livingston, 'The Battle of Hyddgen, 1401: Owain Glyndŵr's Victory Reconsidered', *Journal of Medieval Military History* 13 (2015), 167–78.

8 Adam of Usk, 'Chronicle, Part 2', in *Owain Glyndŵr: A Casebook*, ed. Livingston and Bollard, pp. 65–67.

9 Iolo Goch, 'When His Authority Was Greatest', trans. Bollard, in *Owain Glyndŵr: A Casebook*, ed. Livingston and Bollard, p. 71.

10 The exact location of the battle remains uncertain. I have attempted a reconstruction based on the traditional site, but until archaeological confirmation can be found this must remain tenuous at best. See Livingston, 'The Battle of Bryn Glas, 1402', in *Owain Glyndŵr: A Casebook*, ed. Livingston and Bollard, pp. 451–72.

11 The artefact does not survive, but its existence is recorded in the margin of a copy of Thomas Walsingham's *Chronica Maiora*: Cambridge, Corpus Christi College MS 7, fol. 3r.

12 Gower, 'Presul ouile regis', in Gower, *The Minor Latin Works*, ed. Yeager, p. 50; translation my own.

13 *Historia vitae*, in *Owain Glyndŵr: A Casebook*, ed. Livingston and Bollard, p. 79.

14 Edmund Mortimer, 'Defection to Owain', in *Owain Glyndŵr: A Casebook*, ed. Livingston and Bollard, p. 71.

15 Translation my own, from Prince Henry, 'Razing of Owain's Homes', in *Owain Glyndŵr: A Casebook*, ed. Livingston and Bollard, p. 82.

16 For a selection of sources telling this tale, see Sumption, *The Hundred Years War IV: Cursed Kings* (University of Pennsylvania Press, 2015), p. 366.

17 Quoted in ibid., p. 83.

18 For the text of this letter, written from the hand of Louis II de Bourbon, see *Owain Glyndŵr: A Casebook*, ed. Livingston and Bollard, pp. 104–05.

19 Among the duties keeping him busy was active military engagement in other directions; see Kelly DeVries, 'John the Fearless' Way of War', in *Reputation and Representation in Fifteenth Century Europe*, ed. Douglas L. Biggs, Sharon D. Michalove, and Albert C. Reeves (Brill, 2004), pp. 39–55.

20 For texts of all these agreements, see 'Confederation Between Wales and France', in *Owain Glyndŵr: A Casebook*, ed. Livingston and Bollard, pp. 105–13.

21 Livingston, 'Owain Glyndŵr's Grand Design: The Tripartite Indenture and the Vision of a New Wales', *Proceedings of the Harvard Celtic Colloquium* 33 (2014), 145–68.

22 'Battle of Grosmont', in *Owain Glyndŵr: A Casebook*, ed. Livingston and Bollard, p. 117.

23 *Chronicle of Owain Glyndŵr*, in *Owain Glyndŵr: A Casebook*, ed. Livingston and Bollard, p. 175.

24 Adam of Usk, *Chronicle (Part 3)*, in *Owain Glyndŵr: A Casebook*, ed. Livingston and Bollard, p. 149.

25 Pintoin, *Chronicle of Charles VI*, and Thomas Walsingham, *St. Alban's Chronicle*, in *Owain Glyndŵr: A Casebook*, ed. Livingston and Bollard, pp. 155 and 165, respectively.
26 Henry IV, 'Resisting the French Invasion', in *Owain Glyndŵr: A Casebook*, ed. Livingston and Bollard, pp. 119–21.
27 For a popular account of the murder and the remarkable investigation that followed, I highly recommend Eric Jager's *Blood Royal: A True Tale of Crime and Detection in Medieval Paris* (Little, Brown, 2014).
28 Sumption, *Cursed Kings*, p. 366.
29 My translation, from *Le Procès de Maitre Jean Fusoris*, ed. Léon Mirot (Paris, 1900), p. 244.
30 Sumption lays out what little we know about the letters in *Cursed Kings*, pp. 374–76.
31 John Strecche, a canon of Kenilworth Priory during the king's life, tells a similar tale of frustrated French negotiators saying that they would send such a gift. E.F. Jacob, *Henry V and the Invasion of France* (The English Universities Press, 1947).
32 *Issues of the Exchequer, Being a Collection of Payments Made Out of His Majesty's Revenue, from King Henry III to King Henry IV Inclusive*, ed. Frederick Devon (John Murray, 1837), p. 327.
33 I am happy to acknowledge my debt to Sumption's marvellous account of this entire embassy in *Cursed Kings*, pp. 423–28.
34 Henry V, 'Licence to Treat with Owain', in *Owain Glyndŵr: A Casebook*, ed. Livingston and Bollard, p. 151.
35 Translation my own, from *Mémoires de la Société de l'histoire de Paris et de l'Ile-de-France* (Paris, 1900), pp. 248–49.

PART THREE: THE AGINCOURT CAMPAIGN

1 'Give thanks to God, England, for victory!'

CHAPTER 6: THE SIEGE OF HARFLEUR, 13 AUGUST–22 SEPTEMBER

1 Bibliotheque Nationale MS Français 25709/722, from Anne Curry, *Agincourt: A New History* (Tempus, 2005), p. 73.
2 For an absolutely splendid introduction to the muster rolls of 1415 and much of the detailed work that can be done with them, see Michael P. Warner, *The Agincourt Campaign of 1415: The Retinues of the Dukes of Clarence and Gloucester* (Boydell, 2021).
3 Curry, *Agincourt: A New History*, p. 66.
4 No one has done more to lock down the specific breakdown of the numbers and names of the men in the Agincourt campaign than

Anne Curry – both in her own work and through its extension among her many students and colleagues at the University of Southampton. For a summary of some of this research current to 2005, see her *Agincourt: A New History*, pp. 57–72.

5 Livingston, *Crécy: Battle of Five Kings* (Osprey, 2022), p. 114.

6 For a terrific look at honey in such contexts, see Ilana Krug, 'The Wounded Soldier: Honey and Late Medieval Military Medicine', in *Wounds and Wound Repair in Medieval Culture*, ed. Tracy and DeVries, pp. 194–214.

7 *The Navy of the Lancastrian Kings*, ed. S. Rose (Navy Records Society, 1982), pp. 34–35.

8 Craig Lambert, 'Henry V and the Crossing to France: Reconstructing Naval Operations for the Agincourt Campaign, 1415', *Journal of Medieval History* 43.1 (2017), pp. 37–38.

9 For an overview introducing the *Gesta* and the issues surrounding it, see Anne Curry, *The Battle of Agincourt: Sources and Interpretations* (Boydell, 2000), pp. 22–26. This enormously important book will be cited often in these pages simply as *Agincourt: Sources and Interpretations*. All quotations from this source are reprinted by permission of Boydell & Brewer Ltd.

10 Sumption, *Cursed Kings*, p. 434.

11 Translation my own, from *Gesta Henrici Quinti*, ed. and trans. Frank Taylor and John S. Roskell (Oxford University Press, 1975), pp. 26–27.

12 For an excellent study of these ordinances, see Curry, 'The Military Ordinances of Henry V: Texts and Contexts', in *War, Government and Aristocracy in the British Isles, c.1150–1500: Essays in Honour of Michael Prestwich*, ed. Chris Given-Wilson, Ann Kettle, and Len Scales (Boydell, 2008), pp. 214–49.

13 *Julius Caesar*, III.i.273.

14 *Henry V*, I.Prol.5–8.

15 Michel Pintoin, *Chronique de Religieux de Saint-Denys*, 5.536.

16 Curry, *Agincourt: Sources and Interpretations*, p. 444.

17 Ibid., pp. 445–46.

CHAPTER 7: EDWARD'S FOOTSTEPS, 23 SEPTEMBER–15 OCTOBER

1 The most thorough defence of this position is Clifford Rogers, 'Henry V's Military Strategy in 1415', in *The Hundred Years War: A Wider Focus*, ed. L.J. Andrew Villalon and Donald J. Kagay (Brill, 2004), pp. 399–427.

2 My translation, from *Rymer's Foedera Volume 9*, ed. Thomas Rymer (London, 1739–45), where it is incorrectly dated to 16 September 1415.

3 Quoted in Sumption, *Cursed Kings*, p. 83.

4 Curry, *Agincourt: A New History*, p. 132.

5 Curry, *Agincourt: Sources and Interpretations*, p. 27.

6 Curry, *Agincourt: A New History*, p. 131.

7 Curry, *Agincourt: Sources and Interpretations*, p. 27. I am hardly alone in favouring this smaller number. Sumption regards Curry's number as 'too high' and sets it aside in favour of the *Gesta*'s eyewitness attestation (*Cursed Kings*, p. 814, note 11), and Clifford J. Rogers makes an extended refutation of the higher estimate (and a related argument for the lower estimate of the *Gesta*) in his excellent study, 'The Battle of Agincourt', in *The Hundred Years War, Part II: Different Vistas*, ed. Andrew Villalon and Donald Kagay (Brill, 2008), pp. 114–21.

8 Sumption, *Cursed Kings*, p. 442.

9 That the march was intended as a 'deliberate act of provocation' meant to bring a confrontational battle is the position taken by, for instance, Juliet Barker, in *Agincourt: The King, the Campaign, the Battle* (Little, Brown, 2005), p. 219.

10 Curry, *Agincourt: Sources and Interpretations*, p. 27.

11 Curry, *Agincourt: A New History*, p. 134.

12 Curry, *Agincourt: Sources and Interpretations*, p. 289.

13 Ibid., p. 132. In *Agincourt: A New History*, p. 134, Curry suggests that the main army moved via Fauville, with 'foragers and scouts' perhaps reaching Fécamp. This may be, though the routing of the roads suggests to me that the more northerly route is to be preferred.

14 Translation my own, from *Gesta*, ed. Taylor and Roskell, pp. 60–61.

15 Curry, *Agincourt: Sources and Interpretations*, p. 28.

16 Curry, *Agincourt: A New History*, p. 136, places this event on Sunday 13 October, perhaps misunderstanding *Gesta*'s reference to it happening 'on the night after' the actions of 12 October (*Sources and Interpretations*, p. 28). This does not, however, fit with the prisoners' reports that the French on the Somme were expecting the English to arrive 'on the Sunday or Monday following'. The French cannot have expected the English army to take a week or more to travel the 20 miles that now separated them.

17 At least one explanation for the future William the Conqueror's victory at Val-ès-Dunes in 1047 is his use of the River Orne to separate enemy forces in just this way.

18 Curry, *Agincourt: A New History*, p. 136.
19 Curry, *Agincourt: Sources and Interpretations*, p. 57.
20 Ibid., p. 28.
21 On the discovery of the plan, see Christopher Phillpotts, 'The French Plan of Battle During the Agincourt Campaign', *English Historical Review* 99, no. 390 (1984), pp. 59–66. The plan is translated in *Medieval Warfare*, ed. DeVries and Livingston, pp. 104–05.
22 Another that has survived was made by Jean the Fearless on 17 September 1417, as he marched on Paris. See Richard Vaughan, *John the Fearless* (Longman, 1966), pp. 148–50.
23 Curry, *Agincourt: Sources and Interpretations*, pp. 146 and 129, respectively.
24 Ibid., p. 189.
25 Curry, *Agincourt: A New History*, pp. 144–45.
26 This is, as Curry notes, the probable reason for the variety of places in this region that appear as targets for the English across the chronicles. The English weren't hitting all of them *en masse*, but contingents of the army were searching them all out. See *Agincourt: A New History*, p. 145.
27 Cited by Jacques Godard, 'Quelques précisions sur la campagne d'Azincourt tirées des archives municipales d'Amiens', *Bulletin trimestre de la Société des Antiquaires de Picardie* (1982), p. 132.

CHAPTER 8: DAYS OF DESPERATION, 16–23 OCTOBER

1 Curry, *Agincourt: Sources and Interpretations*, p. 103.
2 Ibid., p. 57.
3 Ibid., p. 77.
4 The finest study of these records is Thom Richardson, *The Tower Armoury in the Fourteenth Century* (Royal Armouries, 2016).
5 Curry, *Agincourt: A New History*, p. 65.
6 Curry, *Agincourt: Sources and Interpretations*, p. 65.
7 As it happens, we actually have the release granted to John Hargrove, sergeant of the pantry, for the loss of salt cellars and other plate at the battle of Agincourt (Rymer, *Foedera*, 1 June 1416).
8 It should be pointed out that although we think of a volley of arrows as if all the archers loosed at once, it's unlikely that this is what happened on the field. If every archer loosed simultaneously, up to half their arrows would probably be fouled in flight by striking each other. Though we don't know the specific solution to this in combat, my own suspicion is that a single call for archers to loose would be

followed by quick waves of shots. If each archer in a company waited a breath after the man next to him shot before loosing his own arrow, space between arrow flights would be sufficiently staggered overall.

9 Curry, *Agincourt: Sources and Interpretations*, p. 30.

10 By coincidence, it may well have been through Boucicaut that knowledge of the tactic reached Henry. See Matthew Bennett, 'The Development of Battle Tactics in the Hundred Years War', in *Arms, Armies and Fortifications in the Hundred Years War*, ed. Anne Curry and Michael Hughes (Boydell, 1994), pp. 15–16.

11 Curry, *Agincourt: Sources and Interpretations*, p. 30.

12 Livingston, *Crécy: Battle of Five Kings*, p. 149.

13 Sumption, *Cursed Kings*, p. 446.

14 For another instance of the desire to give Henry and the English tactical initiative in this situation, Curry suggests that the change of direction was to avoid 'the French gathering at Péronne' (*Agincourt: A New History*, p. 149). It is very much subject to question how much he knew about the French presence there, especially when his men reported their belief that their enemies were at the time gathering well east up the Somme at Saint-Quintin. See below.

15 Curry, *Agincourt: Sources and Interpretations*, p. 44.

16 I have been following the *Gesta* account (as most historians do), but it is worth noting that not every source agrees on the general area of the crossing. For example, two French sources – the Berry Herald and Pierre Fenin – both suggest a crossing of the Somme to the *west* of Péronne, which is nigh inexplicable. Curry nevertheless patiently breaks these possibilities down before rejecting them. See *Agincourt: A New History*, pp. 152–53.

17 Curry, *Agincourt: Sources and Interpretations*, p. 31.

18 Ibid., p. 30.

19 Ibid., p. 31. Sumption suggests that only one of these crossings was at Voyennes, and that the other was two and a half miles down-river at Béthencourt-sur-Somme (*Cursed Kings*, p. 446). To the contrary, the *Gesta* describes the crossings as being close beside one another on the same road and landscape.

20 The *Gesta* says nothing of material being taken from the local buildings, but the French accounts in Waurin, Le Fèvre, and the Religieux had no qualms pointing it out. They are, as Curry notes, more 'brutal' in their depiction than the 'much more gentlemanly' impression given by the *Gesta*. See *Agincourt: A New History*, p. 154.

21 Curry, *Agincourt: Sources and Interpretations*, p. 32.

22 Ibid., p. 104.

23 Ibid., p. 32. Tito Livio Frulovisi has Henry state that he intends to march 'straight to Calais', which in all probability is an addition to match what he in fact did (ibid., p. 58).
24 Ibid., p. 180.
25 Ibid., p. 32.
26 Ibid., p. 104.
27 Sumption, *Cursed Kings*, p. 449.
28 Curry, *Agincourt: Sources and Interpretations*, p. 172. In writing this letter, the French lords surely knew their king would not be coming, but they also knew that this was about the only way to get Brabant to show up: no one else in France had the authority to call upon him.
29 Sumption, *Cursed Kings*, p. 448.
30 Ibid., p. 32.
31 Curry, *Agincourt: A New History*, p. 158.
32 Curry, *Agincourt: Sources and Interpretations*, p. 186.
33 Ibid., p. 180.
34 Ibid., p. 58.
35 Ibid., p. 58.
36 Ibid., pp. 34 and 37, respectively.
37 Curry provides an immensely useful chart of the numbers given for both sides in the major sources in *Agincourt: A New History*, pp. 274–75.
38 Curry, *Agincourt: Sources and Interpretations*, p. 181. For a discussion of similar numbers in other sources, including the *Chronicle of Arthur de Richemont*, the *Chronicle of Normandy*, and the *Chronicle of Ruisseauville*, see Rogers, 'Battle of Agincourt', pp. 57–59.
39 Rogers, 'Battle of Agincourt', pp. 57, 60–62.
40 Curry, *Agincourt: Sources and Interpretations*, pp. 104, 115, and 189.
41 Ibid., p. 157. A vocal proponent of the two to one ratio is Curry, *Agincourt: A New History*, pp. 181–87.
42 Curry, *Agincourt: Sources and Interpretations*, p. 157.
43 It would be cold comfort, but in truth hunger might have been the best treatment for dysentery that could be managed.
44 Rymer, *Foedera*, 5 February 1415.
45 Curry, *Agincourt: A New History*, pp. 69–70.
46 Ibid., p. 71.

PART FOUR: LOCATING AGINCOURT

1 Translation my own, from *Oeuvres de Robert Blondel, Historien Normand du XVe Siècle*, vol. 1, ed. A. Héron (Société de l'Histoire de Normandie, 1891), p. 33.

CHAPTER 9: FINDING AGINCOURT

1 An earlier version of the work in this and subsequent chapters appeared in Livingston, 'A Battle Is Its Ground: Conflict Analysis and a Case Study of Agincourt, 1415', *Journal of Medieval Military History* 21 (2023). For previous examples of my methodology in use, see my books *Never Greater Slaughter* and *Crécy: Battle of Five Kings*.
2 For an example of the abundance of artefacts to be expected – their numbers multiplied by the field-stripping of corpses that is usually trotted out as a reason for their absence – see Veronica Fiorato, Anthea Boylston, and Christopher Knüsel, *Blood Red Roses: The Archaeology of a Mass Grave from the Battle of Towton, AD 1461* (Oxbow, 2000).
3 Philip Preston, 'The Traditional Battlefield of Crécy', in *The Battle of Crécy, 1346*, ed. Andrew Ayton and Philip Preston (Boydell, 2005), pp. 119–21.
4 Michael Livingston, 'The Location of the Battle of Crécy', in *The Battle of Crécy: A Casebook*, ed. Livingston and DeVries, pp. 415–38.
5 Livingston, *Crécy: Battle of Five Kings*, pp. 179–258.
6 The increasing availability of Geographical Information System (GIS) software and publicly available data sets is driving a growing interest in landscape archaeology. As an example of the kind of productive work that can result in an inherently problematic region, see, e.g., Nele Vanslembrouck, Alexander Lehouck, and Erik Thoen, 'Past Landscapes and Present-Day Techniques: Reconstructing Submerged Medieval Landscapes in the Western Part of Sealand Flanders', *Landscape History* 27 (2005), pp. 51–64; and Gerben Verbrugghe, Veerle Van Eetvelde, Steven Vanderputten, and Wim De Clercq, 'Nieuw-Roeselare – Landscape Archaeological and Historical Geographical Research on Deserted Medieval Settlements in the Borderlands of Flanders and Zealand', *Geoscape* 14 (2020), pp. 96–107.
7 For a simplified overview of this approach, see Michael Livingston and Myke Cole, 'All-Source Analysis: The Key to Unlocking the Past', *Ancient Warfare* 11.4 (2017), pp. 10–14.
8 Curry, *Agincourt: Sources and Interpretations*, p. 32.
9 Jed O. Kaplan, Kristen M. Krumhardt, and Niklaus Zimmermann, 'The Prehistoric and Preindustrial Deforestation of Europe', *Quarternary Science Reviews* 28.27-28 (2009).

CHAPTER 10: REACHING AGINCOURT, 24 OCTOBER

1 Curry, *Agincourt: A New History*, p. 161.
2 Curry, *Agincourt: Sources and Interpretations*, p. 68.

3 Ibid., p. 32.
4 Ibid., pp. 32–33.
5 Ibid., p. 33.
6 Ibid., p. 33.
7 The tradition that it was said on the morning of the battle started early. See, e.g., Pseudo-Elmham's account in Curry, *Agincourt: Sources and Interpretations*, p. 70.
8 Curry, *Agincourt: Sources and Interpretations*, p. 33.
9 Ibid., p. 45.
10 Ibid., p. 33.
11 Sanson, *Atrebates: Evesché d'Arras comté d'Artois* (Paris, 1656). Norman B. Leventhal Map Center, ref. 06 01 006630. Unfortunately for us, this map does not mark the site of the battle.
12 Archives départementales du Pas-de-Calais, ref. 3P090/4.
13 Curry, *Agincourt: Sources and Interpretations*, p. 33.
14 Ibid., pp. 33–34.
15 Ibid., p. 34.
16 Ibid., p. 59.
17 Ibid., p. 117.
18 Ibid., p. 153.
19 Ibid., p. 69.
20 Ibid., p. 183.
21 Ibid., p. 186.
22 Ibid., p. 153.
23 Ibid., p. 124.
24 Ibid., p. 351.
25 Ibid., p. 115.
26 Ibid., p. 118.
27 Ibid., p. 159.
28 Ibid., p. 190.
29 Ibid., p. 159.
30 The best studies of the armour and armaments used at Agincourt are Thom Richardson and Karen Watts, 'Armour at the Time of Agincourt', and Robert C. Woosnam-Savage, '"All Kinds of Weapons": The Weapons of Agincourt', both magnificently illustrated in *The Battle of Agincourt*, ed. Anne Curry and Malcolm Mercer (Yale, 2015), pp. 110–37 and 138–54, respectively. For a look at how our popular misunderstandings about armour can change what we think about battle, see Woosnam-Savage's discussion about the alleged armour of Ferri de Lorraine, who died at Agincourt, in 'Of Knights, Cranes, Hoists and Winches ...:

The Myth of How Knights Mounted Horses', *Arms and Armour* 18.2 (2021), pp. 234–35.

31 Curry, *Agincourt: Sources and Interpretations*, p. 59.
32 Ibid., p. 70.
33 Ibid., p. 154.
34 These paragraphs on the numbers and characteristics of the horses on the campaign are heavily indebted to Gary Paul Baker, '"Sitting on a Noble Horse as White as Snow": The English Royal Horses at Agincourt', *Journal of Medieval Military History*, forthcoming.
35 Tobias Capwell, 'The Funerary Helm of King Henry V: A Helm for the Joust of Peace, *c.*1380–1420', in *The Funeral Achievements of Henry V at Westminster Abbey: The Arms and Armour of Death*, ed. Anne Curry and Susan Jenkins (Boydell, 2022), pp. 92–127.
36 Marina Viallon, 'A Saddle from the Funeral of Henry V', in ibid, pp. 128–41.
37 Lisa Monas, 'The Shield from the Funeral Achievements of Henry V', in ibid., p. 156.
38 Mike Loades, *Swords and Swordsmen* (Pen and Sword, 2010), pp. 125 and 146, respectively.
39 Shakespeare, *Henry V*, I.Prol.13–14.
40 Robert C. Woosnam-Savage, '"Our bruised arms hung up for monuments": The Sword of Henry V?' in *The Funeral Achievements of Henry V at Westminster Abbey*, ed. Curry and Jenkins, pp. 157–91.
41 That it was about 'ease of movement' alone is the position taken by Curry, *Agincourt: A New History*, pp. 209–10.
42 Curry, *Agincourt: Sources and Interpretations*, p. 160.
43 Ibid., p. 162. For a discussion of the weapons, see Woosnam-Savage, 'All Kinds of Weapons', particularly pp. 150–53 on the equipment of the archers.
44 Woosnam-Savage, 'All Kinds of Weapons', p. 153.

CHAPTER 11: TESTING THE TRADITION

1 John Keegan, *The Face of Battle: A Study of Agincourt, Waterloo, and the Somme* (Penguin, 1976), p. 78.
2 See Tim Sutherland, 'The Battlefield', in *The Battle of Agincourt*, ed. Curry and Mercer, pp. 196–98.
3 Keegan, *Face of Battle*, p. 83.
4 Curry, *Agincourt: Sources and Interpretations*, p. 51.
5 Ibid., p. 133.
6 Ibid., p. 113.
7 Ibid., p. 174.

8 Keegan, *Face of Battle*, pp. 84–85.

9 Ibid., p. 86.

10 Among the few scholars to take note of the tactical potential of this road running across the traditional site is Rogers, who suggests this as the line for Henry's men-at-arms in what is one of the finest current studies of the battle: 'Battle of Agincourt', p. 90.

11 Woodford's original survey survives as British Library Additional MS 16368, map C. It is reproduced as Figure 2 in Curry's *Agincourt: Sources and Interpretations*.

12 See, for instance, Curry, *Agincourt: Sources and Interpretations*, p. 22.

13 Ibid., p. 27.

14 Curry, *Agincourt: A New History*, pp. 187–88. More precisely, Curry later went on to estimate a count of 8,680 men on the English side; see *Great Battles: Agincourt* (Oxford University Press, 2015), p. 25.

15 In her *Agincourt: A New History*, Curry reckons them as 'small', with the largest losses at one time being seven men on 24 October (pp. 162–63).

16 Curry, *Agincourt: Sources and Interpretations*, p. 60.

17 See, for instance, Rogers, 'Battle of Agincourt', p. 52, who places the archers in an unsubstantiated 'guess' of seven ranks deep.

18 Curry, *Agincourt: Sources and Interpretations*, p. 71.

19 The mean unclothed shoulder width (with elbows tucked in) of male personnel in the United States Army in 1966 was 18 inches. See Robert M. White and Edmund Churchill, *The Body Size of Soldiers – US Army Anthropometry – 1966* (US Army Natick Laboratories, 1971), p. 115. My estimate of 24 inches attempts to account for armour and the need to hold one's arms to the sides of the body.

20 Curry, *Agincourt: Sources and Interpretations*, p. 34.

21 Ibid., p. 158.

22 Ibid., p. 159.

23 Rogers, 'Battle of Agincourt', p. 52.

24 Curry, *Agincourt: Sources and Interpretations*, p. 70.

25 Curry reproduces eight different battle maps in *Agincourt: Sources and Interpretations* (Figures 1–8), dating from 1818 to 1994. Such a wood appears on all of them.

26 Anne Curry, Peter Hoskins, Thom Richardson, and Dan Spencer, *The Agincourt Companion* (Andre Deutsch, 2015), p. 112.

27 The only previous publication of this image that I can locate suggests that the viewpoint is a combination of views from the east and south-west. This would be unusual, as the other paintings in the vast collection are from a single viewpoint. It is also, upon

investigation of the topography, an unnecessary complication to the single viewpoint suggested here. See *Albums de Croÿ, Tome XX: Comté d'Artois IV, Comté de Saint-Pol, Première Partie*, ed. Roger Berger (Crédit Communal de Belgique, 1989), p. 62.

28 This causes enormous problems for those reconstructions that have imagined the English taking a stand at any point between the northern bounds of Maisoncelle's coverage and the rough line of the Rue Henri V. Among many that do so is the reinterpretation recently executed by Michael K. Jones, *Agincourt 1415: Battlefield Guide* (Pen and Sword, 2005), p. 111.

29 For example, the castle appears on the maps (but not the discussions) of the battle in Sumption, *Cursed Kings*, p. 453, and Jones, *Agincourt 1415*, pp. 101–11 – both of which surround the castle with rather enormous choking woods all around the town of Azincourt. See also most of the maps reprinted by Curry (note 21, above).

30 Curry, *Agincourt: Sources and Interpretations*, p. 88.

31 Ibid., p. 164.

32 Ibid., p. 165.

33 Barker, *Agincourt*, pp. 292–93; similarly, see Sumption, *Cursed Kings*, p. 456.

34 For the results of a study of the soil of the area showing how sticky and difficult it could be, see the work of Andrew Palmer, discussed in David Wason, *Battlefield Detectives: What Really Happened on the World's Most Famous Battlefields* (Granada Media, 2003), pp. 70–72, and Anne Curry, *Great Battles*, pp. 195–96.

35 Curry, *Agincourt: Sources and Interpretations*, p. 160.

36 Barker, *Agincourt*, p. 291.

37 Rogers, 'Battle of Agincourt', p. 80.

38 Rogers attempts to avoid these added delays by suggesting that the stakes might have been only loosely set in the ground 'without hammering', or that the hammering was done on 'the stubs of projecting branches' instead of on the ends ('Battle of Agincourt', p. 53). His experiences in the back-country must be different from mine, because I cannot see either option working effectively. If the ground was soft enough to set the stakes without hammering it would be too soft to hold them up; and if pounding was done on 'stubs' it would have stripped them off.

39 Sutherland, 'The Battlefield', p. 201.

40 Tim Sutherland, 'Archaeological Evidence of Medieval Conflict – Case Studies from Towton, Yorkshire, England (1461) and Agincourt, Pas de Calais, France (1415)', *Schlachtfeldarchaologie* –

Battlefield Archaeology. 1. Mitteldeutscher Archaologentag vom 09.bis 11. Oktober 2008 in Halle (Salle), pp. 109–16.

41 Timothy Sutherland, 'The Battlefield of Agincourt: An Alternative Location?' *Journal of Conflict Archaeology* 1 (2006), pp. 245–63.

42 Sutherland, 'The Battlefield', p. 201.

43 Jones, *Agincourt 1415*, pp. 101–12. For a further rebuttal of this interpretation, see Rogers, 'Battle of Agincourt', pp. 122–26.

44 Curry, *Agincourt: Sources and Interpretations*, pp. 365 and 388.

45 Not that I'm inclined to trust de l'Isle unequivocally: he marks Crécy in the traditional site, which I think is completely wrong. Assuming he had sources and wasn't just marking the battles wherever he had room, we cannot assume that his accuracy (or lack thereof) is consistent.

46 Archives départementales du Pas-de-Calais, ref. 3P541/2.

47 Curry, *Agincourt: Sources and Interpretations*, p. 186.

48 Interestingly, an 1827 map of the battle shows something much like this, with French forces both east and west of Azincourt. See *Histoire des ducs de Bourgogne de la maison de Valois, 1364–1477, vol. 14: Atlas des ducs de Bourgogne*, ed. Amable Guillaume Prosper Brugière de Barante (Paris, 1838), n.p.

PART FIVE: THE BATTLE

1 Curry, *Agincourt: Sources and Interpretations*, p. 73.

CHAPTER 12: THE MORNING, 25 OCTOBER

1 Curry, *Agincourt: Sources and Interpretations*, p. 106.

2 Ibid., p. 34.

3 Ibid., p. 51.

4 Ibid., p. 155.

5 Ibid., p. 69.

6 Ibid., pp. 155–56.

7 Ibid., p. 154.

8 Ibid., p. 181. This would be *contra* Monstrelet, who suggests that Orléans had been the one to order Richemont up towards the English encampment and provoke a skirmish on 24 October, and that he was also knighted that night – though, in truth, that order and that act could have occurred *en route* rather than upon the field itself (pp. 155–56).

9 Ibid., p. 186.

10 Ibid., p. 34.

11 These are reproduced in *Albums de Croÿ, Tome XXI: Comté d'Artois V, Comté de Saint-Pol, Deuxième partie*, ed. Roger Berger (Crédit Communal de Belgique, 1990), plates 137 (Maisoncelle) and 202 (Tramecourt). The Tramecourt image, unfortunately, was done from the east side of the village, thus hiding the battlefield from view.
12 Ibid., p. 30.
13 Both of these problems are raised in Keegan's popular *Face of Battle*, pp. 90–91.
14 Though I don't agree with his solutions otherwise, Rogers makes a suitable series of points in exactly this vein ('Battle of Agincourt', pp. 54–56).
15 This is the position taken most famously by Keegan, *Face of Battle*, p. 90.
16 Matthew Bennett suggests that French commanders were deliberately ordering their men to throw their horses on the stakes on the assumption that they would fall over (*Agincourt 1415: Triumph Against the Odds* [Osprey, 1991], p. 77). As Woosnam-Savage observes, this seems an unlikely reading of the sources or any sound military thinking ('All Kinds of Weapons', pp. 153 and 283, note 49).
17 Curry, *Agincourt: Sources and Interpretations*, pp. 132–33.
18 Ibid., p. 133.
19 Ibid., p. 158.
20 Ibid., p. 158.
21 Ibid., pp. 157–58.
22 Ibid., p. 34.
23 Curry, *Agincourt: A New History*, p. 181.
24 Curry, *Agincourt: Sources and Interpretations*, p. 106.
25 Ibid., p. 132.
26 Ibid., p. 118.
27 Barker, *Agincourt*, pp. 275–76.
28 Curry, *Agincourt: Sources and Interpretations*, p. 181.
29 Ibid., p. 35. Edmond de Dynter says the same (ibid., p. 173).
30 Ibid., p. 113.
31 Ibid., p. 35.
32 Ibid., p. 106.
33 Ibid., p. 51.
34 Ibid., p. 60.
35 In his discussion of the battle, Rogers makes an argument for a contemporary standard of 300 yards ('Battle of Agincourt', p. 124). Could arrows reach so far? Absolutely. But because the strength and

accuracy of a bow shot both diminished with distance – and the fact that arrows were not an unlimited resource – I strongly suspect that any average 'bow shot' distance was reckoned far shorter.

36 Curry, *Agincourt: Sources and Interpretations*, p. 59.
37 Ibid., p. 34.
38 Ibid., p. 181.
39 Ibid., p. 104.
40 Ibid., p. 129.
41 Ibid., p. 118.
42 Ibid., pp. 124–25.
43 Curry, *Agincourt: Sources and Interpretations*, p. 159, following Le Fèvre. Waurin says the value of her dowry would be 500,000 francs.
44 Ibid., p. 118.
45 Ibid., p. 125.
46 Ibid., p. 130.
47 Ibid., pp. 104–05.
48 Ibid., p. 105.
49 Ibid., p. 34.
50 For a brief overview of the time, see Curry, *Agincourt: A New History*, pp. 197–98.
51 Curry, *Agincourt: Sources and Interpretations*, p. 35.
52 Curry, *Agincourt: A New History*, p. 198.
53 Curry, *Agincourt: Sources and Interpretations*, p. 34.
54 This last point is well made by Curry, *Agincourt: A New History*, pp. 199–200.
55 Curry, *Agincourt: Sources and Interpretations*, p. 35.
56 Ibid., p. 125.
57 Ibid., p. 135.
58 Ibid., p. 163.
59 Ibid., p. 118.
60 See, for instance, Rogers, 'Battle of Agincourt', pp. 102–03.
61 Curry, *Agincourt: Sources and Interpretations*, p. 163.
62 Ibid., p. 35.
63 Rogers, 'Battle of Agincourt', p. 42, note 13.
64 Curry, *Agincourt: Sources and Interpretations*, p. 35.
65 Ibid., p. 61.
66 Ibid., pp. 35–36.
67 Ibid., pp. 61–62 and 161, respectively.
68 Ibid., p. 35.
69 For an excellent overview of archers performing just this role on other occasions, see Rogers, 'Battle of Agincourt', pp. 48–50.

70 Curry, *Agincourt: Sources and Interpretations*, p. 125.
71 Ibid., p. 36.
72 Rogers, 'Battle of Agincourt', pp. 127–29. By his own admission, this is a rough estimate at best, but I think it quite fair.
73 I use here the approximations of infantry speed at Agincourt provided by Rogers, 'Battle of Agincourt', pp. 80–81.
74 Curry, *Agincourt: Sources and Interpretations*, p. 115.
75 Ibid., p. 61; Pseudo-Elmham speaks likewise, but as Rogers points out, his passage 'is merely a slightly confused paraphrase of Tito Livio's clearer statement' ('Battle of Agincourt', p. 124).
76 Tito Livio Frulovisi, *Vita Henrici Quinti* ['Life of Henry V'], ed. Thomas Hearne (Oxford, 1716), p. 19.

CHAPTER 13: THE BATTLE, 25 OCTOBER

1 For an attempt to pull this off, see Michael Jones, *Voices from the Battlefield: 24 Hours at Agincourt, 15 October 1415* (W.H. Allen, 2015). Though not quite as minute-to-minute, Ian Mortimer takes something of a similar approach in *1415: Henry's V's Year of Glory* (Bodley Head, 2009).
2 Every one of the major historians I have been citing in this book does so.
3 Shakespeare, *Henry V*, IV.iii.41, 47.
4 Curry, *Agincourt: Sources and Interpretations*, p. 157.
5 Ibid., pp. 158–60. On the interpretation of his shout, which is recorded as 'nescieque' and 'nestroque' in these chronicles, I follow Curry's rather clever suggestion (see *Agincourt: A New History*, pp. 201–02). For a different and interesting take, Jones (*Agincourt 1415*, pp. 106–12) suggests that the command calls for the blowing of a horn ('*menée* stroke') used in hunting. Such a command could have been familiar to the nobility on the field, and certainly the larger connection between the realms of hunting and warfare has yet to be sufficiently explored.
6 Curry, *Agincourt: Sources and Interpretations*, p. 161.
7 Ibid., p. 133.
8 Ibid., p. 161.
9 Ibid., p. 125.
10 For the politics behind blaming Clignet in particular, see Curry, *Agincourt: A New History*, pp. 205–06.
11 This experiment, conducted by Tod's Workshop, was posted on YouTube on 22 November, 2022 and ought to be required viewing

to anyone interested in the battle and the longbow more generally: https://youtu.be/ds-Ev5msyzo.

12 This design has on some occasions been called 'hounskull', but current research by Ralph Moffat points to the hounskull being, rather than a bascinet, 'some kind of mail defence for the head and neck'; see his *Medieval Arms and Armour: A Sourcebook, Volume I: The Fourteenth Century* (Boydell, 2022), p. 226. For more detail on the question, see also Moffat's 'A word "I was delighted to meet": Why we must bid Auf Wiedersehen to *Hounskull* as the name for the "pig-faced" basinet', *Arms & Armour* 19 (2022), pp. 20–42.

13 In this respect, the experiments give weight to the arguments of DeVries, who has pushed hard against the idea that technologies of warfare were the primary determinant of the outcome at Agincourt. See his 'Technological Determinisms of Victory at the Battle of Agincourt', *British Journal for Military History* 2 (2015), pp. 2–15.

14 Curry, *Agincourt: Sources and Interpretations*, p. 35.

15 Ibid., p. 161.

16 Ibid., p. 106.

17 Ibid., p. 52.

18 The first serious attempt at running these numbers, one I have gratefully followed as a model for my own discussion here, is in Rogers, 'Battle of Agincourt', pp. 73–78.

19 This experiment, conducted by Tod's Workshop, was posted on YouTube on 1 January 2023: https://youtu.be/Mf7KCqQLw78.

20 See Woosnam-Savage, 'All Kinds of Weapons', p. 147. The Chaplain tells as much, describing the strikes of arrows against the advancing French that 'by their very force pierced the sides and visors of their helmets' (Curry, *Agincourt: Sources and Interpretations*, p. 36).

21 Curry, *Agincourt: Sources and Interpretations*, p. 161.

22 Ibid., p. 130.

23 Ibid., p. 125.

24 Ibid., p. 161.

25 Ibid., p. 36.

26 Ibid., p. 36.

27 This was the position taken by Keegan (*Face of Battle*, p. 83), for instance.

28 Rogers, 'Battle of Agincourt', p. 88.

29 Keith Still has made a study of the flow of human beings in crowds to show exactly this. See Wason, *Battlefield Detectives*, pp. 73–76; and Curry, *Great Battles: Agincourt*, pp. 194–95.

30 Rogers, 'Battle of Agincourt', p. 83. This is beautiful imagery, though it should be noted that a single volley of arrows would not mean all archers shooting at once. See Chapter 8, endnote 8, above.

31 Curry, *Agincourt: Sources and Interpretations*, pp. 160–61.

32 Ibid., p. 52.

33 Ibid., p. 36. See also Walsingham's statement that 'the cloud of arrows flew again from all directions' (ibid., p. 52).

34 Rogers, 'Battle of Agincourt', p. 89.

35 Curry, *Agincourt: Sources and Interpretations*, p. 39.

36 Ibid., p. 47.

37 Ibid., p. 47.

38 Barker, *Agincourt*, pp. 318–19.

39 This had been part of Boucicaut's plan, anyway.

40 On the shortening of the lances, see Waurin and Le Fèvre in Curry, *Agincourt: Sources and Interpretations*, pp. 159 and 161. Woosnam-Savage discusses their effectiveness in 'All Kinds of Weapons', pp. 142–43 and 146.

41 Curry, *Agincourt: Sources and Interpretations*, p. 63.

42 Ibid., p. 36. See also Fenin, in ibid., p. 118.

43 For an interesting treatment of the weapons and the theory that this made the difference, see Rogers, 'Battle of Agincourt', pp. 90–92.

44 See, respectively, also Elmham (Curry, *Agincourt: Sources and Interpretations*, p. 47), Religieux (ibid., p. 107), Pierre de Fenin (ibid., p. 118), and the *Anonymous Chronicle of the Reign of Charles VI* (ibid., p. 115).

45 Curry, *Agincourt: Sources and Interpretations*, p. 37.

46 This would be particularly true if they had back defences as well, which was something that probably only the wealthiest would have at the time of the battle. See Tobias Capwell, 'Arms and Armour at Agincourt: "Furnish'd in Warlike Sort"' in *1415: The Battle of Agincourt, Medieval Warfare Special Edition* (2015), p. 45.

47 Curry, *Agincourt: Sources and Interpretations*, p. 184.

48 Ibid., p. 165.

49 Ibid., p. 352.

50 Ibid., p. 81. Rogers presents an excellent list of similar sentiments across a number of sources, including some not in Curry's sourcebook, in 'Battle of Agincourt', p. 96.

51 Curry, *Agincourt: Sources and Interpretations*, p. 37.
52 Ibid., p. 125.
53 Ibid., pp. 37 and 62.
54 Ibid., pp. 172 and 174. His late arrival is also noted in many of our sources.
55 Ibid., p. 174.
56 Translation my own, from the original in Curry, *Agincourt: Sources and Interpretations*, p. 328. The earliest tradition of the duke's death at the point of surrender is found in Monstrelet's chronicle; see ibid,, p. 168.
57 Ibid., p. 163.
58 Ibid., p. 475.
59 Ibid., p. 37.
60 Ibid., p. 163.
61 Ibid., p. 164
62 Ibid., p. 174. That he was found some distance away is evidence, Curry notes, that prisoners were 'being taken to a collecting point, but it also fortifies the argument that the battle was already deemed to be over well before the killing of the prisoners was ordered' (*Agincourt: A New History*, p. 219).
63 Curry, *Agincourt: Sources and Interpretations*, p. 37.
64 Ibid., p. 47.
65 Ibid., p. 163.
66 Ibid., p. 62.
67 Ibid., p. 108.
68 Ibid., p. 33; he again notes their being mounted at the end of his narrative when he expresses the rumour that they would attack (p. 37).
69 Rogers appears to be similarly confident in the relative prospects of the rearguard had it engaged ('Battle of Agincourt', p. 102).
70 Curry, *Agincourt: Sources and Interpretations*, p. 115.
71 Ibid., p. 118.
72 Ibid., p. 88.
73 Ibid., p. 125.
74 Ibid., p. 174.
75 Ibid., p. 187.
76 Ibid., p. 131.
77 Ibid., p. 475.
78 Ibid., p. 118. This timing is frequently misunderstood, as it is by, for instance, Rogers, 'Battle of Agincourt', pp. 102–03. See above for

the placement of the baggage raid in its proper position at the outset of fighting, as attested to by the man who was there.

79 Curry, *Agincourt: Sources and Interpretations*, p. 164.
80 Ibid., p. 37.
81 Ibid., p. 125.
82 See Woosnam-Savage on the possibility that the mutilation was intentional, with reference made to mutilations done to unhelmeted men at the later battle of Towton ('All Kinds of Weapons', p. 154). The evidence from Towton is indeed important, though its status as a civil conflict may play a role in the cruelty exacted upon the dead.
83 Curry, *Agincourt: Sources and Interpretations*, p. 131.
84 Livingston, 'Counting the Dead at Crécy', in *The Battle of Crécy: A Casebook*, ed. Livingston and DeVries, pp. 485–88.
85 Curry, *Agincourt: Sources and Interpretations*, pp. 193–94.
86 Ibid., p. 53.
87 Curry provides an excellent accounting of the range of numbers in an appendix to her book *Agincourt: A New History*, pp. 276–79.
88 Ibid., p. 245.
89 Barker, *Agincourt*, p. 320.
90 Curry, *Agincourt: Sources and Interpretations*, p. 164. Barker has rightly raised the question of whether the adding of 1,000 to Monstrelet's number is a scribal mistake that was promulgated through the tradition (*Agincourt*, p. 421, note 2). It seems likely.
91 Curry, *Agincourt: Sources and Interpretations*, p. 37.
92 Ibid., p. 63.
93 Ibid., p. 164.
94 Ibid., p. 164.
95 Ibid., p. 165.
96 My translation, from Book 21, chapter 4.

CHAPTER 14: THE DAYS AFTER, 1415–22

1 Curry, *Agincourt: Sources and Interpretations*, p. 63.
2 Ibid., p. 166.
3 Ibid., p. 119.
4 A terrific survey of what is known and, perhaps more importantly, unknown in the matter is Anne Curry and Glenn Foard, 'Where Are the Dead of Medieval Battles? A Preliminary Survey', *Journal of Conflict Archaeology* 11 (2016), pp. 61–77.
5 Curry, *Agincourt: Sources and Interpretations*, p. 109.
6 Ibid., p. 127.

7 Ibid., p. 170.

8 This would be improbably short. The mean height of male personnel in the United States Army in 1966 was just over 68 inches. See White and Churchill, *The Body Size of Soldiers*, p. 73.

9 For comparison, the mean chest depth of male personnel in the United States Army in 1966 was just over nine inches. See White and Churchill, *The Body Size of Soldiers*, p. 109.

10 See Rowena E. Archer, 'War Widows', in *The Battle of Agincourt*, ed. Curry and Mercer, pp. 216–25.

11 An excellent example of shedding light on these oft-neglected aspects of history is in Barker, *Agincourt*, pp. 322–31. See also Rowena E. Archer's 'War Widows', in *The Battle of Agincourt*, ed. Curry and Mercer, pp. 216–25.

12 Curry, *Agincourt: Sources and Interpretations*, p. 166.

13 Ibid., p. 167.

14 Ibid., p. 113.

15 Ibid., p. 354.

16 Ibid., p. 194.

17 Rogers, 'Battle of Agincourt', p. 69.

Index

References to maps are in **bold**.